Praise for Step... ...essay collection,
When Words Deny the ... *Reshaping of Canadian Writing.*

* * *

"Crucial reading for anyone concerned about Canadian writing or, for that matter, our sense of identity."

—Kenneth J. Harvey, *The Globe and Mail*

"The most clear-sighted, bracing and provocative collection I have read in years."

—Ken McGoogan, *Winnipeg Free Press*

"Some of the most blistering and erudite pieces of Canadian literary criticism ever published."

—James Grainger, *Quill & Quire*

"This is criticism that is non-academic, readable, respectful of genuine literary accomplishment and merciless towards pretence and muddle. How badly we need it."

—Philip Marchand, *Toronto Star*

"A riveting read – something one hardly says of literary criticism every day!"

—Noah Richler, *The National Post*

Also by Stephen Henighan

A REPORT ON THE AFTERLIFE OF CULTURE

STEPHEN HENIGHAN

A Report
on the
Afterlife of Culture

ଔଓଃ

BIBLIOASIS

FIRST EDITION

Library and Archives Canada Cataloguing in Publication

Henighan, Stephen, 1960-

   A report on the afterlife of culture / Stephen Henighan.

ISBN 13: 978-1-897231-42-5
ISBN 10: 1-897231-42-3

   1. Culture. 2. Literature—History and criticism.
3. Globalization—Social aspects. I. Title.

PS8565.E5818R46 2008   C814'.54   C2008-900200-8

Edited by Daniel Wells

Canada Council   Conseil des Arts
for the Arts   du Canada

ONTARIO ARTS COUNCIL
CONSEIL DES ARTS DE L'ONTARIO

We gratefully acknowledge the support of the Canada Council for the Arts and the Ontario Arts Council for our publishing program.

PRINTED AND BOUND IN CANADA

CONTENTS

I:

A REPORT ON THE AFTERLIFE OF CULTURE

afterlife / n./ **1**. life after death. **2**. life at a later time

—The Canadian Oxford Dictionary

1.

The people of Todos Santos Cuchumatán are the kindest in Guatemala. Nowhere else in the Americas, perhaps, do family ties and traditional culture retain the force they do here. In April 2000, members of this community united to save the souls of their children. Satan was roaming the undulating main street of their mountain town, harvesting children's souls and preparing to make off with them. Like other marauders, Satan wore Western clothes. His contorted face, neither indigenous nor that of a gringo tourist, eliminated any doubt as to his identity. Directing Satan up the steep streets where drunken men incapable of coming to their children's rescue staggered through the high-altitude chill, was a Guatemalan dressed in Western clothes. The people of Todos Santos, one of the last communities in Guatemala where not only women but also men wear traditional Native dress (which here means red-and-white striped leggings, shirts with ornately embroidered collars, colourful jackets and broad-brimmed hats) were aware of the threat posed by mixed-race Guatemalans who had been assimilated into Western culture. Unlike other forms of Latin American Spanish, Guatemalan speech does not use the word *mestizo* to denominate a person of mixed European and Native American heritage: here one is either *indígena* or *maya* or *indio*, or else one is *ladino*, a person presumed to be of European culture; there is no third term, no allowance for the possibility of bridging cultures.

Once you become *ladino*, by abandoning Mayan customs and ceasing to speak a Mayan language, you are a foreigner; you make this fact clear by expressing your disdain for *indios*, even if your own skin is brown. In most of the Mayan languages spoken in Guatemala, the word for "foreigner" and the word for "Spanish-speaking Guatemalan" are identical. During the 1980s the people of Todos Santos Cuchumatán survived a brutal occupation by the Guatemalan military, whose officers, in their eyes, were foreigners: assimilated Guatemalans similar to the man directing Satan through their streets.

Unlike the soldiers, Satan did not carry a Galil rifle, only the box in which he was capturing their children's souls. The men gathered near the alabaster arches of the town square, overlooking the main street. They looked again at the face of the figure pursuing their children. There could be no doubt: it was Satan. They knew what they must do. Speaking in Mam, men who were sober rallied others who were drunk. It was their duty, according to their Mayan culture, to subordinate personal concerns when the survival of the community was under threat; the syncretized Catholicism to which their ancestors had been converted told them that they must put Satan behind them. At the moment in which they acted, these men were not conscious of being guided by the fused imperatives of a hybridized culture: they were reacting to a threat. The fact that, historically speaking, they were the products of the mingling of Mam traditionalism with Western influences that had been impacting Guatemala since the 16th century, was not apparent to them as they watched Satan stride through their streets, stealing the souls of their children. They knew only that they must seize the devil, break open the box in his hands and release their children's souls so that they might return to their bodies. As news of the danger spread through the town, men came from all around to help. They caught up with Satan and surrounded him. When the Westernized Guatemalan protested, men struck him down with their bare hands. Then they struck down Satan and broke open the box he was carrying. The children's souls were freed and returned to their bodies. The men had saved the community's future. In this way a Japanese tourist and the guide he had hired to help him take photographs were beaten to death.

* * *

There are many versions of the Japanese tourist story. Most concur that the victim arrived on a tour bus. In one version, perhaps the most reliable, he was an elderly Japanese man who began to pursue a little girl, trying to take photographs of her. Never having seen an elderly Asian, the Mam mistook him for Satan. The Guatemalan who died with the tourist, in this account, was the bus driver, who tried to come to the old man's rescue. In other versions the tourist was young and spry and penetrated into parts of the town where tourists, particularly those with Asian features, were not a common sight. Some versions shift the emphasis from children's souls to their internal physical organs. Local radio stations, it is said, had been running scare stories about foreigners stealing children to harvest their kidneys, hearts and livers. According to another account, a child from Todos Santos had disappeared a few days earlier. When local men saw the Japanese tourist pursuing the little girl they assumed that they had found the culprit. The element that remains consistent in all of these stories is that what the foreign Satan wanted from the Mam lay inside them. Whether conceived spiritually, as a soul, or physically, as internal organs, the outsider was trying to steal the most intimate part of the Mams' beings.

By 2003 everyone had grown more circumspect. The men held most responsible for beating the tourist to death were in jail. The locals were repentant and mournful. Tour buses had abandoned the three-hour drive up to Todos Santos from the northern Guatemalan city of Huehuetenango, leaving the town to the trickle of anthropologists, hardy backpackers and high-altitude hikers who had first made it legendary. The Japanese, it was said, had crossed

Guatemala off their list of tourist destinations, a source of rejoicing to their arch-enemies the Koreans, who run many of Guatemala's sweatshops. Yet none of this had stopped the absorption of Todos Santos Cuchumatán into Westernized modernity.

If, in older cities, artists are "the shock troops of gentrification," in Guatemala hippies have been the shock troops of globalization. During the 1960s they began arriving in the small colonial city of Antigua, less than an hour from Guatemala City. By the 1970s they had made their way upcountry to Panajachel, located on a small shelf of land on the edge of Lake Atitlán, the sacred lake of the Maya, plunged deep into a volcano-ringed valley three hours up the Pan-American highway from the capital. The heaviest fighting of the 1980s drove the hippies out of Panajachel and back down to Antigua, but long before the 1996 Peace Accords concluded Guatemala's civil war, they had returned. Like big-city bohemians, Western hippies in underdeveloped countries first make destinations popular then make them too expensive for people such as themselves. The process they set in motion inundates local cultures with Westernized concepts and gadgetry and contributes to squeezing locals off their land. Once initiated, this dynamic dispatches the agents of modernity deeper and deeper into the hinterland. The first time I visited Antigua, in 1994, the town was full of $4-a-night flophouses crammed with permanently stoned hippies. Men in traditional Mayan dress still appeared in the town's streets. By 2003 the few remaining dirt-cheap dives had been pushed to the wrong side of the avenue dividing the market from the heart of the town; the guests at these cheap hotels tended to be earnest, clean-cut young workers from non-governmental organizations. The average price of a house in central Antigua had risen to US$300,000 in a country where US$100 is a good monthly wage. One no longer sees men in traditional Mayan dress in Antigua, or anywhere in the surrounding region. The shores of Lake Atitlán, meanwhile, have acquired a tiled appearance as wealthy Americans, many of them in show business, have built mansions beneath the Mayas' sacred volcanoes and landscaped the terrain in a style influenced by North American suburbia. The hippies continue to forge northward. The Ixil triangle, cut off from the rest of Guatemala by a wayward branch of the Cuchumatanes mountains, is one of the most isolated regions of the country. In much of Guatemala, people refrain, out of shame, from speaking Native American languages in urban areas. The three large towns of the Ixil triangle are remarkable in that one hears Ixil, a particularly difficult Mayan language, spoken in restaurants and banks. During the civil war, the Ixil triangle was the site of some of the worst slaughters of Mayan people; a notorious scene in Rigoberta Menchú's memoir, *I, Rigoberta Menchú*, takes place in the town of Chajul. Today well-off young Americans devoted to "alternative culture" – the yuppie form of hippiedom – are buying up tracts of land in the Ixil triangle at cheap prices. An outpost of this culture has set up business in the main Ixil town of Nebaj. Known as "El Descanso" ("Rest"), it consists of the usual multi-purpose restaurant, café, bookstore, handicraft shop and language school. El Descanso provides a base and a meeting-point for gringos who are pioneering the Westernization of the Ixil triangle. The owner is an affable, open-minded gringo. A process has been set in motion that will almost certainly lead to Nebaj being transformed in ways that resemble the changes which have occurred in Antigua and Panajachel.

In Todos Santos Cuchumatán the murder of the Japanese tourist had slowed this process. Even so, in May 2003 I discovered a young foreign woman running a down-at-heel vegetarian restaurant, and a small language school offering courses in Spanish and Mam. Interaction with the outside world is actually more extensive than it appears. The steep mountainsides rising above Todos Santos, some of them cresting at over 3000 metres, are overpopulated. Lacking land on which to practise traditional agriculture, men from the community travel all over Guatemala, and sometimes farther afield, in search of work – usually agricultural labour – that will provide them with a cash income. The first trip out of the valley is said to be psychologically harrowing. The moment the bus arrives in dusty Huehuetenango, a city whose shabby modernity and mustached, mixed-race men wearing white cowboy hats make it feel more like part of Mexico than Guatemala, the Mam man, dressed in his striped leggings and embroidered collar, his Spanish vocabulary limited, feels the force of the modern world's disdain. He perceives his own customs and language as evidence of backwardness. "You never recover from that first trip out," a Mayan activist told me. The pulverization not only of the individual's vision of life, but of that of his parents and grandparents and ancestors, reduces existence to a black pit devoid of boundaries, moorings or any obvious route back to a sense of self-worth. The gods who have escorted the man through life, lending shape and resonance to his existence, become as trivial as plastic toys. Having plunged into this pit, economic migrants from traditional areas fall prey to desperate remedies for their alienation, particularly the twinned self-annihilations of alcohol abuse and its purported antidote, evangelical Christianity. Yet staying put in Todos Santos offers no solution; even here, the negation of all that life means if you are from the valley is encroaching. This negation is imported by backpackers, and by hippies and their vegetarian restaurants. But it is threaded even more profoundly into the warp of the fraying Mam culture by men who leave the valley to find work, then return. These returnees come back with quetzals or Mexican pesos, or even U.S. dollars, but they also bestow a more troubling gift on their community: a sense of deep nihilism, a terminal uncertainty about who they are, a feeling that Mam life is incoherent, that perceptions once taken as natural are false. The men who stumble along the main street of Todos Santos in a drunken stupor are often those who have worked outside the valley. "They come back not knowing who they are," I was told by a man who had spent nearly thirty years working with indigenous communities.

One evening in May 2003 I was walking around Todos Santos with a friend. On a street clinging to the mountainside we found a low-set wooden lodge that announced itself as a restaurant. To enter the building we had to walk downhill through a kitchen where women were cooking in near-darkness over steaming pots. Below the kitchen was another low doorway that opened onto a balcony offering an excellent view of the central part of the town and the vast flank of the opposite side of the valley. Two Mam men in traditional dress were sitting at a table on the balcony drinking the ubiquitous Gallo beer and chatting in Mam. My friend and I sat down at the next table and ordered supper. We ate, speaking to each other in English between bites. We spoke to the woman serving us in Spanish. As we finished our meal, the two men at the next table said goodbye; one of them left the restaurant. The man who remained turned to us. In a Spanish that was several social classes above that normally spoken by a Mam man in traditional dress, he said: "I have a Master's degree in biology from the University of Texas."

The confession was so incongruous that I assumed this man was more drunk than he looked. But as he continued to speak, I realized he was telling the truth. He was a lecturer in biology at San Carlos University in Guatemala City, the oldest university in Central America. He had left Todos Santos in his late teens, assimilated into *ladino* society, pretended not to know anything about *indios*, or to speak their "dialects," as middle-class Guatemalans call the Mayan languages. Having completed a degree at San Carlos, he won a scholarship to do his Master's in Texas. "This weekend," he said, "I came back for the first time in fourteen years."

He looked down at his pink jacket and striped leggings. My friend and I glanced at each other, and I knew (and the biologist must have known also) that we were refraining from asking him how difficult it had been to put those clothes on again.

"A weekend, that's all," he said. "After fourteen years! At eight o'clock tomorrow morning I'm catching the bus to Guatemala City. Where nobody knows anything.... That's another life..."

"Another world," I suggested.

"But it's important for me to come back, important for me to visit all my family," he said. His voice faltered. He looked away. Without speaking, he got up and hurried out of the restaurant.

* * *

We are all Mam now.

In José Saramago's novel, *Baltasar and Blimunda*, a rustic young couple are recruited by Father Bernardo de Gusmão to build a flying machine. The machine is made of iron and cloth, in the shape of a bird. It is powered by captured human souls stored in bottles (*"frascos"*). No friend of the Catholic church, Saramago skirts vocabulary that might bear connotations of religious belief, using the neutral word *"a vontade"* – literally "the will" – to describe the souls that Baltasar and Blimunda harvest while walking through Lisbon at a time when many people are dying of the plague. By setting his novel in the early 18th century, when rationalist modernity was beginning to slice into traditional belief systems, Saramago captures the tension that arises from the intersection of the religious past and the technological future. The flying machine, which projects humans into the heavenly realm that was previously the uncontested domain of deity, symbolizes this tension. I had assumed that the novel's plot was entirely the product of Saramago's imagination until, ambling around the castle district in Lisbon one evening, I found myself on a sidestreet named "Bernardo de Gusmão"; beneath Gusmão's name was the explanation *"precursor da aviação."* As a priest, this "forerunner of aviation" turns to a divine source of energy for his new technology. Like the Japanese tourist as perceived by the Mam nearly four centuries later, he insists that a purely spiritual essence, the soul, can be contained in a material form: a bottle, a camera. In both cases, this paradoxical belief signals a point of crossover between a culture that is communal, cyclical, local and animist (as Christianity in early modern Europe remained in many ways an animist religion, particularly in Catholic countries and rural areas), and a culture that has technology as its motor, individualism as its mantra and the acquisition of material goods as its ideal. The extrapolation of this final characteristic is that experience itself must become an object which, through technology, can be individualized, objectified and acquired. It is for this reason that the photographic image epitomizes modernity. In its various incarnations – as billboard poster, magazine illustration, film, television program, video cassette and digital snapshot swapped on the internet – the photographic image becomes the essence of a materialist culture that contests the validity of the spiritual longings that inspired written culture: a culture which, in nearly every national or linguistic tradition, had its origins in, or was fostered by, embryonic forms of organized religion. Visual art, like classical music, also has roots in the church, but the Judeo-Christian ban on graven images limited the range of themes that could be addressed by painters or stained-glass artists; the word, in theory, could address any aspect of creation.

We are not all Mam now in that we necessarily endure the deep psychological crisis that Mam culture is experiencing as globalized modernity inundates it, nullifying its belief systems. Most people capable of reading these words would be miserable living anywhere other than at the heart of globalized modernity. But we do resemble the Mam in our longing to free the captured souls from Satan's box in order to resituate our own lives, actions and experiences within a meaningful, coherent social order that will lend our existences a resonance capable of being transmitted to succeeding generations. The tangible form of this anxiety is evident in the "hothouse" upbringings ambitious yuppie parents inflict on their children, compensating for the fading claims of cultural traditions with a regime of lessons, courses or activities which, because they are expensive and therefore not available to all, become material objects, as the children themselves become both "acquisitions" and "investments." Sustaining the consumerist status of the family into the next generation becomes a substitute for the cultural, religious or linguistic heritages sacrificed in order to fit into globalized modernity. Inheritance no longer concentrates on the "great estate" but on the possibility of transmitting the potential for a prosperous, if culturally neutral, "lifestyle." The "great estate" inherited by the landowner's son consisted of cultural tradition as much as of woods or herds of deer; the son or daughter of the peasant on the estate, meanwhile, inherited distinctive speech patterns, folk knowledge, a confirmed place in the community, a strong religious tradition: a coherent culture, if one weighed down by poverty and oppression. In all but the most remote corners of the world, the question of the transmission of cultural values (how many of these do most of us have left?) has become a source of growing anxiety. This fear becomes concrete in the oppressive codes of Islamic or Christian or Hindu or Zionist fundamentalism. Yet no amount of aestheticism, prohibition, self-assertion or proselytization can restore us to a world where souls cannot be collected in bottles or boxes. We are all Mam now because we live in a world where our experience and our cultures, down to the spiritual depths of our lives, are commodities.

The Mam who attacked the Japanese tourist hoped that by releasing their children's souls from the small box of his camera they could restore their children to their cultural roots. Their action may be read metaphorically (although it is important not to forget the two men lying dead on the ground). In the late 1990s, after the end of the civil war in Guatemala, satellite television began to spread throughout the northwest highlands. Children soon grasped that the languages spoken by their parents were not heard on television, which was dominated by Spanish and English. In recent years significant numbers of Mayan parents have despaired of children who refuse to speak the language of the household; the shame that used to infect Maya only when they visited predominantly Spanish-speaking towns or cities has insinuated itself into the home. Even the robust Quiché language, which has one million speakers, is suffering from children who, like immigrant kids on new continents, reply in the language of power when their parents address them in the language of the community. Many Maya fear that their children's souls have vanished already. In this sense, Satan's arrival on the streets of Todos Santos confirmed anxieties that were already present in the town. By breaking open the tourist's camera, the Mam men were trying to wrest their children from an alien grip, to claim their offspring as their own, not as creatures of the image.

In Saramago's novel, it is the release of souls that makes the image available to characters who have lived circumscribed traditional lives. Father Gusmão and his helpers take to their flying machine in order to escape the Inquisition, the Catholic form of rigid reaction against the emerging technological world. The souls they release to power their flight, gathered from people who were dying, will not return to living bodies; in the place of reintegration, Saramago offers a flight into the first glimpse of the characters' objectification of their environment. Baltasar and Blimunda, knocked down when the flying machine takes off, get to their feet: "... they could barely see the farm, soon lost among the hills, and that over there, that's Lisbon ..." The rural environment shrinks from sight. In the world as viewed from the platform of technology, the city dominates the horizon. The city's values gain greater influence by virtue of the impressive silhouette of its skyline. The transition from a sacred world defined by the word to a technological world defined by the image promotes the primacy of urban life.

At its peak, the tension between spiritual and technological conceptions of the world, between ritualized localism and systematized, commercialized industrialism, became hugely creative, engendering the questing visions that elevate Western cultural production between the Renaissance and the end of the Cold War. But in the margins of this long arc of creativity – in its early stages, where Father Gusmão died a madman, and in its epilogue, where Mam men who have worked in the outside world stumble down the streets of Todos Santos unable to believe in their own perceptions – the disjuncture between spirit and mechanism grows unendurable.

The tension between the sacred and the technological lies nestled in all human cultures from their outset, even non-Western cultures such as that of the Maya, in which oppositions are perceived as complementary rather than antagonistic. It was rampant building and the exhaustion of natural resources that led, around 900 AD, to the collapse of the theocratic Mayan civilization in its Classical form, and to the loss of most of its written literature. Five centuries earlier, St. Augustine, writing *City of God* in North Africa, argued: "God wanted rational man, made to His image, to have no dominion except over irrational nature." Reason was a threat because it offered the individual the potential to extend his power. Holy men, Augustine said, should be shepherds, not masters of cities: they should rule animals, not other people. While God could make humans in his image, humans, in the Judeo-Christian tradition, were not permitted to make images of God. From an early stage, city life and technological presumption link arms; the image becomes the battleground on which the struggle to define the place of life's spiritual dimension is fought. Leonardo da Vinci, a master of religious art, anticipated Father Gusmão by sketching designs for flying machines, in addition to detailed portraits of human bodies, which many of his contemporaries considered blasphemous. From the Renaissance onward (and arguably as far back as the Middle Ages) Western culture generates creators who oscillate between the sacred and the secular, and creations that fuse the competing demands of these two realms, each of which asserts its own totalizing vision of human life and neither of which can be completely suppressed or ignored in the manifestations of the other.

The fretting of the technological against the spiritual is most evident in literature, which first developed as a means for expressing spiritual belief. Literature and music are the two art forms that hold off the avalanche of technologized modernity because the images they forge dwell within the imagination of the listener or reader and, in and of themselves, do not exist in a marketable visual form. Of the two, literature offers the more radical possibilities for repelling technologized modernity. Music, from its earliest days, was not only a score but a spectacle; a visual aspect was implicit in its production. The experience of going to hear the Vienna Philharmonic Orchestra was partly social and visual: the ladies in evening dress, the noble families in the balcony, the conductor gesturing with his baton. The listener was also a spectator, and in the experience that the spectator carried away at the end of the evening the rhythms of the music of, say, Brahms and the sheer visual grandeur of the orchestra, the glimpses of great personnages and the sound of the audience's applause remained jumbled. The popular music of our own era has accentuated this tendency. Stadium rock bands do not necessarily inspire the loyalty of fans on the basis of their recorded music, which sometimes, as in the case of the Rolling Stones or the Grateful Dead, is less popular than their live performances. Other bands have become successful on the strength of their videos, or are remembered because of their lyrics, the literary component of their work, rather than as composers of striking music. The advent of the DVD has fused music and performance to a point where, at least in their most popular forms, they have become increasingly difficult to distinguish from one another.

Medieval literature, as is often pointed out, included illuminated manuscripts which, in their festooning of text with bright images, resembled Web pages. Some would contend that, in the on-line mingling of text and image, written literature has returned to its point of origin. Yet during the middle period of the long arc in which the sacred and the secular coexist in a tensed clasp, the text is autonomous. There are notable exceptions, such as the illustrations that appeared in the original editions of the novels of Charles Dickens. But what distinguishes literature during what one might characterize as the period of "high literacy, " starting somewhere around 1610 – *Don Quixote,* the first great modern European novel, is published in two volumes in 1605 and 1615, the *King James Bible* in 1611 – and concluding at an endpoint that is probably too recent for us to discern it, is the primacy of the text, the dynamic power of the word. Reading, as a private experience in which each traveller who crosses the terrain of a given collection of pages experiences the same words yet internalizes them differently, underlies the democratization of hierarchical medieval society, the levelling of the Great Chain of Being. At the same time, in its enforcement of solitude and its cultivation of an individualism based on divergent interpretations of the same text, or eclectic individual reading choices, reading begins the work of shearing away the assumed common heritage of Western culture even as it seeks to extend, define and catalogue the range of this culture's achievements. The marginalization of oral culture, particularly in Europe after the advent of Gutenberg, ruptures the wholeness of the tribe, lifting storytelling out of the public domain and implanting it in the individual psyche. The result is an inexorable internalization of the subject matter of fictional narrative that begins in the satirical collision of the Knight of the Sad Countenance's chivalric fantasies with unyielding reality in Miguel de Cervantes's *Don Quixote* and concludes in the miring of the reader in the linguistic flux of the psyche in James Joyce's *Finnegans Wake*. Released from its dependence on the image (though still, of course, sculpted by developments in technology and commerce), literature becomes the field where the claims of the imagistic-technological drive may be assessed against those of the spirit. Stendhal's novel *The Red and the Black* expresses this dual pull with exemplary Cartesian clarity; but it is present in nearly all of the great writers of the 18th, 19th and early 20th centuries. Readers isolated themselves for hours or days to participate in the protagonists' searches for meaning in the landscape between life's two poles. They did so in the confidence that, in spite of the solitary individualism they were cultivating through their reading, they were contained within a coherent, integrated society. Their radical individualism was possible, in other words, because they benefitted from a cultural "safety net." No matter how eccentric reading might render their perceptions, they continued to be marked by language, descent and custom as members of a given nation, a defined social class, a recognized community.

Part of the work of the great novelists is to chart the disintegration of these certainties. Tolstoy's *War and Peace* shows us characters searching for spiritual meaning through love, religion,
immersion in the vast natural world, and the tests of courage
found on the battlefield. But the frame of the novel's plot is the
attempt by Europe's first centralized, self-consciously modern
nation-state, that of Napoleonic France, to subordinate Europe's
last remaining feudal oligarchy, primitive, serf-holding Russia.
The invaders are eventually driven out, but their ideas are not. The
novel concludes with Nikolenka, Prince Andrei's son and a proba-
ble future instigator of the 1825 Decembrist plot to assassinate the
Czar, vowing to undertake a great idealistic action. On the final
page of the sheaf of essays that follow the conclusion of the novel's
story, Tolstoy invokes the rationalism of Voltaire, who believed
that the discovery by Copernicus and Newton of the laws of
astronomy had put an end to religion. Tolstoy asserts the paradox
that, far from serving to "destroy the concept of the soul," rational
analysis of history and the revelation of its patterns "rather
strengthens the foundation on which the institutions of church and
state are founded." This ingenious manoeuvre enables Tolstoy to
wriggle free of the closing vise-grip whose two prongs are spirit
and mechanism; yet it is France, where "the institutions of church
and state" are formally separated from one another, that embodies
the future. The uncoupling of church and state first stimulates the
environment in which literature thrives, then suffocates it. As
France is the epicentre of the rupture between church and state,
this process occurs most rapidly and decisively in French literature. The French novel, losing its command of the social panorama
that was the natural territory of Balzac, Stendhal, Flaubert and
Zola – the inheritors of the consolidation of the centralized state
that rendered society uniquely susceptible to being understood
through the realist novel – retreats in the early 20th century from
the modernism of Proust, which paints the society of *la belle époque*
through an extravagant subjectivity, to the fusion of narration and
philosophy in novels by Jean-Paul Sartre and Albert Camus, then

to literature as the exposition of theories of subjective perception in the *nouveau roman* of Alain Robbe-Grillet, Nathalie Sarraute and Michel Butor in the 1950s and early 1960s. In May 1968 in Paris the final uprising against the spiritual sclerosis of the technological society, an uprising that enshrines spirituality carnally in the student revolutionaries' cries for sexual freedom, fails. The French novel is swallowed whole by philosophy and literary theory. For the next thirty years one hears next to nothing of French fiction, while the dense diction of the theorists – Jacques Derrida, Michel Foucault, Roland Barthes, Louis Althusser, Michel de Certeau, Jean-François Lyotard, Hélène Cixous, Luce Irigaray, Tzvetan Todorov, Julia Kristeva, Gilles Deleuze, Jean Baudrillard – does battle with the technological imperative without defeating it. When the narrative impulse returns to French fiction, in the novels of Michel Houellebecq, it has consumed technology, conceiving the immortality that the characters seek not in terms of their inscription into the pageant of a culture destined to be passed on to future generations, but in the most literal sense, as genetic modification or surgical intervention that will enable them to bypass the horror of death and physical decay. Houellebecq's characters do not possess spirits. They are flesh and matter that have learned the subterranean lesson of 1968 – the selfish lesson that was lurking behind the revolutionary chants – that the human organism is happiest when young and most fully realized in moments of sexual intercourse. The characters in Houellebecq's novels are matter flayed of spiritualty and culture: the human conceived as mechanism and defined by the image. Houellebecq's novel *Les particules élémentaires* (1998; translated as *The Elementary Particles*) concludes with the disappearance of humans of "the old race." People created in the laboratory, as Houellebecq writes, "in man's image," come to dominate the human population. The technological revolution has snapped the leash that linked our species to obsolete "humanity." In the ultimate self-realization, humans have appropriated the image, and, pushing aside St. Augustine's God, have remade themselves in a way that leaves them with no spiritual debt to a creator nor a bond with a community. If women and Muslims are portrayed unsympathetically in Houellebecq's fiction, it may be because their concern for, respectively, children and spiritual rectitude makes them prone to resist this reductive definition of existence. Yet however much one may wish to reject Houellebecq's nastiness, his insights contain a prickly truth about where we are going. We are no longer alienated by technology. Little by little, we are ourselves becoming the alienating force.

* * *

In May 1989 Poland was in upheaval. The elections that had been planned as a formality to renew the power of the Communist Party took on an unexpected energy. Suddenly the country was facing the unimaginable: a potential victory by the opposition Solidarity movement. As the campaign grew more frenzied, I saw young people in conservative, Catholic Cracow, home of Pope John Paul II, take to the streets in bohemian clothes – the young women in short skirts and tight-fitting black leggings that imitated current London fashion, the young men unshaven and shaggy – chanting: "*Sovietski Go Homu! Sovietski Go Homu!*" In the lengthening, almost Scandinavian evenings of the northern Solidarity heartland of Gdynia and Gdańsk the streets were full late into the night. Solidarity banners were draped everywhere. An activist had only to set up a table offering anti-government leaflets to be surrounded by an avid crowd. A naval officer running for the Communist Party, his campaign poster plastered to the glass window of a restaurant, had adopted as his slogan the beseeching: "*Give me a chance!*" The young men showing me around town scoffed. "Give you a chance? We gave you forty-five years!"

Everywhere, I heard Poles arguing with one another. I wished I could understand their language in order to follow their arguments, in which the words "*Sovietski*" and "*Americanski*" were repeated again and again as they struggled to define the boundaries of the independence they were about to gain. But, as exhilirating as I found the fervour that gripped the country, the stern Catholic nationalist messianism I encountered during a Sunday morning service at the Gdańsk church attended by Solidarity leader Lech Wałęsa made me recoil. Was one brand of dogmatic uniformity to be supplanted by another? Yet it was Warsaw's old city that gave me greatest pause. More than fifteen years later, the Stare Miasto ("Old Town") rises from among the conflicting impressions of that turbulent time as the true harbinger of the future.

Warsaw's historic centre was built during the 17th and 18th centuries. By 1795 Poland had been overrun by Russia, Prussia and Austria; it disappeared as a nation until 1918, when, having slid several hundred kilometres to the west, it returned to the map. For more than a century the Poles kept their language and culture alive underground. Enforced Russification and Germanification in the areas occupied by these powers (the Austrian occupation of the south was less draconian) was resisted by families and communities who taught children Polish language and history in secret. The Stare Miasto survived the long occupation as a symbol of the history that Poles hoped one day to reclaim. But in the final battles of the Second World War, the Stare Miasto was obliterated. With the exception of two or three battered churches, the heart of Polish nationhood was a littered field.

After the war the Poles created a perfect copy of their past.

As Poland had been occupied by the Soviet army and absorbed into the Soviet Bloc (whose military alliance, to their discomfort, was named the Warsaw Pact), much of the city was rebuilt according to bruising Stalinist aesthetics. The centrepiece of the Stalinist reconstruction, completed in 1955, was the hideous thirty-storey Palace of Culture. Yet, in the place where the Stare Miasto had stood, the Stare Miasto was reconstructed. After the war, I was told, a call had gone out for photographs, paintings and sketches of the Stare Miasto. Thousands of citizens mailed in images. Extending the surviving maps and plans with the images they received in the mail, the architects developed a meticulous record of the appearance, inside and out, of nearly every building in the old town. The 17th- and 18th-century buildings were replicated using original materials and were painted their original colours. Every window, cobblestone, eave and mantle was recreated exactly as it had been in 1939. The fact that this was achieved under a government installed by a foreign power determined to blemish Warsaw with gargantuan reminders of its own ideological dominance – a government that construed Polish nationalism as a threat – raised the feat to the status of a near miracle.

In May 1989, the Stare Miasto felt removed from the turmoil that prevailed elsewhere. Nothing happened there. Tourists ambled about in the sunlight; politics felt far away. There was little evidence of the anger I found in Cracow, or the non-stop hyperactivity of the opposition movement in Gdynia and Gdańsk. No blob-lettered red-on-white *Solidarność* banners marred the perfect procession of tall, narrow buildings – one painted green, the next one pink – that lined the Rynek Starego Miasta, the central square. Poles pointed to this place, where they had imprinted a fixed vision of Polishness on the featureless, much-invaded plain across which their country was spread, as the place where their national soul had revived. But you only had to glance around the square to know that in the Stare Miasto the image had defeated history.

* * *

In *La condition postmoderne* (1979) the French philosopher Jean-François Lyotard, who is often credited with defining the term "postmodernism," traces the beginning of contemporary culture's separation from the great narratives of Western civilization to the late 1950s. Lyotard identifies this as the moment when Europe completes its post-Second World War reconstruction. The severing of continuity with the past, represented by featureless office towers and apartment blocks that occupied lots swept clear of the rubble of buildings that had stood for centuries, sets the stage, Lyotard contends, for a more fragmented, provisional way of knowing, unhitched from the centuries'-old narrative that had constituted "Western civilization." Yet the Europe whose post-war reconstruction Lyotard witnessed was "Western Europe," itself a concept minted by the Cold War, and one that would disappear after 1989. The reconstruction that surrounded Lyotard was directed by leaders such as Konrad Adenauer and Charles de Gaulle, older men saturated in 19th-century ideals of "Western civilization." By contrast, the Stare Miasto, a tenacious attempt to reclaim history by a nation crushed by the Stalinist ideology of its occupier, teaches a lesson more relevant to our time: that, under the pressure of an ideology that admits no alternatives, when the soul can be captured in a tangible space (the tourist's camera, the would-be early aviator's bottles, the perfect copy of a building from an earlier century) the image (the tourist's snapshot of a Mam child, the individual's first aerial glimpse of his landscape that reveals the dominance of the city, the window and lintel that replicate 18th-century contours unsupported by 18th-century culture) replaces cultural engagement with a simple proliferation of material objects – the condensed form of images – and cuts us off from meaningful engagement with history.

This may sound like an exercise in wordplay, or a mere restatement of the postmodernists' belief that we are condemned to create either pastiche-like imitations of past cultural forms or images based on an ahistorical popular culture: Andy Warhol's paintings of Campbell's soup cans, for example. According to this view, we lack the existential authenticity necessary to generate our own spontaneous yet culturally coherent responses to the world around us. But I think the examples I've given lead to different conclusions, dictated by the particular historical circumstances in which we live.

Postmodernism developed during the Cold War. Its belief that the artist, severed from meaningful connection with a coherent tradition, could not produce but only reproduce reflected the duality of a politically bipolar world. The insistence that the present-day act of narration takes precedence over the content of that which is being narrated (such as stories that link the individual to the past), which lies at the heart of many of the textual assaults launched by postmodern literary theorists, springs from an acute consciousness of the competing political rhetorics of communism and capitalism that manipulated the past in order to paint the present as both inevitable and desirable. After 1990, when the Cold War ends, a single ideology dominates, a reduced repertoire of consumer products is manufactured in larger quantities and distributed in more countries, the spread of email and the internet refutes the boundaries of time and space, transnational corporations and continental trading blocks infringe upon the borders of the nation-state, and money flees from Moscow to Kuala Lumpur at the press of a button. As a result, both our relationship with the past and the channels by which culture is disseminated change.

What does this have to do with the Stare Miasto?

Built against the grain of an ideological project dedicated to eradicating Polish history, the imitation 17th- and 18th-century houses of Warsaw's Old Town reproduce the past perfectly and therefore remain politically neutered. They do not annihilate the past, like the Stalinist Palace of Culture on the other side of Warsaw, or the faceless pedestrian shopping district in the centre of Cologne, Germany, which is built on land once occupied by neighbourhoods that were destroyed by the bombers of the Royal Air Force. At the same time, restrained by the Stalinist and neo-Stalinist context in which they were built, the houses of the Stare Miasto advertize in their immaculate cornices and pristine mantles the fact that, unlike the rest of post-1945 Poland, they have not been processed by the mill of history. The rebuilt Stare Miasto did not threaten Poland's Soviet-installed dictatorship because it did not provide a living, vital channel back to the reality of an autonomous Polish nation. In fact, by converting the past into an obviously fabricated spectacle, the born-again Stare Miasto may have defanged Polish historical consciousness. The movement to overthrow Soviet rule was nurtured by the Catholic church, which had its stronghold in Cracow, and most of whose principal edifices –

including those within the Stare Miasto – bore the scars of having weathered centuries of turbulence and disaster, and by the dissident trade unions and rebellious youth of the open Baltic coast stretching between Gdynia and Gdańsk, where weekend shopping trips made by ferry to neutral Sweden renewed minds and ideas throughout the Cold War (when I asked directions in this part of Poland in 1989, people would sometimes reply in halting Swedish). It was not the perfectly preserved "history" of the Stare Miasto, but a dissonant concert of conservative religious dogma and stray chords of Westernized modernity that energized the opposition movements to renovate the Polish state. The fact that Poles, at least until very recently, memorized the major events of their national history like a religious catechism, has its roots in history, particularly in the one-hundred-twenty-year Russian-Prussian-Austrian occupation that preceded the Soviet occupation, but also in the preponderant role played by the Catholic church in coordinating national resistance. The form in which the Stare Miasto was rebuilt sidelined it as an effective focus for the opposition to Soviet domination.

The impact of the Stare Miasto on pre-1990 Poland is not dissimilar to the way in which the internet perpetuates the prevailing hierarchy of the post-1990 world while purporting to negate its existence. The internet's champions – which, these days, includes most of us – proclaim it to be "borderless." Yet my email address concludes in ".ca," indicating my geographical position in the world; those of my old friends in Italy end in ".it," those of people in Moldova end in ".md" and those of friends in Great Britain end in ".co.uk" or ".ac.uk," depending on whether they work in business or academe. Yet when I send a message to someone in the United States, the address ends in ".com" or, if the person is an academic, in ".edu." The internet's dynamics assert the refusal of the contemporary United States to define itself as a nation among others; its insistence on being not a country, but the ahistorical Jerusalem or black hole (depending on your point of view) towards which mere nations are being swept. By definition, the United

States is that place which has transcended nationness, downgrading the national histories of other countries to disposable detritus. The enforcement of U.S. norms on the internet can be unremitting. A few years ago a former student of mine moved to Holland, where she had family. She wrote me occasional email messages asking about possibilities for pursuing a Master's degree upon her return to Canada. As our correspondence progressed, I noticed that when my former student returned my messages with her replies at the top, the spelling in my earlier messages had been Americanized. Where I had written, "Don't forget to practise your Spanish," the email program had rewritten: "Don't forget to practice your Spanish." My earlier messages were revised until they brimmed with "centers" and "travelings." Infuriated by this mauling of my language, I went through the old messages and rewrote them in Canadian spelling. In the next reply they had been re-Americanized. My former student eventually lost interest in doing a graduate degree and our correspondence ended. A few months later, when she returned to Canada, the young woman explained that during the time we were corresponding she had been dating an American who had encouraged her to use a U.S. version of Yahoo. This version rewrites all messages received in "American usage." One of the supposed emblems of "cyberspace democracy," Yahoo.com was eliminating any trait that diverged from U.S. norms. As with numerous historical examples of U.S. campaigns to bring "democracy" to the outside world (Iran, Guatemala, Indonesia, the Dominican Republic, Greece, Chile, Nicaragua, Grenada, Panama, Iraq, Haiti . . . the list is endless), this virtual form of "borderless democracy" admitted only American dominance.

The Stare Miasto is the precursor of our dismissal of history in the post-1990 era. It is not precisely what the postmodernists might call a "simulacrum": a shadowy likeness of the past. Its construction dependent on the image – on the photographs, sketches and paintings sent in by thousands of Polish citizens – the Stare Miasto, in its dissidence against Soviet-era homogenization, insists on a kind of defiant independence. It demands to be understood as an inclusive, democratic attempt to reinstate the past with hyper-realist accuracy; yet, disconnected from the culture that gave birth to the forms it reproduces, these new old houses of the new Old Town become themselves the bottle or the camera from which the soul can never return. The rebuilt Stare Miasto is not an extension or direct emanation of early modern European tradition: it is, rather, the afterlife of that culture.

In its subordination to the image and its appeal to a putative democratic inclusiveness (the individual citizens mailing in photographs and paintings, the individual tourist taking a photograph of Mam children that differs from all other photographs) the Stare Miasto incarnates the type of object that is produced during the afterlife of culture. It resembles the hybrid novels, both literary and commercial, that characterized the first wave of post-1990 English-language publishing. Many of these novels are meticulously researched historical tales that depict the past through a marshalling of detail yet twist the cultural and moral codes of past eras to make them acceptable to our present through the insertion of individualist, egalitarian, feminist or anti-racist sensitivities that characters inhabiting the close-knit traditional societies of the past would not have had, or would have expressed in very different ways (or, conversely, by portraying past society as hopelessly restrictive in order to highlight by contrast the moral superiority of the present). These contemporary novels diverge from the underlying assumptions of works created during the period of "high literacy" that reaches from the Renaissance to the conclusion of the Cold War.

The impact of globalized commerce on culture has been to transmute democratic ideals into the I-express-my-individualism-by-shuffling-a-personal-selection-of-products-available-at-the-shopping-mall mass consumerism. This "mass" element pervades all contemporary cultural activity, from the cherry-picking of downloaded tunes on a teenager's iPod that expresses her "individuality" to the book club reading lists that try to fill the void left by the disintegration of literary culture by establishing a common ground for literary discussion. It is evident in the weblog, where people put forth opinions, and others respond to them: an untutored exchange that is often touted as the "democratization" of culture, but which could be characterized as the penetration of the mass individualism of the shopper in the mall into political, social and intellectual debate. At its best the weblog provides a conduit into the public domain for issues ignored or under-reported by the conventional media, or develops arguments for debunking the palaver of politicians. More often the weblog is sloppy, fractured, grammatically tangled, intellectually malnourished, responsible only to a coterie of correligionists: in its universal visibility and the brevity of its entries, it epitomizes the word sapped of energy by its framing within the field of the visual image. The weblog, unlike a book on the same topic, is rarely held accountable to past debates in the field it is discussing; in this way it furthers the excision of the eternal present of the contemporary era from the progressive chronology of past eras. This difference becomes clear in a case such as that of Riverbend, the notorious "girl blog from Iraq," an online favourite the value of whose insights into her society were widely and seriously debated only after a selection of her blogs was published in book form as *Baghdad Burning: Girl Blog from Iraq* (2005). The book was judged not only by different standards, but within a broader historical context, than her original blog.

Mass culture promotes film, now transmitted on DVD, as the dominant narrative form. The widespread installation of DVD drives in laptop computers means that film must be sufficiently intellectually challenging to withstand multiple viewings; since visual language is crude, simplistic and over-obvious by comparison with written language, complexity is achieved through variant endings, collections of bloopers or outtakes, "director's cuts," or willful obscurity. The consumer may choose a preferred version of the film from among those offered by the DVD, as he or she would choose favourite products from among the repertoire available at the mall. The consumer's personal extraction of meaning from the

film, however, remains less active, and less predicated on the sub-
tleties of a given type of language, than the reader's construction of
meaning when reading a novel. Meaning becomes a question of
selecting combinations of options rather than of the development
of an imagination. The reader of a novel must supply the basic
images of the story, down to the characters' appearances; this exercise renders the reader's imagination robust. None of us sees
Heathcliff's dark allure exactly as our fellow readers do. In film, by
contrast, appearances are imposed on us: we all view the same
image of the male and female leads gazing into each other's eyes;
the only exertion that we can be obliged to make is to disentangle
the plot, and here at best a handful of options are available. The
mass consumption of "culture," its conversion into an ahistorical
commodity, may not be unique to the post-1990 era; but in its distinctive present form, the "mass" quality erases both the eccentric
individuality of the past and the pillar that upheld original perceptions: privacy.

Culture, by definition, is now a question of personal prefer-
ences, expressed in a public context, and based on "feelings" rather
than aesthetic judgements made within a tradition consciously
mastered or painstakingly adopted. When I board the bus to the
downtown core of the city where I live, half the passengers, and
nearly all of the younger passengers, have wires trailing from their
ears. I transfer to the intercity bus and, while some people are reading or conversing or talking on their cellphones, others are watching movies on their laptops; the ubiquitous wire may funnel the
sound into the spectator's ear alone, but people in three or four different seats can view the images flashing on the movie-watcher's
screen. The distracting presence of these images makes it difficult
to concentrate on anything else.

The books discussed in book clubs become public in the same
way: they are read for a shared deadline, discussion may be channelled by the "Questions for your reading group" section at the
end of the paperback edition, the level of literary debate descends
to whether members of the group "liked" characters or regarded

them as laudable models for behaviour, or saw them as raising salient public debates in a congenial way; appreciation of literary form or original uses of language sinks below the horizon. The effect is to reverse the intense introspection that distinguished the individual within the organic post-tribal society of early modern Europe; almost six hundred years after Gutenberg set in motion the implacable deterioration of the tribe, our solitude is punctured and we are restored to the community.

But after centuries of modernity and the recent breakneck acceleration of global commercialism the tribe to which we are restored is hollow. It is a bottle from which the soul has been released, a smashed camera lying on a highland street, a never-inhabited house that was built to be admired by visitors, in perfect replication of a house that was built to be lived in. The book club, the public forum for the expression of literary culture, dissolves the private spiritual dimension of the literary experience, as the muzak playing on the elevator, the rap lyrics thumping from a car halted at the intersection, winnow away this dimension of music. The book club absolves literature of non-conformist reclusiveness by projecting it into the neon-lit glare of the mass world (the most famous book club of all, that of Oprah Winfrey, is televised). Having originated in the cultivation of private, solitary perceptions in the context of uncompromising post-feudal societies, the book has descended to the role of being a social facilitator among a random collection of people who ultimately have little in common other than the "universal" values of very late modernity (whether they belong to a women's book club or a Braille book club or a Pentecostal or Marxist book club). What they talk about when they talk about culture is a tamed package one step removed from lived experience. A telling cartoon in *The New Yorker* portrayed a group of disconsolate-looking women sitting on a couch with books in their laps; one woman says: "Well, instead of discussing the book we could discuss why none of us had time to read it." This cultural afterlife is shared by literature, music and the visual arts. We persist in reading, or listening to classical music (while washing the dishes and talking about recycling with our mother-in-law) because we possess a vestigial historical memory that these things are good for us; residual associations link these experiences to pleasure and spiritual elevation. Books and music help to sustain our identities as people enjoying the best that life can offer; by passing on these hobbies to our children we certify our offspring as members of a superior class (in a society that feigns blindness to the concept of social class). We know that being "cultured" is part of our social heritage as people who have attained a certain level of material success; we believe that children who read will advance in life, and that we must set a good example for our children. Yet our focus is on the public experience: the book club meeting, the lifestyle, the children's careers. The actual act of reading, in a sub-urban house where nearly every room offers the enticement of a screen of some sort and other people's music washes through the walls, often proves to be an ordeal.

We inhabit the afterlife of culture because the forms we use to express ourselves possess only a vestigial relationship to the real-ity that gives them birth. The artist imagined by postmodernism, who creates a simulacrum or pastiche of an older work of art, re-mains nonetheless steeped in that tradition and is struggling, however ironically, to acknowledge his or her relationship to it. In the afterlife of culture, the connection withers. Like primitives dwarfed by the ruins of a collapsed civilization whose language and history they have forgotten, we imitate without being fully conversant with the traditions that we are copying; we simplify, we dumb them down to our level. In our case, the tradition that looms over us is one predicated on the assumption of broad swathes of silence and solitude. Our public print culture had its origins in the scholasticism of the middle ages, in the silence of monasteries; even a medieval writer who was a busy public fig-ure like Geoffrey Chaucer – one of his era's most important diplo-mats – would find himself hyper-stimulated by the rapid-fire distractions of our era. It is not that reading groups, for example, have not existed in the past. Chaucer himself probably read sections of *The Canterbury Tales* aloud at the court of Richard II. One thinks of Victorian families where the novels of Sir Walter Scott or Anthony Trollope were read aloud in the evenings, or Cuban factories in the early years of the Revolution, where official "readers" edified the workers by reading the novels of Cervantes, Dickens and Pérez Galdós to them as they refined the sugar. But these events were supplements to the central culture of private reading (or, in the Cuban case, a way of stimulating interest in acquiring literacy during a period in which adult literacy classes were being promoted). Today, by contrast, we are never alone anywhere. To imagine past cultural, and particularly literary, events in a present-day context is to predict their annulment. Would Arthur Rimbaud's flight to Abyssinia have made the same dramatic impact if the guardians of the French poetic milieu he abandoned had been able to contact him by email? Messages from Verlaine picked up at the internet café in Harrar might have persuaded impetuous young Arthur to forego gun-running and inveigled him to return to France to live out his career as an ordinary working poet. Flaubert would not have been left alone at the country house in Croisset, nor Faulkner in Oxford, Mississippi, nor Chaucer in his writing retreat in Kent, long enough to gestate their masterpieces. Televised news reports of the bubbling of talent in Paris in the 1920s would have precipitated a tidal wave of tourism and inflated Paris property prices to the point where James Joyce, Gertrude Stein, F. Scott Fitzgerald, Ezra Pound and Ernest Hemingway would have had to decamp from Montparnasse. Alfred Lord Tennyson would have been distracted from getting down on paper his mourning for his friend Arthur Henry Hallam by the string of condolence calls coming in on his cellphone. The spread of satellite television into remote areas of Yorkshire would have deprived the Brontë sisters of both the time and the imaginative originality to fill notebooks with stories of passionate young women. Jack Kerouac, rather than pursuing ecstatic enlightenment, might have been content to play computer games.

The Stare Miasto was rebuilt beneath the aegis of totalitarian Stalinism, which was able to point to its reconstruction as evidence that Poles were allowed to express themselves after all. The book club, under a triumphant 21st-century global capitalism that denies the existence of ideological alternatives (a denial rendered more effective by casting its sole threatening opponent in irrational religious, rather than rational political, terms), claims to perpetuate humanistic culture. Yet, as the economics of globalization shrink the middle class, the participants in most book clubs are likely to belong to a more privileged stratum of society than in the past. It should not be surprising that they seek out books that raise prominent public issues without ruffling very many well-preened feathers. The culture of the book club novel is sentimental, "life-affirming," deflected from engagement with the world around it, and often obsessed with the therapeutic reconstruction of the individual psyche – think of Oprah Winfrey's promotion of Wally Lamb, think of book-club standards, such as *Captain Corelli's Mandolin* – or with outdated solutions to social problems that have since acquired more nefarious dimensions. The revival in the United States of Harper Lee's *To Kill a Mockingbird* (1960), a gawky period piece about white liberals who try to help oppressed African-Americans in the pre-Civil Rights era South, coincided with the media blanket on discussion of the detention and abuse of thousands of Arab and Muslim men in U.S. or U.S.-run prisons. The mere fact that Oprah Winfrey can present writers such as Tolstoy and Faulkner as though they were new underlines the problem. It is impossible not to applaud Winfrey for trying to reconnect these writers with the diaphanous non-tradition of post-literate society, but the earnestness of her efforts lays bare our sundering from an organic web of culture.

In radically ethnically diverse developed societies, such as contemporary urban and suburban Canada, the commercial imperative conspires with the desire for integration and social peace to subordinate an awareness of historical continuity and imprison us in a cultural afterlife that we dare not rupture for fear of exploding the tranquil circumstances in which we live. When I moved from a rough neighbourhood on the east side of London, England, where ethnic diversity was fractious and no intercultural interaction failed to chafe on both parties, to suburban southern Ontario, my first thought was that here, contrary to what prevailed in London, ethnic diversity promoted cultural uniformity. The Canadian model may be more desirable from a purely public order point of view, but, in its present form, it accentuates our disconnection from culture. Since we do not talk about history in order to avoid discussing the fact that your ancestors were slaves and mine were slave-owners, that your ancestors were victims of the Holocaust and mine were collaborators in it, that your parents do not drink alcohol and mine come from a culture of whiskey, the commercial ground becomes the common culture in which we meet. This is particularly evident in urban Canada, which until about 1990 was believed by many sociologists to harbour the most conservative, insular immigrant communities in the Western world – the famous "Canadian mosaic" – and which, almost overnight, has begun to pride itself on effortless interculturalism. The central trope of this new interculturalism is the shopping mall, with its commercial values, its architecture unconnected to any past or tradition, its food court serving commercially streamlined falsifications of national cuisines full of sugar and extra calories absent from these meals' prototypes, its dozens of stylized, logo-branded shops offering variety within the strict limitations imposed by production lines, the mass market and the relentless tyranny of seasonality. I once tried to buy ping pong balls in June, only to be told by Canadian Tire, Zellers, SportChek and Sport Mart, that ping pong balls were "seasonally discontinued." Reflecting the consumerist conformism that is the ideology of contemporary youth, teenage clerks regarded me as though I were a dangerous misfit for wishing to play ping-pong in the summer.

The shopping mall is an apt metaphor for the terrain on which contemporary cultural mixing occurs; but it is also, in the most literal sense, the ground where the next generation of young people meet and mingle. Canada loves to vaunt its "multiculturalism." The reality is that Canadian society is increasingly multiracial rather than multicultural: a multiracialism rendered feasible by the downplaying of cultural differences rooted in historical consciousness and their replacement by the unifying ethos of consumption. Different communities and different regions experience this phenomenon to different degrees. In some cases, the parents suffer and suppress their values to permit the children's integration; in others the parents discover that the authority they assumed would be theirs by right is not recognized by their offspring, who live their lives as their friends do. The children, defining themselves as Canadian yet knowing almost nothing about Canadian history, perceive their ancestral cultures as fashion accessories, like a ring in the nose or a blouse that exposes the navel. It becomes easy to "respect other people's cultures" when these cultures do not imply substantial differences in spiritual or moral outlook, as they did, for example, in my East London neighbourhood, where unassimilated Nigerians and Turkish Cypriots and Bangladeshis and Cockneys and Irish were so riven by incompatible visions of history that they never tried to speak to each other about anything serious.

"In her culture they light candles when they give each other their presents," the young woman in front of me in the line-up says to her friend during Christmas shopping at the mall. "Cool!" the friend replies. The two young women, who speak with identical accents, are of different racial backgrounds; the friend they are discussing is probably of a third. Their unselfconscious integration is admirable, yet whether you call the gift-giving season Christmas, Diwali, Ramadan, Hanukkah or Kwanza, it is all the same celebration of consumption, the god who unites the young women and their friends.

This scenario is not pervasive, even if it appears to be on the way to becoming dominant. Some immigrant cultures retain their traditional values; some parents bring up their children in their ancestral languages and enforce their marriages to members of their own ethnic or religious groups. Groups who feel that their efforts at integration have been rebuffed, such as young men of African ancestry who cluster together in street gangs with other young men of their own race (even if they have different cultures, the parents of one having immigrated from Trinidad, another from Somalia and a third from Ghana), suffer the paradox of being rejected on the basis of their race by a multiracial mainstream. The key to their exclusion lies in their failure – a failure that is often enforced on them by the host society – to subordinate race to consumption. In response to their impoverishment in a wealthy society, these young men funnel their consumerist ambitions through the racial conduit of the gang, whose defiant specificity – a portmanteau "Black culture" that fuses Jamaican, African-American and generic pop-culture elements – insists on the primacy of culture in a society founded on its negation. The gang, in this sense, is marginalized for being retrograde enough to assert that culture matters. In some parts of the Western world, such as London or Los Angeles, integration-through-consumption occurs more slowly than in urban Canada; due to long-established local cultural barriers, the state of fusion predicted by the indicators in the Canadian shopping mall may never be realized in these cities. The meshing of ethnic diversity and cultural uniformity, however, is likely to win out in the end (though it may continue to exclude certain groups) because it is consistent with the economic structures of contemporary globalization. The more definitively this multiracial ahistoricism establishes itself, the clearer it will become that in our ritualized diversions it is no longer culture itself that we experience, but its afterlife.

* * *

It is a long-standing, unfair tradition to criticize young people for not being as knowledgeable, respectful or well-educated as young people "in the old days." As far back as Petronius Arbiter's masochistic novel *The Satyricon*, which was written in about 62 AD, we read that: "Young men did not learn set speeches in the days when Sophocles and Euripides were searching for words in which to express themselves . . . . This windy and high-sounding bombast, a recent immigrant to Athens from Asia, touched with its breath the aspiring minds of youth, with the effect of some pestilential planet, and as soon as the tradition of the past was broken, eloquence halted and was stricken dumb." Rootless, migratory Western thought is always lamenting paradises lost. The Romans mourn their tenuous inheritance from the culture of classical Greece, the Renaissance looks back to Rome, Henry James both yearns for and fears an impossible communion with European culture, African-descended New World writers from Nicolás Guillén in Havana to Langston Hughes in Harlem look back to Africa to mourn a wholeness they can never recover, Joseph Roth's creativity is inseparable from his exile from an Austro-Hungarian Empire whose destruction by the First World War left him without a nation. The inferiority of today's young people is invariably portrayed as a consequence of the breaking of a link with history and the perversion of tradition by "foreign" influences (such as "immigrant," "Asian" rhetorical customs). In the contemporary world, immigrant parents, educated in the ancestral theology, philosophy, literature or music of their homelands, often regard their imperviously happy, sexually unfettered, know-nothing children, assimilated into an ahistorical consumerism, in this way. It is important not to lapse into the repetition of these complaints; it is equally important not to ignore real change when it occurs.

All art forms are appreciated most fully by those who understand their histories; all provide an entry into the larger panorama of human history. Literature, however, provides the best test case for our eviction into the afterlife of culture because literature and history are two strands tangled beyond separation from one another. Neither of these ways of understanding the past through the written word makes sense without a knowledge of the other; an apprenticeship in literature instills an acquaintance with history and vice versa. Literature's articulation of historical consciousness as framed in specific epochs, its reinforcement of a sense of historical chronology, its utter independence from the image, its demand for total concentration on the part of its audience and its inscription in written language, the organizational foundation of most advanced societies over the last two thousand years (the Incas of Peru were perhaps an exception), makes it the most sensitive gauge of our relationship (or lack thereof) with history.

Yet history is a concept that is increasingly difficult to explain to young people. In a sense, history has been collapsed into the category of "culture." Young people grasp the notion of a culture, understood as a set of customs observed by your friend's parents, which lend your friend a portion of her "identity": the kind of jewellery she wears, the sort of food her mother cooks, or what takes place at her family gatherings in late December. It is the next link in the chain, the fact that these customs represent part of the outcome of a particular chronological development, that has been purged by the invasion of the image. A picture, contrary to the popular dictum, is not worth ten thousand words: a picture squelches ten thousand words of tightly argued complexity with a tendentious one-dimensional visual stamp. It is striking that the computer and internet revolution has barely grazed the dominance of television. In spite of the long hours many of us now spend in front of the tiny screens where we do our work, pay our bills, check our bank accounts, reply to email, catch up on the national news, shop for books or CD's or vacations, surf for pornography, or hunt for a date for Saturday night, the average citizen now watches slightly more television than was the case a decade ago. In addition to the obvious conclusion that this mounting accumulation of hours spent in front of the two small screens means that other aspects of our lives – outdoor activity, time with family, reading, conversation – are being eroded, one must consider the consequences of the dominance of these screens (which appear destined to merge into a single screen) in shaping the conception of reality, and specifically of history, of young people raised in this environment. The most concise description of the impact of these trends that I've found appears in Manuel Castells's book *The Rise of Network Society* (1996). "The timelessness of multimedia's hypertext is a decisive feature of our culture," Castells writes, "shaping the minds and memories of children educated in the new cultural context. History is first organized according to the availability of visual material, then submitted to the computerized possibility of selecting seconds of frames to be pieced together, or split apart, according to specific discourses . . . . The whole ordering of meaningful events loses its internal, chronological rhythm . . . . Thus, *it is a culture at the same time of the eternal and the ephemeral.*"

Everything is in the present; nothing lasts. How can we empathize with Jane Austen heroines who must choose the right partner the first time around when we no longer have access to the historical chronology that generated the cultural context in which the social morality of Jane Austen novels – to say nothing of their language, wit or irony – was nurtured? The fact that today's young readers do not feel themselves to be propelled forward within the fast-moving net of historical chronology is intimately linked to the downgrading of literature to a form of mental jogging. To say this is not to fall into the "history-has-ended" fallacy popularized by Francis Fukuyama; rather, it is to recognize that one of the vital tools for understanding our human condition has been sheared away. The prevailing ideological keyword of our present is "terrorism," a word that slices acts out of the historical contexts that gave them birth, reframing them as spectacles that can be understood only as outbursts of fanatical irrationality.

I teach a course on Spanish American prose written between 1900 and 1940. This was a period of transition in South and Central America: the positivism and aping of Parisian fashions that had dominated the upper classes during the late 19th century was shaken by the Spanish-American War of 1898, in which the United States seized control of Cuba and Puerto Rico. Facing the threat of an aggressively expansionist northern neighbour, writers turned their attention inward, trying to fortify and define the nation. The cultures they discovered beyond the boundaries of the then-Europeanized capital cities of Latin America – mixed-race cowboys, hardbitten peasants, Mayas and Incas and Afro-Cubans – were converted by literature into emblems of the nation; the racist vocabulary of positivism, of necessity, receded. But it receded by contradictory fits and starts; fresh intellectual concepts and a renovated artistic language emerged slowly and awkwardly during the 1920s and 1930s. We sometimes have good discussions in my class after reading the essays, short stories and novels of Spanish American writers of this period, but at the end of each semester I discover that for a significant proportion of my students, the very notion of historical development is too foreign to be fathomed. Trained to perceive human culture as a flat, ahistorical plane, they struggle to assimilate a concept such as the evolution in mindset that occurred during the slow retreat of positivist thinking in Central and South America between 1898 and the 1920s or 1930s. The idea of historical and cultural change almost lies beyond their mental scope. Disciplined by the two screens, they see – literally – what is as always having been. The mere use of dates befuddles them; concepts such as "the 19th century" are meaningless and antithetical to their perception of reality. The closest most students can come to understanding the discussions that animate a society in flux, such as that of early 20th-century Latin America, the slow evolution of ideas and actions that constitutes history, is to state that people used to be racist and sexist, then they became normal like us. The students cannot enter into the details of historical change, and the many contradictions it enfolds, because they do not perceive historical change or feel the force of the ideological debates, most of them conducted by way of the written word, that was the accomplice in bringing it about. To a young adult born at the end of the Cold War, the ideological movement of history is an old person's fantasy. The study of the history or literature of past times serves merely to certify the rightness of the present and the irrelevance of all human activity prior to about 1990. An individual who has no memory of the Cold War (the last time that competing visions of history threw into relief the reality of different, book-based ideological interpretations of chronological change), sees the idea of lives shaped by chronological change as being as alien as quasars would have been to a medieval pope. The extinction of historical consciousness is inseparable from the weakening of the grip exerted on readers by great literature. The struggles and agonies of literary protagonists, from Odysseus or Gilgamesh or Hunahpu and Xbalanque to Hamlet to David Copperfield or Raskolnikov or Dorothea Brooke to Mrs Dalloway or Aureliano Buendía, reel us in because we perceive that we, too, are the makers of our lives within a community; we, too, are balancing the spiritual stasis of the eternal and the drive of the progressive, ever more codified and mechanical world transformed, in some microscopic measure, by our own efforts within a defined historical context. Once the historical context becomes invisible, once the souls captured in bottles are deep-discounted at the mall, the relevance of history to illumining our lives can no longer be self-evident. Delacroix's *The Raft of the Medusa*, Cézanne's paintings of Mont Saint-Victoire, Picasso's guitars and Piet Mondrian's jazzy abstracts may all strike us as "nice pictures," but we lose the capacity to understand how one leads to the next, or even, in many cases, to arrange them in the correct chronological order. Purcell, Bach, Mahler, Rachmaninov are all "classical music," now understood as an ahistorical genre category, posed against pop, rock, folk, rap, grunge, soul, head-banger, jazz or country and western. All these entities are distractions that hum in the backgrounds of our lives while we get down to the business on the screen – while talking on our cellphone, which rings incessantly. The logical next development in this chain is presaged by the *Têtes-à-claques* mini-videos that people in Quebec watch on their cellphones – and which are now being retooled for English-speaking markets – which compress narrative into two minutes of denuded imagery accompanying monologues whose brutal satire depends on the crudeness and lack of expressive range of a post-literate vernacular.

In eras when the telephone rang less often and we hoped to catch our friends at home during an unhurried moment, telephone conversations were about time ("How are you doing? It's been ages since we talked. What's going on? What's been happening in your life?"); now that many phone conversations are conducted in public, an increasing number of them are about space ("Where are you? I'm on the bus! I'm in the mall! Where do you want to meet?"). In this way, too, a reflective dimension has been stripped away, reducing our telephone exchanges to their instrumentalist aspect. We make arrangements by phone, but are less likely than in the past to get down to intimacies: we are too busy communicating to share our impressions of our passage through life.

Since reading demands total concentration, and prose narrative is inseparable from history, the evaporation of large blocks of silence in our lives, combined with the terminal thinning of an organic conception of history, debilitates literature more seriously than other art forms. Literature's plight becomes the canary in the mine for future cultural unravelling. It is not, at the risk of falling into Petronius-like crankiness, that people born into the world dominated by the image are illiterate. In spite of the obscene inequalities that rack our divided planet, there have never been so many literate people on earth as there are at present. Yet, more and more often, literature fails to sink its claws into these literate young people's spirits. One man told me of his exasperation with his teenage son, who was intelligent and literate but did not read books. The son preferred to play computer games, watch television and surf the internet. One summer, when the son was sixteen or seventeen, the father connived to arrange a family vacation at a cottage in the woods that had no television or computer or internet connection. He stocked the son's room at the cottage with classic novels dealing with young men and coming-of-age themes. After a few days of swimming, canoeing and getting bored in the evenings, the son took one of the novels off the shelf and began to read it. The father rejoiced. His son was reading great literature! Unaccustomed to reading novels, the son read slowly. At the end of the week, when the family returned to the city, the son still had a hundred pages of the novel left to read. He read avidly in the back seat of the car all the way home. As soon as the car pulled into the driveway, the son, who was approaching the novel's climax, sat down at his computer and did not open the book again.

Perhaps his actions are not surprising. Studies show that children who do not become self-motivated readers by the age of twelve or thirteen are unlikely to develop the habit in later life. Yet the young man's approach is emblematic of the outlook that prevails during the afterlife of culture: the technical capacity to read coexists with an indifference to literature (or painting, or older musical forms) as a means of understanding contemporary life, of reconciling our spiritual and instrumental urges. Literature fails to captivate most young readers; they can admire it in an impersonal and half-comprehending way, as I may admire a medieval Japanese temple, but it does not get under their skin. Much of the culture that surrounds us is homeless; like souls released from bottles, it forges on into empty air, persisting in weaving elaborate designs beyond the exhaustion of the context that lent those designs meaning.

2.

How do we experience culture once we have moved beyond the tussle between the spiritual and the mechanical that made cultural expression vital to us? What is the form of the bottle emptied of the soul, the Mam man who no longer knows who he is, the stucco 18th-century house that was built in 1950? Literature offers the surest guide. To understand the place and function of literature in the contemporary world one must return to that largest of reading venues, the book club.

In August 2005 a seven-month survey of forty-eight of the estimated 10,000 book clubs in the United Kingdom released an exhaustive list of what, in the view of the more than five hundred members of these forty-eight book clubs, were the world's fifteen greatest novels. They were: *The Handmaid's Tale* (1985) by Margaret Atwood; *Captain Corelli's Mandolin* (1994) by Louis de Bernières; *The Name of the Rose* (1980) by Umberto Eco; *Birdsong* (1993) by Sebastian Faulks; *The French Lieutenant's Woman* (1969) by John Fowles; *Memoirs of a Geisha* (1997) by Arthur Golden; *The Curious Incident of the Dog in the Night-Time* (2003) by Mark Haddon; *Catch-22* (1961) by Joseph Heller; *Brave New World* (1932) by Aldous Huxley; *To Kill a Mockingbird* (1960) by Harper Lee; *Atonement* (2001) by Ian McEwan; *The Time Traveller's Wife* (2003) by Audrey Niffenegger; *Star of the Sea* (2003) by Joseph O'Connor; *All Quiet on the Western Front* (1929) by Erich Maria Remarque; and *One Day in the Life of Ivan Denisovich* (1962) by Aleksandr Solzhenistyn. Only three were written in languages other than English; nine of the fifteen were published since 1980. Four of the novels – those by Remarque, Solzhenitsyn, Huxley and Heller – would be strong contenders for inclusion in a more literary assessment of classic fiction, although Fowles, Eco and possibly Atwood might count as also-rans. The inclusion of Faulks and O'Connor, who are not well known in North America, betrays the list's U.K. provenance, but what is more surprising is the emerging uniformity of taste: this list would have differed little had the book clubs surveyed been located in Winnipeg or Tucson or Melbourne or Cape Town, or even in some cities outside the English-speaking world (book clubs, friends tell me, are becoming all the rage in Germany and France). Nor did these readers choose contemporary works out of base ignorance of the literary fiction of past decades: during the evaluation process the forty-eight reading groups read and discussed novels by writers such as Franz Kafka, William Faulkner and Virginia Woolf. They simply reached the conclusion that Louis de Bernières and Arthur Golden were better writers.

The crucial point is less how recent the majority of the novels' dates of publication are than the ways in which the contemporary novels on the list arrogate to themselves the privilege of commenting on a past which they view from a vantage point that enables them at once to romanticize and denigrate it. The underlying message of these books is that having severed ourselves from the history that bred us, we may declare our autonomy from preceding epochs of human life and our moral superiority to them. History ceases to be what shaped us and becomes simply the raw material for new book-shaped consumer products. We package it up in the forms of popular entertainment in order to dispense with it. Some of the novels even articulate an explicitly anti-innovative, anti-chronological critical ideology; nearly all abdicate the realist novel's responsibility to engage with the present. I'd like to trace how this works in one of the novels on the list, Ian McEwan's *Atonement*.

McEwan, Julian Barnes, Martin Amis and Graham Swift, all born in the late 1940s, established themselves at an early age as the dominant white male British novelists of their generation. Of the four, McEwan had the least privileged background; in the long run he has become the most commercially successful. The son of a Scottish sergeant-major, McEwan was born on the Aldershot military base in the south of England in 1948. While Barnes and Amis were studying at Oxford, and Swift at Cambridge, McEwan attended the University of Sussex, a "redbrick university" that was then the home of Great Britain's most politically radical English Department. He went on to the University of East Anglia, known in British academic circles as "the University of Easy Access" due to its less-than-rigorous entrance requirements. McEwan earned the M.A. in "Modern Fiction," an experimental program that combined literary studies with creative writing workshops, becoming in the estimation of some the first person in Great Britain to earn a Master's degree in Creative Writing. In his twenties, McEwan spent the money he earned from his first published short stories to buy a hippie bus and make a psychedelic overland pilgrimage to Afghanistan. His first two short story collections, *First Love, Last Rites* (1975) and *In Between the Sheets* (1978) (the latter title is a quote from a Rolling Stones song) combined a counter-culture ethos of soft drugs and sexual freedom with gothic perversity – pickled penises bought at auctions, two women acting out the ritual castration of a philanderer – of a sort that both revelled in sexuality and brandished it as a weapon against the patriarchal underpinnings of British society. McEwan was soon adopted as "a voice of his generation": the generation that was twenty years old in 1968, which was arguably the last middle-class generation in the English-speaking world to seek its self-definition through literature. His declared "feminist male" outlook, which became more pronounced during the 1980s – Angela Carter once hailed McEwan as "a born-again feminist" – secured his base among the crucial market of well-educated younger women readers. (McEwan, who read Ian Watt's *The Rise of the Novel* as a student, likes to express his awareness that the novel is a form sustained by women who read.)

Like many other younger British writers, McEwan was radicalized by Thatcherism. He wrote an anti-nuclear libretto and a film script that dramatized the Suez Crisis of 1956 in order to reflect on the Falklands War of 1982. *The Child in Time* (1987), in which McEwan's growing interest in feminism and physics were played out against the search for a way to move from the sexual freedom of the 1960s and 1970s to a responsible model of parenting that would obviate the restrictive gender-roles of the traditional British family, struck a chord across the Atlantic, providing McEwan with his first major international success. But *The Child in Time* also displayed some of McEwan's weaknesses. Like his later *Enduring Love* (1997), *The Child in Time* proceeds from a dazzling opening to an uncertain development and a forced, over-explained resolution. The scientific and political themes are imperfectly integrated into a personal story about a faltering marriage. The novel portrays the public domain as hateful yet inescapable; in the "public" portion of the novel's action a Margaret Thatcher-like figure appears as a character in an asexual guise, counterpointed against the feminist wish-fulfillment figure of a beautiful, grey-haired middle-aged woman physicist.

The political forces at work during the death throes of the
Cold War exerted a powerful influence on McEwan in both his
public stances and his fiction. McEwan was an early supporter of
Charter 88. Modelled on the Czech dissident movement Charter
77, this initiative of Harold Pinter and Lady Antonia Fraser
equated Thatcherism with totalitarianism and called for a written
British constitution that would limit the Prime Minister's power.
Like other left-wing British intellectuals during the late Thatcher
and early John Major years, McEwan sought an outlet from the
suffocation of Britain's revived class system in engagement with
Europe. Both *The Innocent* (1990), a thriller that moves into John le
Carré territory, but with a distinctive dose of McEwan gore – the
hero and heroine are obliged to chop a human body into pieces in
order to smuggle it out of a Berlin apartment – and *Black Dogs*
(1992), were set in Europe. The latter novel, which strings together a series of critical moments in recent European history, asserts the merging of British history with that of the continent, in a
direct challenge to Thatcherite declarations of British hostility to
Europe based on the primordial importance lent the "special relationship" with the United States. The mythology of the black
dogs that attend moments of historical disaster (a symbol that
Goethe introduced into *Faust* as one of the forms taken by the
devil) becomes a pan-European myth in which Great Britain
shares. Yet, as an Englishman deeply in tune with the evolving
mood of the English-speaking world, McEwan did not adhere
naturally to a European conception of historical chronology. *Black
Dogs* is one of McEwan's most ambitious and least commercial
novels; ultimately, though, its central thesis feels forced. No
resonant vision capable of counteracting Thatcherite trans-
Atlanticism coheres from the novel's disparate scenes. A similar
awkwardness surfaces in the final sentence of *The Innocent* where
the protagonist, whose life underwent a crucial transformation
in the Berlin of the 1950s, imagines returning to the city in 1987
with the woman he loved in his youth to "take a good long look
at the Wall together, before it was all torn down." In 1987 no one

expected the Berlin Wall to be torn down at any point in the fore-
seeable future. The sentence betrays the fusion of McEwan's English imperviousness to historical chronology with his populist
instincts, which require him to wrench historical perceptions into
alignment with the present-day outlook of his audience. This tendency, a minor irritant in McEwan's earlier work, was destined to
swell into one of the defining traits of his fiction as the memory of
the Cold War, and the allegiances it inspired, passed out of the
spotlight.

Having been overlooked by the Booker Prize shortlist for
Enduring Love, another novel that begins with a throat-grabbing
scenario (in this case a ballooning accident in the countryside near
Oxford) only to fall back onto a predictable psychological case-
study as the source of its resolution, McEwan won the Booker for
the short novel *Amsterdam* (1998). Almost certainly the weakest of
his novels, *Amsterdam* is schematic, heartless and emotionally
superficial from beginning to end. The only explanation for
McEwan's crowning for this trivial piece of work is that the heated
media coverage of his failure to appear on the previous year's
shortlist made the next batch of jurors so wary or contrite that they
felt compelled to compensate for their predecessors' lack of acu-
men. The Booker Prize threw into relief the tensions between
McEwan's literary ambitions and his populist instincts. The persis-
tent murmuring that *Amsterdam* was not a very good book appears
to have fuelled McEwan's ambition to write a novel that would be
longer, more complex and fit less obviously into the gothic or
thriller category; a book that would justify his bracketing with literary writers such as Barnes, Swift, Amis, Salman Rushdie and
Kazuo Ishiguro. The result, rather than an undeniable literary success such as Barnes's *A History of the World in 10½ Chapters*, or
Swift's *Waterland* or *Last Orders*, or Amis's *Money*, or Rushdie's
Midnight's Children or Ishiguro's *The Unconsoled*, was *Atonement*, a
book club "classic."

Atonement alludes to classics of the English novel, such as Jane
Austen's *Northanger Abbey* (itself a pastiche of tendencies in 18th-

century fiction), from which it contains a lengthy epigraph, and
L.P. Hartley's *The Go-Between* (1953), from which McEwan bor-
rows the central plot device of an adolescent carrying letters
between illicit lovers at a big country house. Yet *Atonement* fails to
transmit the gristle of history in the way a good novel does.
McEwan wrestles with the 1935 setting of the novel's opening section. (The blurb on the paperback erroneously gives the date of the
action as 1934.) The reader can hear the resonant opening sentence
of *The Go-Between* – "The past is a foreign country: they do things
differently there" – murmuring in his ears as he writes. The chronological disjuncture between the customs of the present and
those of the past, the consciousness of how the present continues to
be warped by past traumas, however, which Hartley takes such
care to establish (his novel, set in 1900, is narrated from the perspective of the early 1950s), is precisely what McEwan struggles to
capture. McEwan first exaggerates the social restrictions of 1935,
then opts for a soft slide into the middlebrow haze of the war-
time-romance-that-lives-forever. The first three sections are narrated in the third person; the fourth section, set in 1999, consists of
a first-person confession by Briony Tallis, the adolescent literary
prodigy of the opening section, that she, now an aging novelist of
substantial reputation, is the narrator. The novel is the story of her
atonement. But for what is she atoning?

On a simple plot level it is the offence of having precipitated a
disaster in the lives of her older sister, Cecilia, and her lover,
Robbie Turner, a young man of working class background whose
Cambridge education has been paid for by Briony and Cecilia's
father. During the hottest day of 1935 – the motif of rising tempera-
tures foreshadowing cresting social tensions is borrowed from *The
Go-Between* – Robbie writes a jesting note to Cecilia, who in spite of
being his Cambridge classmate remains, as his social superior, an
inappropriate object of his affections. "The truth is," Robbie writes,
"I feel rather light-headed and foolish in your presence, Cee, and I
don't think I can blame the heat! Will you forgive me?" This typically elliptical British statement of affection does not make it into

the envelope. By mistake, in an improbability that lumbers the novel with an air of formula fiction contrivance, Robbie puts the first draft of his note into the envelope that he hands Briony. Expressing the earthy working-class nature that his refined education has suppressed, this draft says, "In my dreams I kiss your cunt, your sweet wet cunt." Robbie is horrified when he discovers what he has done, but the note unfreezes the frigid Cecilia, leading to a bout of raucous stand-up lovemaking against the bookshelves of the library, the concluding seconds of which Briony witnesses, possibly prompting *coitus interruptus*. By fucking the bookcases with impunity, Robbie wreaks symbolic retribution for the fate of Leonard Bast, the lower-class insurance clerk who makes futile efforts to become cultured in E.M. Forster's novel *Howards End* (1908). Poor Leonard dies when he makes a grab for a bookcase and pulls it down on top of himself. By contrast, Robbie and Cecilia's coupling is an act of triumphant defiance against the historical prohibitions on sex between people of different social classes: prohibitions incarnated in the heritage represented by leather-bound books. The literary-historical heritage itself, in McEwan's portrayal, is subordinated to the whim of the aggressive individual. History becomes a succession of clichés to be manipulated from the knowing-but-sentimental vantage point of the present.

Unlike the characters of *The Go-Between*, where an interclass love affair continues to impact the lovers' descendants two generations later, the people we meet in *Atonement* are creatures of an author who, feeling detached from history, may caricature it. The class boundaries in *Atonement* are too rigid. It is not that Britain was not, and does not in some quarters remain, a society of straightjacketed social insularity. The problem is that McEwan has overlooked the material that would have intrigued a contemporary chronicler of the society of 1935: the contradictions, the chinks in the armour of the class system, the weird exceptions that prevail in spite of apparently immutable laws. A glimpse of this is evident in *The Go-Between* where the narrator, thirteen-year-old Leo, the son of a déclassée middle-class single mother, manages to feign an air of upper-class self-assurance that earns him an invitation to spend the summer at the grand country estate of the Maudsley family. Robbie Turner in *Atonement* is a similar sort of in-between – or "go-between" – figure who disrupts class categories. Such figures begin seeping into the English novel at least as far back as the appearance of Jewish characters in late Victorian works such as Anthony Trollope's *The Way We Live Now*, Charles Dickens's *Our Mutual Friend* and George Eliot's *Daniel Deronda*. These characters are dramatically interesting precisely because they stretch the British class system into unexpected shapes. By contrast, McEwan, writing from the secure redoubt of culture's afterlife, takes the stereotypes as unbreakable moulds. When a second letter is discovered, a semi-literate letter in which two little boys who are being harboured at the estate while their parents divorce announce that they have decided to run away, the ensuing search scatters the characters through the twilit parkland. Briony's precocious adolescent cousin is sexually molested by a half-seen assailant, and Robbie is blamed. The class system instantly condemns him because of his humble origins (even though the attacker's true identity will be evident to most readers).

The first part of the novel closes, with emotive simplicity, with Robbie's working-class mother screaming, "Liars! Liars! Liars!" at the Humber car in which Robbie is being taken away by the police. A willful flattening of the complexity of the past animates this scene. It is so much easier, when we are enmeshed in a society committed to forgetting its history, to see those who preceded us in one-dimensional terms. Grace Turner's words make us feel the hypocrisy of the system that sends Robbie to prison with an emotional immediacy that is one of the keys to McEwan's talent and his success. In fact, though, even in 1935, the case would have been far from open and shut. Robbie may be the son of a widowed cleaning woman, but he has just earned a First at Cambridge, an achievement that elevates him to the pinnacle of British society. The accusations against him would have carried more weight than if they

had been levelled against the man who turns out to be the real culprit (whose class status is unimpeachably more elevated than that
of Robbie); even so, the case would have been complicated. As
someone marked to join the next generation of the British elite,
Robbie would have been able to enlist a prominent barrister to
defend him; testaments to his fine character from his Cambridge
tutors and classmates would have made most judges reluctant to
sentence him. The prosecution case, resting on the testimony of
two adolescent girls (Briony is a partial witness to the assault),
would have been weakened by the average British judge's mis-
trust of the "flightiness" of young girls. McEwan, the one-time
"born-again feminist," stresses the class aspect of Robbie's
dilemma at the expense of his memory that, if the society of 1935
was resolutely class-bound, it was also irredeemably patriarchal
and sexist. Beneath the emotional vein milking our sympathy for
Robbie, the novel appeals to the surreptitious superiority that
most of McEwan's readers, as people firmly situated in the upper-
middle-class, feel towards a striving scholarship boy. The letter
Robbie sends to Cecilia by mistake, with its use of the word "cunt,"
alerts us that his educational attainments have not erased the
"crude" working-class elements in his make-up; an echo sounds of
the gamekeeper Mellors in D.H. Lawrence's Lady Chatterley's Lover
(1928), a book which, after realizing his mistake, Robbie remembers having read. Mellors also has sex with a woman above his
social station, and exhibits a similar fondness for "cunt." As readers, we feel a half-buried strain of condescension towards Robbie
even as we rage against the (implausible) injustice that is done to
him.

Why has McEwan shifted the focus of his criticism from gen-
der and big-picture politics to social class? And what has led him
to willfully oversimplify a class system whose knotted intricacies
most British people imbibe at birth? Where L.P. Hartley wrestles
with the strangeness of the "foreign country" that is the past at the
same time that he portrays the tangible legacies of that past in the
present, McEwan rewrites Hartley's novel for the post-1990 era by

flattening the past into a place where people were just like us except that they were a little dim in being sexist/ racist/ classist – take your pick; a place whose only connection with now is that we must get over it and consign it to oblivion. The *difference* of the past, the hard fact of the evolution of outlooks and experiences over time, the fact that our predecessors were equal to us in intellect but that their perceptions were geared to different settings than ours, becomes the reality that cannot be acknowledged, the contradiction that contains the potential to make the frail yet alluring edifice of our consumerist eternal present come tumbling down. It is not surprising that much of our recent popular art, in both film and fiction, purports to depict "universal values" and "the eternal human spirit": code words for denying the specificity of cultures that preceded ours and those that coexist imperfectly with globalized consumerism. But this does not explain why McEwan, a long-time progressive with a demonstrated interest in the development of British society, would move towards this sort of position. The key to the transformation of McEwan's outlook, I suspect, lies in his position in the literary world. The love affair of Robbie and Cecilia, which in the novel's second and third parts spreads out across readable but all-too-familiar scenes evoking Second World War battlefields and London during the Blitz, may be the novel's romantic, narrative core; but the connective tissue that gives the book its shape clings to the development of the young writer Briony.

The novel opens with a long, awkward sentence describing the mock-artistic agonies with which thirteen-year-old Briony composes her seven-page play, *The Trials of Arabella*. The play has a moral and a rhyming prologue, an evil count, a virtuous prince disguised as an altruistic doctor, a bout of symbolic disease and concludes with a happy marriage. Briony's models, in other words, come from late Victorian or Edwardian popular art. The cousins she recruits to act in the play treat it with indifference; in the end Briony abandons the rehearsals and the play is not performed. Her frustration with the actors' appropriation of her script, their insistence on inserting their own meanings into it, causes her to retreat to prose. But what sort of prose? Her initial impulse to abandon drama for fiction springs from the appeal of more direct communication with an audience: "Reading a sentence and understanding it were the same thing . . . . There was no gap during which the symbols were unravelled." This blockish refutation of the modernist play of perspectives (and of most literary theory) lays the groundwork for a stout defence of the precepts of popular fiction.

No sooner does Briony formulate this aesthetic principle than it is challenged by events outside her window. Her sister Cecilia strips to her underclothes in front of Robbie Turner, who has just taken her hand, and dives into the fountain in the park. Briony tries to place these events within the context of the tropes of Edwardian melodrama, where they do not fit: "The sequence was illogical – the drowning scene, followed by a rescue, should have preceded the marriage proposal. Such was Briony's last thought before she accepted that she did not understand and must simply watch." Briony does not understand this scene because she has missed a crucial event: Robbie and Cecilia have broken a vase, two sections of which have fallen into the pond; Cecilia dives in to retrieve the lost shards. From this scene, Briony derives the morality that will propel her literary career: the need to "grasp the simple truth that other people are as real as you. And only in a story could you enter into these different minds and show how they had an equal value. That was the only moral a story need have."

Briony has discovered the pseudo-egalitarian ethos of "universal values," which purports to underlie mass consumerism, sixty years prior to its heyday. Yet her purchase on this point of view is tenuous and remains to be consolidated. McEwan sets up middlebrow populism as a philosophy that must be earned through hard experience, and to which one cannot simply accede. A jarring interruption in this smoothly narrated scene vaults the reader ahead to the late 1990s:

Six decades later she would describe how at the age of thirteen she had written her way through a whole history of literature, beginning with stories derived from the European
tradition of folk tales, through drama with simple moral in-
tent, to arrive at an impartial psychological realism which she
had discovered for herself, one special morning during a heat
wave in 1935. She would be well aware of the extent of her
self-mythologising, and she gave her account a self-mocking,
or mock-heroic tone. Her fiction was known for its amorality,
and like all authors pressed by a repeated question, she felt
obliged to produce a story line, a plot of her development
that contained the moment when she became recognisably
herself . . . . She also knew that whatever actually happened
drew its significance from her published work and would not
have been remembered without it.

Eschewing the European tradition (an allusion to McEwan's
own experiments with European themes in *The Innocent* and *Black
Dogs*), and having abandoned her moralizing play, Briony adheres to a psychological realism "known for its amorality," a description that fits some of McEwan's own work, such as the
non-judgemental account of brother-sister incest in *The Cement
Garden* (1978), or the sexual transformations of the characters in
The Comfort of Strangers (1981), or the downbeat description of the
lovers slicing up the corpse in *The Innocent*. In Briony, McEwan
forges for himself a forerunner and model: a writer a generation
older than he, and better yet a woman, who certifies the rightness
of his populist aesthetic choices, sealing the superiority of a brand
of "psychological realism" that is essentially crowd-pleasing and
populist. The literary modes that McEwan has espoused throughout his career represent the culmination of Briony's hard-won
development: the arc of her creative life concludes with the realization that the Ian McEwan aesthetic is the right one. The fictions
generated by this aesthetic will erase history – "whatever actually
happened" – and replace it with the overmastering narrative of

popular fiction. The penultimate section of *Atonement* concludes with the notation "BT/ London 1999." It is Briony who has narrated the story of Cecilia and Robbie's love affair; this romantic tale exemplifies the amoral and ahistorical "psychological realism" (for which, in McEwan's rendering of this term, read: "middlebrow fiction") that enshrines the literary ideals of Briony and her creator. At the same time, the flash-forward alerts the reader that the novel is also the bearer of "a story line, a plot of her development that contained the moment when she became recognisably herself." This tale of the book club novel's will-to-power, however, is entitled *Atonement*. Again one must ask: atonement for what?

In the novel-behind-the-novel, the place where McEwan's deepest concerns reside, Briony fails to remain true to her insight. It is tempting to use the word "epiphany" to describe the revelation she experiences while looking out over the garden. This word, popularized by James Joyce to describe the aesthetic development of the short stories in *Dubliners* (1914) and intimately associated with literary modernism, encapsulates her moment of truth.

Briony knows that "psychological realism," cool, impartial observation, is the path to truth: "she accepted that she did not understand and must simply watch." Yet in the hours that follow, she deviates from this path. In two subsequent scenes, Briony allows her subjectivity to slant her interpretations of events. The first scene occurs when she enters the library when Cecilia and Robbie are copulating against the bookshelf. Briony's first glimpse of the intertwined bodies gives her the impression that Robbie is attacking Cecilia.

> He had pushed his body against hers, pushing her dress right up above her knee and had trapped her where the shelves met at right angles. His left hand was behind her neck, gripping her hair, and with his right he held her forearm which was raised in protest, or self-defence.

He looked so huge and wild, and Cecilia with her bare
shoulders and thin arms so frail that Briony had no idea what
she could achieve as she started to go towards them . . . .
Robbie moved in such a way that her view of her sister was
completely obscured.

Beyond the obvious point that thirteen-year-old Briony's sexual innocence leads her to misinterpret the scene before her, lies
her first deviation from the populist aesthetic of "simply watching" when one cannot understand. Briony concludes that her sister
needs to be rescued even though her view of her "was completely
obscured." As she makes her way into the library, Cecilia flees and
Robbie hastily straightens his trousers. Having diverged from the
amoral psychological realism afforded her by close observation,
she compounds her error later in the evening, when she comes
upon her cousin Lola in the park just as Lola's sexual aggressor is
fleeing. In the dim play of trees, shrubbery, distant lights from the
manor house and muted blue underwater lighting installed in the
fountain, Briony retreats into a realm of fluid, subjective perception. Aware of movements in the dark, she believes she has
encountered the two boys who have run away.

She walked directly towards the temple, and had gone seven
or eight steps, and was about to call out the names of the
twins, when the bush that lay directly in her path – the one
she thought should be closer to the shore – began to break up
in front of her, or double itself, or waver, and then fork. It was
changing its shape in a complicated way, thinning at the base
as a vertical column rose five or six feet. She would have
stopped immediately had she not still been so completely
bound to the notion that this was a bush, and that she was
witnessing some trick of darkness and perspective. Another
second or two, another couple of steps, and she saw that this
was not so. Then she stopped. The vertical mass was a figure,
a person who was now backing away from her and begin-

ning to fade into the darker background of the trees. The remaining darker patch on the ground was also a person, changing shape again as it sat up and called her name.

Succumbing to a modernist stream-of-consciousness, Briony gets it wrong. When Lola sits up and calls her name, Briony does not verify the facts. She imposes her subjective interpretation, born of the scene she has witnessed in the library, on events in the park. Having fallen into the thrall of the internal logic of a string of subjective images that dictate that Robbie is a "maniac," she projects her private vision onto public circumstances, ascertaining from Lola merely that her attacker was "him" before asserting with conviction that, "I saw him. I *saw* him." Her determined repetition of this certitude to the police dooms Robbie. The logic that leads Briony to moral disaster is the modernist logic of unity forged by a succession of internally resonant images. Briony must spend the rest of her life atoning for having perceived reality as modernist writers perceive it. The modernist subjectivity that overwhelms her in the park becomes an explicit allegiance. Working as a nurse during the Blitz, she comes to believe that: "The novel of the future would be unlike anything in the past. She had read Virginia Woolf's *The Waves* three times and thought that a great transformation was being worked in human nature itself, and that only fiction, a new kind of fiction, could capture the essence of the change." When she submits a Woolfish reworking of the moment when Robbie and Cecilia break the vase, under the title *Two Figures by a Fountain,* to Cyril Connolly's literary magazine *Horizon*, her manuscript, rescued from the slush pile by Elizabeth Bowen, prompts a lengthy reply from Connolly himself. In the letter Connolly offers advice that will prove crucial to Briony in rewriting her modernist novel, based on the premise that "only fiction, a new kind of fiction could capture the essence of the change," into a piece of simple popular storytelling: *Atonement*, the novel we hold in our hands. Connolly works from notes prepared by Bowen, a writer whose career in some ways presages that of Briony. Beginning as a late modernist writer whose lush prose, influenced by Virginia Woolf and Henry James, is on its most intimidating display in *The Death of the Heart* (1938), Bowen veered towards what might be described as an amoral psychological realism – albeit still decked out in a rather ornate style – in her best-known later novel, *The Heat of the Day* (1949), which is about a woman in wartime London who falls in love with an eminently decent man who turns out to be a Nazi spy. (The man Bowen fell in love with in wartime London was the Canadian diplomat Charles Ritchie.) Under Bowen's influence, Connolly steers Briony away from the "crystalline present moment" towards a more democratic appeal: "Your most sophisticated readers might be well up on the latest Bergsonian theories of consciousness, but I'm sure they retain a childlike desire to be told a story, to be held in suspense, to know what happens." The more modest novel that emerges from Briony's rewriting does not assert the primacy of fiction in understanding the world; it is, rather, a piece of popular entertainment that advances a claim for the superior utility of popular entertainment and dismisses pretensions to higher truth, whether artistic or psychological. It is clear that Briony has incorporated some of Connolly's suggestions into the final version of the novel. Connolly writes: "If this girl has so fully misunderstood or been so wholly baffled by the strange little scene that has unfolded before her, how might it affect the lives of the two adults? Might she come between them in some disastrous fashion? . . . . Might the young people come to use her as a messenger?" What we are reading, then, is not what "really" happened; it is an arrangement of events calculated to satisfy our "childlike desire to be told a story."

McEwan focuses on social class in order to pursue a literary vendetta. Working-class Robbie is imprisoned by evil literary modernism, his life ruined by the stream-of-conscious technique. Briony's atonement for having abused her upper-class position to condemn him and her atonement for interpreting reality through modernist subjectivity are the same process. In the final pages of

Atonement the reader learns that Briony has spent her entire life rewriting *Two Figures by a Fountain*: "The earliest version, January 1940, the latest March 1999 . . . . I've regarded it as my duty to disguise nothing . . . . I put it all there as a matter of historical record . . . . What are novelists for? Go just as far as is necessary, set up camp inches beyond the reach, the fingertips of the law." She finally confesses that Robbie and Cecilia's wartime romance is pure invention. Both protagonists died during the war, without having consummated their love. No shred of a pretence to verisimilitude, or the capturing of fleeting individual perceptions, remains; there is only "a story." The refutation of "the crystalline moment" is complete; the shining modernist image has been lanced like a boil. And in McEwan's eyes, modernism is a boil.

Atonement displays the powerful influence exercised on McEwan by John Carey's utilitarian polemic *The Intellectuals and the Masses* (1992). Carey, like McEwan a man from a modest social background, rose to become Merton Professor of English at Oxford. He chaired the Booker Prize jury in 2003, chaired the first Booker International Prize jury in 2005, and was for many years the lead book reviewer for *The Sunday Times* of London. Carey has praised McEwan's work lavishly, beginning with *The Child in Time*. During the 1990s both men lived in Oxford, McEwan in North Oxford, Carey in nearby Headington: two accomplished literary outsiders in a world of privilege into which neither of them had been born. From the vantage point of North Oxford's secluded homes, it is not always easy to distinguish between artistic aspiration and social pretension. As the narrator of *Enduring Love* recounts during a visit to a house in the district: "I knew this kind of north Oxford interior . . . This was the austerity once thought appropriate to the intellectual life, unsensually aligned to the soul of English pragmatism, unfussy, honed to the essential, to the collegiate world beyond the shops."

The Intellectuals and the Masses recruits "the soul of English pragmatism" into a rebellion against the grand exteriors of large houses and the class system they celebrate. Carey proposes that literary modernism was a form of social snobbery designed to create a literature that would reinforce class privileges by remaining incomprehensible to the working class. The core of Carey's argument is that:

> The intellectuals could not, of course, actually prevent the masses from attaining literacy. But they could prevent them from reading literature by making it too difficult for them to understand – and this is what they did. The early twentieth century saw a determined effort, on the part of the European intelligentsia, to exclude the masses from culture. In England this movement has become known as modernism . . . . Realism of the sort that it was assumed the masses appreciated was abandoned. So was logical coherence. Irrationality and obscurity were cultivated.

Carey's argument works well when he applies it to arrant social snobs such as Virginia Woolf and E.M. Forster – *Atonement*'s two most obvious targets – and some of their associates, such as T.S. Eliot. But his treatment of working class modernist writers such as D.H. Lawrence and James Joyce (denounced by Virginia Woolf as "a self-taught working man, and we all know how distressing they are, how egotistic, insistent, raw, striking and ultimately nauseating") is not convincing. Carey concedes that in Leopold Bloom Joyce has shown us more about an ordinary man's daily life than has ever been dramatized before, but he still maintains that Joyce was a snob for having used modernist techniques to achieve this. His treatment of D.H. Lawrence ignores the class tensions imbuing Lawrence's work, concentrating on an alleged philosophical debt to Friedrich Nietzsche to the exclusion of almost all other aspects of Lawrence's fiction. Carey does not even mention modernism's vital legacy: the fact that, exported to the margins of the West, it supplied a technical repertoire and a vocabulary that enabled writers from Latin America, India and Africa to breathe creative life into the national identities suppressed by the colonialism that provided the comfortable economic circumstances in which the European intelligentsia (and even the European working class) thrived. Carey's book fails to address Joyce as the remaker of trampled Irish nationhood and the transformer of modernism into the mythologizing apparatus of marginalized cultural identities; it does not contain a single reference to William Faulkner, whose novels popularized modernism among Third World intellectuals. Without the modernism of Joyce and Faulkner, there could be no Gabriel García Márquez, João Guimarães Rosa, Salman Rushdie, Amitav Ghosh, Miguel Ángel Asturias, Mario Vargas Llosa, Carlos Fuentes, Juan Carlos Onetti, Patrick Chamoiseau, Ben Okri, Mia Couto or dozens of others. Both Carey and McEwan elide the fact that in societies that are on the margins, rather than at the centre, of global power dynamics, modernism and its various national descendants provide not a flight from engagement, but the tools for the artistic resuscitation of local realities crushed by colonialism. Stream-of-consciousness revives animist cultures; magic realism, the inheritor of the "crystalline moment," mythologizes oral storytelling; the subjective play of points-of-view enables the retelling of history from the perspective of those who were defeated by the conquering narrative of European colonialism. The English pragmatism that purports to defend Europe's masses, when evoked in the post-1990 context, can fuel only a reactionary suppression of the realities of poorer and weaker continents. In attempting to write a longer, more ambitious, deeper novel, McEwan produces a refutation of modernism that morphs into a justification for a brand of popular fiction that severs all tangible links with the past, depicting history in formulaic ways in order to gut its influence on the eternal present and repel fiction's aspirations to high art. McEwan's demolition of innovation includes a disdain for the novel's vitality on the margins of the West. It is hardly surprising that when McEwan returns to the English present, in *Saturday* (2005), he does so from a conservative point of view. Like Mrs. Thatcher, the McEwan of *Saturday* subscribes to the view that the quest for social justice is useless and that, as Thatcher claimed, "society does not exist." *Saturday* depicts human behaviour as the exclusive product of genetic inheritance and individual physiology: "it's down to invisible folds and kinks of character, written in code, at the level of molecules . . . No amount of social justice will cure or disperse this enfeebled army haunting the public places of every town." Though Henry Perowne, the surgeon who is the protagonist of *Saturday*, is described as "reductive" for harbouring these beliefs about homeless people, the adjective sticks out from the faultless surface of McEwan's prose. It is difficult not to see this "reductive" as a self-defensive shield raised by the author after following his character, whose stern complacency is undisturbed by narrative irony, to the logical conclusions of views which, the rest of the novel suggests, Perowne and McEwan share. The novel provides no sustainable opposing view to that of the protagonist. Perowne, turning his back on the anti-war protesters who fill the streets of London on Saturday February 15, 2003, symbolizes McEwan's estrangement from the social concerns that once animated his fiction. (At one point Perowne ridicules a scene from *The Child in Time*.) The anti-war voice in the novel, Perowne's daughter Daisy, is furnished with weak versions of the anti-war arguments that are inferior to Perowne's pro-war disquisitions (the novel does not, for example, mention the issue of national sovereignty). As if in punishment for her views, Daisy undergoes a peculiar sexual humiliation during the novel's climax. Having thrashed modernism in the name of the masses in *Atonement*, in *Saturday* McEwan derides the masses in the name of the successful professional's right to the financial privileges accorded him by his genetic superiority and his 7000-square foot house at the core of the world's most overheated property market in Central London. Perowne lives in this luxury, as does McEwan, who moved to Central London on the strength of his earnings from *Atonement*. It is not surprising that, after much waffling (he once said that his head supported the invasion but his heart was against it), McEwan himself became a supporter of Great Britain's participation in the United States invasion of Iraq.

And perhaps that is the best place to leave Ian McEwan: spurning the 35 million people, including two million in London, who, in a single day, united to march against U.S. plans to invade Iraq. Never had the world's masses exercised their intelligence in a such a truly global grass-roots repudiation of the policies of a rogue state. The Mozambican novelist Mia Couto echoed the thoughts of millions when, in an open letter to George W. Bush that was published around the world, he wrote: "We, the poor people of small countries, have a weapon of mass construction: the ability to think." Yet these foreign masses failed to earn McEwan's sympathy; nor did he respect their ability to think. On November 20, 2003, during a visit to London by the U.S. president and his wife, McEwan turned down the opportunity to join the 100,000 people, including many of his oldest allies such as Harold Pinter, who went into the streets to protest. McEwan chose instead to accept an invitation from Prime Minister Tony Blair to join the president's wife, Laura Bush, for dinner. She wanted to meet him because, while preparing to launch a new book club, she had read *Atonement*.

* * *

The dominance of the mass has expelled the spectre of the masses. Unlike the masses, the mass has no revolutionary potential: it confines us within the translucent, infinitely elastic sheath of consumption, in mental uniformity, in a pseudo-democracy of objects for purchase. In denial of the widening chasm between rich and poor, both within Western societies and between wealthy nations and nations beset by poverty, we see ourselves as belonging to a single class. In a shack in the jungle, malnourished children are watching television, while Bill Gates, for ten years the richest man in the world, talks like an ordinary guy and sometimes appears in public in garish T-shirts. This is the afterlife of culture, where the common currency of image and object has blinded us to many distinctions that matter. Our consignment to this afterlife has not yet snuffed out all meaningful engagement between art and history: some of the essays that follow trace the sparks that continue to fly between the clashing of the imperatives of progress and spirit. But the advance of the afterlife of culture appears to be unstoppable. Here we are all ghosts. We may long to reclaim meaning for our actions, but if we strike out at the devil, seeking to liberate our souls, we will open our eyes to find that the most we have achieved is the banal murder of a tourist.

Sections of "A Report on the Afterlife of Culture" appeared in different form in *The Eden Mills Literary Festival Programme 2007*.

II:

REPORTS FROM THE WORLD

1. THE USES OF ENGLISHNESS

In Oxford all the best writers are dead. The walls of the upper reading room of Oxford University's august Bodleian Library are lined with mosaics portraying the immortals of Western literature; lecture halls and seminar rooms resound with discussions of these writers' masterpieces. Yet for a city whose vast libraries contain more than 10 million books, Oxford's writing community remains remarkably elusive.

A newcomer in search of literary ferment might assume that, as in Canada, writers lounge in the corners at readings held in gloomy cafés. But cafés are unknown here and the city's many pubs are raucous dives devoid of artistic pretensions. Readings in Oxford take place in plush bookstores, such as the immense Blackwell's.

On a raw, chilly night in late 1992, English writer Julian Barnes prepares to read with impeccably ironic disdain from his novel *The Porcupine*, a satire on the collapse of communism in Eastern Europe. A hum of conversation animates the small Blackwell's crowd.

As the reading is about to begin, a short man wearing glasses slips into the room. The crowd falls silent. In a reverential hush every head turns to watch novelist Ian McEwan, who lives in North Oxford, take a seat in the back row. McEwan, author of the recent *Black Dogs* and four other well-received novels, is only 44, his reputation still in the making. Yet given the treatment accorded him by the crowd, his face might as well be enshrined on the wall of the Bodleian's upper reading room.

A tendency to hold writers at a distance also bedevils student literary activity. Editorial meetings of the *Phoenix*, the university literary magazine, take place in a frigid cell at ancient New

College. The inaugural meeting attracts a medley of voices. Poems and short stories, some of them impressively accomplished, are read out in an eclectic variety of accents – not just English, but Irish, West Indian, West-Coast American. Each reading is meant to be followed by constructive criticism. But the three editors' calls for comments, issued in lofty upper-class English voices impervious to human warmth, bring conversation to a halt. By the magazine's second meeting, many of the most original writers have disappeared. During the third meeting a woman from Rome reads a daring experimental short story. The rhythms of her non-native English reduce the editors to snickers; two of them start chortling so hard that they have to leave the room. This, it becomes clear, is not the place to find literary community.

The novelist Martin Amis has also made the complaint that Oxford is full of highly literate people who enjoy little shared literary life. Recalling his undergraduate days at Oxford, Amis lamented that there had been "no sense of the new generation of minds or talents coming up. No little meetings at coffee bars where we hammered out our New Aesthetic."

In the absence of supportive peers, writers will do what they always do: retreat into stealth, cunning and solitude. In time, some of them will create good work – or at least get their revenge on the peculiar chilliness that sometimes infects the Oxford scene. Few writers have wreaked a more effective revenge than Javier Marías.

Marías is a Spanish novelist who spent two years in Oxford as a visiting lecturer. His invitation to teach at the university was extended on the strength of his success in translating ferociously difficult English novels, most notably Laurence Sterne's 18th-century puzzlebox *Tristram Shandy*, into pristine Spanish. Oxford's Spanish faculty decided to overlook the fact that Marías also wrote fiction. They should have known better.

Not only did Marías not enjoy his stay in Oxford, he based a novel on his experiences. When *All Souls* was published in English in December 1992, telephones began ringing all over Oxford as

London journalists tried to find out how many of the novel's scandalous anecdotes about Oxford's Spanish faculty were true. The answer: all of them.

Marías has made little effort to shield the models for his characters. The department head in the novel writes lurid horror stories under a pseudonym; the same is true in real life. Yet *All Souls* is not easily dismissed. In spite of passages of trivializing farce, this is a serious, well-written novel of considerable power.

As the mood of the grey, ancient city seeps into the narrator's skin, the satirical scenes of the opening chapters begin to alternate with sombre meditations on time and mortality. The narrator starts a hopeless affair with a married woman. He learns that his only friend among the faculty members is dying of AIDS (here Marías transfers the illness of one real-life Oxford Spanish lecturer to the character of another). The married woman and the dying lecturer, less transparently based on real people than the caricatured dons, give the narrator's predicament significance that resonates beyond the narrow boundaries of academic comedy.

"Having lived my life in the world," Marías's narrator writes of his adaption to Oxford, "I now found myself outside the world, as if I had been transported into a foreign element, such as water." Beneath the sure grip of Marías's prose, Oxford, with its eccentrics, its serrated spires and bone-chilling mist, becomes a compelling vantage point from which to reconsider life back in the busy world. *All Souls* shows that with the right treatment the notorious Oxford sense of distance – distance between people, distance between Oxford and the world – can be transformed into a source of insight.

* * *

In 1998 a pub in my East London neighbourhood lowered the Union Jack. In place of the layered crosses of England, Scotland and Ireland, the pub hoisted the St. George cross, representing England alone. Surveying the denuded-looking red-on-white flag, my neighbours and I, all of us foreigners, wondered what this could mean.

For centuries the chore of managing the British Empire enabled "Britain" and "England" to remain comfortably synonymous. But the Empire is gone: even Scotland and Wales have elected their own legislative assemblies. The obsession with social class that once defined English society has been diluted by immigration and new fortunes earned in the global market. Satellite television has eroded England's cultural particularity, turning small English boys into experts on NFL football, while political and economic integration into the European Union beckons. The English are both uncertain and uncharacteristically assertive about who they are.

In Search of England finds Michael Wood, creator of the successful PBS series *In the Footsteps of Alexander the Great*, seeking a stable English identity in the distant past. An Englishman demanding definition, Wood can also be a beady-eyed sceptic. Visiting the New Age mecca of Glastonbury, he observes that, in historical terms, most of the claims made for the spot's mystical antiquity are rubbish. Wood's respect for the needs fulfilled by the popular romanticization of Glastonbury's and England's past does not deter him from a dispassionate sifting of historical evidence. After scouring a range of manuscripts, he concludes that King Arthur is a complete fiction. He never existed, and neither did anyone like him.

Wood excels at this sort of archival detective work, guiding the general reader through thickets of historical debate. Yet when his attention shifts from legendary figures such as King Arthur to the Saxon monarchs he adores, his bracing scepticism evaporates.

The notion of the Norman Yoke – the idea that the invasion of the Norman French in 1066 permanently warped English society – is close to Wood's heart. His authentic England is Anglo-Saxon England. Wood marshals an arsenal of linguistic evidence to defend a heroic biography of the Saxon King Alfred that has been attacked as a forgery. But Wood's real hero is Alfred's grandson, King Athelstan. "Athelstan," Wood writes, "turned the kingdom of England into a fact . . . . He was the most powerful ruler since the Romans, and to a degree he was aware of it."

King of the West Saxons from 924 to 939, Athelstan came to power in a world blighted by the Dark Ages, where the collapse of the Roman Empire had extinguished most general knowledge and even basic literacy. His victory over Celtic and Norse forces at the Battle of Brunanburh in 937 expanded England's borders to their present outlines and established the West Saxons as the dominant culture of the British Isles.

Athelstan returns in the book's final section. Ostensibly devoted to English people and landscapes, these chapters plunge into the Saxon past. Wood traces the site of the Battle of Brunan- burh to a post-industrial wasteland. Other landscape chapters are devoted to the survival of Anglo-Saxon crafts in English villages and a visit to the abbey where the 8th-century historian the Venera- ble Bede lived as a monk.

Wood's Saxon triumphalism is not always easy to stomach. Crammed with information, *In Search of England* becomes repeti- tive in its ancient obsessions. Is recovery of the Anglo-Saxon past the key to English identity? My former neighbours in multicultural East London would not think so. Wood scrupulously refutes the anti-immigrant racism of ideologues such as the late Conservative politician Enoch Powell. Yet even readers who share Wood's despair at globalization's destruction of our links to the past may balk at his narrow focus. A vision that decries the Norman inva- sion of 1066 as the destruction of essential Englishness is a spuri- ous foundation for a 21st-century society.

Edward Rutherfurd, though sharing Wood's idealization of rural England, perceives 1066 as the birth of Englishness, not its death. Rutherfurd's mammoth novel *Sarum* (1987), which concen- trated on the territory around Stonehenge, established his reputa- tion as a titan of documentary fiction. *The Forest* is a chip off the old neolith. Weighing in at 600 pages, each as long as a normal short story, Rutherfurd's novel narrates the history of the New Forest, a wedge of immemorial wilderness extending from near Stonehenge down to England's south coast. Located, like Wood's West Saxony, in England's deep south, the New Forest becomes a microcosm of the English nation. The novel opens in 1099, with a story that culminates in the marriage of a Norman noblewoman to a Saxon hunter. This union of Saxon and Norman would be contested by Wood, who insists that the two cultures rarely intermarried for at least 250 years after 1066; Rutherfurd makes this fusion his book's symbolic core.

In a novel whose narrative spans nearly 1000 years, Rutherfurd deals not with individual characters but with families typifying the social classes of rural England. The Martells are haughty aristocrats, the Albions represent the emerging middle class, the Prides are stout yeomen, the Furzeys dull-witted peasants, and the troll-like Puckles live deep in the woods. Each section of the novel hinges on a well-known historical period or event. *The Forest* offers a painless, if lengthy, refresher course in English history, supplemented by digressions on the breeding habits of deer and the intricacies of forest management. The book's episodes are highly dramatic, skilfully constructed and narrated in clear, unobtrusive prose. Unfortunately, the continuity of traits among the families, necessary to sustain reader identification from one century to the next, mutates into a biological determinism that flattens the characters. Though the Furzey family is allowed to sprout an intellectual branch in the 18th century, the reader soon learns to interpret the characters' surnames as banners announcing how they will behave. Describing a character from the Victorian era, Rutherfurd writes: "Colonel Godwin Albion would have been pleased to know that he resembled his Saxon ancestor Cola the Huntsman and, in all probability, would have agreed with him on most matters of importance."

Ethnocentric complacency of this sort contributes to a loss of momentum in the final chapters. The novel ends in 2000 with a London journalist discovering her New Forest ancestry and reinaugurating her bond with the region's human and natural life. Like Wood, Rutherfurd rejects the city, defining Englishness as the unbroken continuity of pastoral customs and rural genetic and social traits. This is one version of England. But as a visit to urban England reveals, much more than a revival of the rural past will be required to fill the blank spaces on the flag where the St. George cross flies alone.

* * *

Until the St. George cross was raised on our street, my neighbours and I thought we had seen the end of that sort of Englishness. The year before, Tony Blair had won a landslide election victory that brought to a close the seventeen years of social destruction under Margaret Thatcher and John Major. By the morning after the election, public discourse had changed. The casual racial slurs that had been the daily currency of Tory Members of Parliament gave way to the reasoned open-mindedness of young, middle-of-the-road New Labour MPs. Nobody expected an economic revolution from the Blair government, but the social climate seemed poised to take a leap into the 21st century. On election night in 1997 I sat in my basement room beneath the small shop (known as an "off-licence"), and listened in amazement as Labour made its first incursion into the Tory heartland: a young German immigrant woman, who spoke English with a clipped accent, had defeated an incumbent Conservative Member of Parliament in a stodgy suburb of Birmingham. Could this be the end, not only of Toryism, but of British xenophobia? As the trend consolidated, the silent streets outside woke up. I heard scattered, rowdy voices in the darkness. The rowdiness gradually turned to rhythmic chanting. The dangerous streets that we avoided at night, where all of us had been mugged on occasion, filled with people. Lights went on above the folded awnings and bolted-down metal security screens of the shopfronts. At two in the morning the street was glowing with light. Irish, Bulgarian, Bosnian and eastern

German immigrant workers, French students who had come to London to learn English, dozens of Nigerians and Ghanians, Turks from Turkey and Turks from Cyprus, old Bangladeshi men with beards and white skull-caps, and clean-shaven young Bangladeshis in black leather jackets, mingled and yelled and finally united their shouts into a delighted chant: "The racists are gone! The racists are gone! The racists are *gone!*"

When I returned to Canada, I delighted in telling people how the bad old England had been vanquished. Blair might not be doing much to alleviate the gap between rich and poor, I was fond of saying, but he was creating an atmosphere in which a multicultural society could thrive. I told my British-born mother and stepfather, who had avoided the U.K. since the rise of Thatcherism, that they should go back for a visit. Alas, I should have paid more attention to the St. George crosses that were sprouting all over the country.

I returned to England for much of 2004 and 2005. Oxford had filled up with restaurants and cafés, but literary life remained as elusive as ever; the selection of books in Blackwell's bookshop had grown thin and ephemeral. Service jobs were filled by young Russians or Ukrainians or Poles or Bulgarians or light-skinned Brazilians. Even prior to the al-Qaeda-inspired bombings in London in July 2005, it was clear that the Blair government was playing a double game on immigration, manipulating Britain's role within the European Union in order to draw young Eastern Europeans – the world's prized "last wave of white immigrants" – to London before Germany or France could clear the bureaucratic hurdles to admit them legally. This was done in the shadows; in public, the legacy of the West Saxons had fused with the born-again Christian Islamophobia of the Bush administration. Britain had its own peculiar word for refugee claimants. Known as "asylum seekers," they were reviled in most newspapers as the greatest plague experienced by humankind. During the 2005 election the Conservative leader, Michael Howard, whose Romanian Jewish father lied his way into Great Britain after his own mother was murdered in the Holocaust, announced that if elected he would withdraw Great Britain from the United Nations Convention on Refugees. Howard went on to place a sustained assault on British Gypsies at the core of the Conservative election campaign. Blair made desultory gestures in the direction of the high road, only to end up playing to the same base instincts as Howard. The "anti-terrorist" policies Blair introduced after July 2005 fenced off Muslims from the rest of British society, guaranteeing a delay of at least a generation in any sustained multiracial integration. It is difficult to dampen the spirits of a city as vivacious as London, but by the time I left Great Britain in September 2005, buoyant London street life had grown wary and hesitant. Perhaps it is not suprising to discover that a country that is reviving the mythology of a racially pure past by replacing a layered flag with one that starkly celebrates a single heritage is in fact a crossroads between the world and the village, Europe and the Americas. Commercialized Americana permeates every pore of contemporary British life. Having learned British English as an infant, and being in the habit of reverting to British vocabulary almost without thinking about it when I find myself in the U.K., I've discovered in recent years that some of my traditional British usages are becoming archaisms. Ten years ago if I talked about a "vacation," English people would correct me by forcefully saying, "holiday." Today the English speak among themselves about "vacations." Every important leader in the country's two major political parties cherishes the "special relationship" with the United States above all other policy considerations including, as Blair's decision to invade Iraq made clear, those of internal social peace. Yet, in spite of its obsession with "America," which it brandishes as an illusory alternative to the European Union, Great Britain remains profoundly European in its ancestral presumptions, which echo the rhetoric of far-right nationalisms in Austria and the Netherlands more closely than any form of national self-assertion known in the Americas. The Empire having receded, Britain has been exposed as a culturally incoherent mid-Atlantic platform on the globalized stage. It may be decades before the British realize that they are all the flotsam and jetsam of immigrations, from both before and long after 1066, and that it is in the cohesion of these different layers of human sediment that their identity lies.

"The Uses of Englishness" includes sections from "Alienated at Oxford: writing about it is author's best revenge," Montreal *Gazette*, 17 April 1993, and "Ye olde England swings," Montreal *Gazette*, 15 July 2000.

2. MEXICO AGAINST ITSELF

It is common for first-time visitors to Mexico City to become disoriented. The thin mountain air, the suburbs and shantytowns whose populations exceed those of entire nations, the snow-smudged peaks of the volcanoes shimmering through the poisoned smog, all contribute to the visitor's bewilderment. But for many people the most striking feature of a first visit to Mexico City is the inescapable presence of history. From the grandiose monuments to the heroes of the Mexican Revolution of 1910-1920 to the vast European-style boulevard of Paseo de la Reforma, laid out by the Hapsburg emperor Maximilian, who ruled in the 1860s, past and present meld. No city in the Americas feels more laden with history than Mexico's capital. Spanish colonial churches crowd the 17th-century city centre. The exposed ruins of the Great Temple of the Aztecs stand next to the presidential palace, while a short drive away the pyramids of Teotihuacán, predating the Aztecs by nearly eight centuries, dominate an arid landscape.

Mexico's omnipresent history has forged a culture whose customs, food, art, architecture and literature are utterly distinct. Michael C. Meyer and William H. Beezley, the editors of *The Oxford History of Mexico* (2000), underline an important paradox: "Mexico today has a relationship with the United States in which the cultures are converging through mass media, tourism and economics, yet it has become increasingly recognized throughout the world as a unique culture." This long-overdue volume forms part of the paradox. A readership exists for a detailed history of Mexican distinctness precisely because Mexico is becoming less foreign to English-speaking readers. To package tourists, Mexico is a hotel-studded beach; to business people, it is a NAFTA-integrated market of 100 million customers fuelling the world's tenth-largest economy; to Mexicans themselves, the country is a source of pride and exasperation; and to scholars, as this huge, detailed history demonstrates, Mexico is a reservoir of inexhaustible fascination: a country whose obsession with history exists in ceaseless counterpoint to its quest for modernity.

Nowhere else have indigenous civilizations of the Americas mixed so thoroughly, both genetically and culturally, with the waves of Europeans and Africans who began arriving in the 16th century. In Mexico the indigenous cultures, though often embattled, retain a unique centrality to national identity. Advances in archeology, assisted by the recent deciphering of some of the pre-Columbian scripts, have expanded our knowledge of the Olmecs, Mayas and Aztecs.

Mexico's indigenous cultures borrowed and learned from each other, reaching the pinnacle of their achievements in astronomy, mathematics, sculpture, sport and architecture around 800 AD. These "classical" civilizations collapsed between 900 and 1000 AD. When the Spanish conquistador Hernán Cortés invaded in 1519 he confronted the more authoritarian, militaristic "post-classical" face of the Aztecs of central Mexico and the neo-Mayan cities of the south. Ross Hassig's chapter narrating Cortés's two-year military campaign to overthrow the Aztecs is engrossing. Hassig emphasizes both the decisive role played by European diseases and the cunning manoeuvres of native commanders. Conventional images of compliant indigenous leaders melting away before the bearded white conqueror yield to a picture of a patchwork of cultures that had been subjugated by the Aztecs astutely playing off their two conquerors against each other.

The three centuries of colonial rule that succeeded Cortés's triumph have often been portrayed as a time of despotic inertia. *The Oxford History of Mexico* highlights the vigorous cultural mixing that occurred during these centuries, from the flowering of Mexican baroque architecture, which drew upon both Spanish and Aztec styles, to the growing proportion of the population that could claim mixed racial ancestry. The piety of a colony living in the shadow of the Spanish Inquisition coexisted with a climate of interracial sexual experimentation and acceptance of children whose parents were not married. The indigenous population, which plummeted from more than 12 million in 1520 to just over one million in 1600, began to recover, but was soon surpassed by Mexico's new majority, the mixed-race *mestizo*. By ushering Mexico into the world economy, the conquest brought Spain silver, sowing the seeds of the Spanish empire's destruction. Spain's Mexican silver reserves spared the country the pain of modernizing, dooming it to be overtaken by England and France. Trade reforms in the 18th century came too late and by 1821 Mexico, like most of its Spanish American neighbours, was independent.

The chaos and misery of 19th-century Mexico are almost indescribable. The four chapters devoted to this period do a valiant job of disentangling decades where governments changed so rapidly that the strongman General Santa Anna served eleven terms as president and the U.S. invasion of 1845-1848 lopped off half of the country's territory (including Texas and California). During the French invasion of the 1860s, Benito Juárez, the Zapotec Indian who became a revered reformist president, governed from a horse-drawn carriage perpetually ready to flee for safety. Little wonder that Mexicans welcomed the stability of the 35-year dictatorship of Porfirio Díaz, who ruled until 1910.

Díaz, a dark-skinned *mestizo* who used makeup to lighten his complexion, paid a high price for success: by 1910 foreigners owned nearly one-third of Mexico's land and 90 per cent of its industry. Culture came from Europe; despising their compatriots, privileged Mexicans worried little about a cavernous divide between rich and poor. In his chapter on the ten-year civil war that destroyed the old order and created modern, culturally assertive, nominally left-wing yet politically authoritarian Mexico, John Mason Hart resists the temptation to depict the Mexican Revolution as an orgy of carnage. Hart's understated account of the competing revolutionary forces sets the stage for an engaging chapter by Helen Delpar on the post-1920 reimagining of Mexican culture, including the glorification of the indigenous past, and compelling accounts by Thomas Benjamin and John W. Sherman of the state-driven politics and economics of the mid-20th century. By 1982, 80 per cent of Mexico's economy was under state control. In the 1990s, under the presidency of the tough, criminally corrupt and possibly homicidal Carlos Salinas de Gortari, neo-conservative economics took over, baring the increasing hollowness of the government's revolutionary rhetoric.

This history ends weakly. The decision to send the book to press before the July 2000 elections that closed the seventy-one years of post-revolutionary rule of the Machiavellian Party of Revolutionary Institutions (PRI) by bringing to power the conservative opposition candidate Vicente Fox does not justify the clumsiness of Roderic Ai Camp's repetitive chapter on contemporary politics. The closing chapter, Anne Rubinstein's lacklustre account of Mexican comic books and soap operas, is a poor advertisement for the current academic fad of "cultural studies." Most chapters are meticulously researched and cleanly written, yet, although this is Oxford University Press, the editing is shockingly lax. Typos abound, and factual errors (many of them contained in the captions to the scores of illustrations) glare from the pages. We are told that the haunting Mayan city of Yaxchilán is in Guatemala, when it is in Mexico; that the neo-Mayan confederation of Mayapán collapsed in 1221, when this date marks its foundation; that the Hapsburg Empress Carlota was six years older than her husband, when she was thirteen years younger; that José Iglesias was a 19th-century president, when he was Chief Justice of the Supreme Court; that Benito Juárez criticized Porfirio Díaz at a time when Juárez was dead, and many more. *The Oxford History of Mexico* is a very good idea, but readers should wait for the second edition.

By contrast, readers of English had to wait far too long to experience Elena Poniatowska's *Here's to You, Jesusa!* (2000). If, as the translator Alastair Reid once suggested, the translation process is a lottery, Poniatowska has been unfairly bilked out of a winning ticket. After Carlos Fuentes, Poniatowska is Mexico's best-known living writer. One of the most influential intellectuals in Latin America, she was prominent among the international group of celebrities who welcomed Subcomandante Marcos and the Zapatista rebels when, recreating the arrival of the indigenous leader Emiliano Zapata in the capital during the Mexican Revolution, they entered Mexico City in March 2001. Yet few of Poniatowska's forty books have been translated into English. She does not fit our model of the Latin American writer: she is a woman who does not write magic-realist romances of the kind that have made Isabel Allende popular; she is an immigrant writer, having arrived in Mexico as a child refugee from Europe during the Second World War. And Poniatowska's best work lies in a difficult-to-market middle ground between fiction and journalism. All of these factors conspired to prevent *Here's to You, Jesusa!*, one of the milestones of modern Latin American literature, from appearing in English until twenty-eight years after its publication in Spanish.

In the 1960s, Poniatowska met an older working-class woman named Josefina Borquez in the slums of Mexico City. She overheard Borquez speaking and asked to hear more of her stories. Poniatowska spent months taking notes on Borquez's life, transforming the material into a "testimonial novel" narrated in the first person by a woman named Jesusa Palancares. The result, while neither as formally elegant as a traditional novel nor as factually grounded as good journalism, has a compelling immediacy. During the political violence of the 1980s in Latin America, *Here's to You, Jesusa!* became the model for a wave of "testimonial" books, such as *I, Rigoberta Menchú* (1982), which mobilized the voices of the downtrodden to dramatize horrific events.

Jesusa, born in 1900, is a child when the Mexican Revolution begins and a traumatized widow when it ends. Her early life in the Tehuantepec region of southern Mexico is tumultuous. Her mother dies, she loses touch with her older siblings, and her stepmother stabs her. Jesusa is rescued by a severe but decent godmother. After her beloved brother is murdered at the outset of the Revolution, Jesusa rejoins her father, now a revolutionary soldier.

The women who travelled with the troops have been excluded from much writing about the Mexican Revolution. Jesusa gives voice to women who marched and fought alongside the soldiers, and also had to cook for them. She exposes an environment of crushing *machismo*. At fourteen, she is forced to marry a seventeen-year-old captain she barely knows. After their wedding, he locks her in a room for a week while he goes off partying. "When Pedro was on a campaign," Jesusa says, "since there weren't any women around, he satisfied his urges with me, but in the ports he forgot about me."

Jesusa meets most of the famous revolutionary generals and dismisses them as bandits exploiting the poor. Her disparaging attitude towards the Revolution, its leaders and its lauded social advances shocked many Mexican readers when the book was first published. But it is Jesusa's voice, foul-mouthed and distrustful yet driven by a ferocious bravado and the quest for a rich spiritual life, that carries the story. At the end of the war, with her husband and father both dead, Jesusa is put on a train home to Tehuantepec, where a widow's pension awaits her. Passing through the Mexico City train station, she is robbed, ends up on the street and spends the rest of her life in the slums of the capital. Illiterate and knowing nothing of the city, Jesusa cannot even identify a "Help Wanted" sign. After months of near-starvation she learns how to find work. She entertains herself drinking, dancing and, especially, brawling. "I was an animal," she reports, recounting one of the occasions on which she beats up a man who has designs on her. Spurning men, Jesusa nonetheless makes painful attempts to adopt and bring up children. Her greatest fulfillment comes from her involvement in a mystical form of Christianity that preaches reincarnation and spiritual healing. The clash between her no-nonsense vitality and her mysticism makes Jesusa a fascinating, contradictory character.

Here's to You, Jesusa! was written in a more innocent time, before debates about the ethics of writers reworking the voices of the poor. (Elisabeth Burgos, the editor of Rigoberta Menchú's memoirs, has been harshly criticized for some of her editorial choices.) Poniatowska addresses these issues, albeit indirectly, by including a new introduction describing her friendship with Josefina Borquez. The book that emerged from the meeting of these two women from opposite ends of the social scale has made an ignored part of Mexico's history, that of poor women, unforgettable.

The part of Mexico's history that has been most widely reported in recent years is the uprising of the indigenous Zapatista guerrillas in Chiapas and the ironic utterances of their hyper-literate middle-class press secretary, Subcomandante Marcos. Launched on January 1, 1994, the date of the implementation of the North American Free Trade Agreement (NAFTA), the Zapatista revolt is a new, if as yet unimitated, phenomenon in Latin America: an insurgency against an international trade accord, a movement that seeks to assert ethnic and regional rights rather than trying to overthrow a corrupt dictatorship or promote a more dignified identity for the nation-state; an insurgency whose conduct combines land seizures and sporadic armed confrontation with the authorities with press releases, conferences, publicity stunts, newspaper guest editorials and ceaseless activity at the fount of the cherished Zapatista website. On the ground, however, the Zapatista uprising is no joke. Mayan peasants suspected of collaboration with the Zapatistas are harassed, driven off their land and sometimes killed. Anxious to avoid the kind of international condemnation that isolated Guatemala during the 1980s, when the government responded to the recruitment of the Maya into a long-standing guerrilla insurgency with a campaign that has been defined by the United Nations as genocide, Ernesto Zedillo, the Mexican president from 1994 to 2000, found more devious ways of combating the Zapatistas. Sections of the Lacandón Forest, where the Zapatistas are believed to have their base, were clear cut; land grants in Chiapas were given to landless *mestizo* peasants from northern Mexico, who were brought in to compete for scarce resources with the Zapatistas' Mayan base, often by cutting down more trees; and, as I saw during the summer of 2000, everywhere in Chiapas, large highways were under construction. Drawing on the work of sociologists who link highways to the erosion of traditional cultures, the Mexican government had decided to pipe the modern world into Chiapas to dissolve the sense of wholeness and community that nurtured Mayan resistance to globalization. And where there were not yet highways, there was always the Army.

San Cristóbal de Las Casas, the historic mountain town briefly taken over by the Zapatistas on the day NAFTA was implemented, is named after the 16th-century Archbishop of Guatemala, Father Bartolomé de Las Casas, who wrote a famous defence of the Indians. One of the keys to understanding the tensions in Chiapas is that it is not historically part of Mexico. Originally falling within the colonial viceroyalty of Guatemala, Chiapas was annexed by Mexico from independent Guatemala by stages, through a combination of legal chicanery and brute military force, between 1823 and the early 1880s. Highland Chiapas (the lowland area around the state capital of Tuxtla Gutiérrez is different) still feels like part of Central America. Like Central America, and unlike the rest of Mexico, the region did not participate in the struggle for independence from Spain at the beginning of the 19th century. Chiapas was largely bypassed by the Mexican Revolution, the defining event of modern Mexican history: while left-wing radicalism was taking charge elsewhere in Mexico, a reactionary local government came to power in Chiapas. This intangible sense of apartness, combined with the strength of the Mayan culture, has made the mountainous part of Chiapas attractive to tourists. San Cristóbal's streets of small restaurants and souvenir shops stuffed with Subcomandante Marcos T-shirts – a form of homage to the insurgency that epitomized its contradictions – seemed to be geared almost entirely to tourism. In spite of the presence of numerous European visitors (mainly Italians and Germans), and groups of backpacking young middle-class Mexicans, the residents I spoke to bowed their heads and said that times were hard because tourism had declined. Each time I asked whether this decline was due to the insurgency, my interlocutor would become mute. It was clear that adverse publicity in the United States had scared off the Americans, for whom San Cristóbal had once been a favourite hangout. I did not meet a single American during my stay.

I spent a few days soaking up the highland colonial ambience of San Cristóbal, and riding out to nearby tourist attractions in the minivans that Mexicans call *combis*, before I decided to visit Larraínzar. The town of San Andrés Larraínzar is famous for two reasons: it is the home of intricate weaving techniques that are unique in the world; and it was the location of the arduous, heavily armed and ultimately futile peace negotiations between the Zapatistas and the Mexican government in 1995 and 1996. I have a long-standing amateur interest in traditional weaving, and I was curious to see how Larraínzar was faring four years after the failed peace talks. I walked to the back of the San Cristóbal market and asked around for a *combi* going to Larraínzar. Even as I was sitting in my seat waiting to leave the tiny roofless concrete minivan station, I noticed a difference from other *combis*: no one spoke to me. No one even wanted to speak Spanish. The day before, on the way to Zinacatán, the driver had made his announcements bilingually, in Spanish and the Mayan language of Tzotzil. From the moment I entered the *combi* to Larraínzar, everything was in Tzotzil only.

We followed the road past San Juan Chamula, home of a famous "syncretic" church that enshrines a blended Mayan animist and Roman Catholic form of worship, and continued on through the bright cone-shaped hills yoked together by sagging spurs whose tops and steep sides were sown with corn. Blue-clad Mayan women carried firewood on their backs in harnesses that hung from bands stretched around their foreheads. The yards in front of the small houses were crowded with children and dust and chickens, but the hills behind looked higher and emptier than the dense, multi-crop cultivation surrounding San Juan Chamula. In the distance, bright green summits were bannered with white cloud. The driver took the ill-banked curves in daredevil sweeps. An enormously broad green-glistening valley opened up. Spreading over a wide pan on a spur vaulted up off the valley floor, lay San Andrés Larraínzar.

The road forked at the entrance to the town. The Mexican Army guarded both forks. The knoll between the forks was fenced in with barbed wire and appeared to have become a military base. The *combi* stopped and the soldiers ordered me out of the van. As I got out, seven men in uniform surrounded me. I handed my passport and tourist card to the soldier in front. Soldiers standing on opposite sides of me lifted cameras and took complementary side-angle photographs of my face. One of them stepped in front of me and snapped again. The soldier holding my passport said, *"Buenos días,"* and wrote my last name and first name in large letters at the top of a lined, photocopied sheet. He filled in all the other information that could be gleaned from my documents. The other soldiers stood staring at me, swinging their rifles with extremely serious expressions. Behind them the valley shimmered. The military, I reflected, always gets the best view.

A man in an officer's uniform stepped up. "Where are you from?"

"Canadian."

"You're going to Larraínzar?"

"Yes, to see the market." I put on a gringo accent as I spoke to him. Already that summer a number of visitors to Chiapas had been deported from Mexico for being "foreign agents" of the Zapatistas; excessive competence in Spanish would only heighten suspicions.

They let me get back into the *combi*. We drove down an alley of unfinished-looking concrete houses with filthy yards. Soldiers patrolled the streets. The locals were invisible: this was a town under military occupation. Or, rather, it was a divided town. As we climbed the hill to the *zócalo* (the central square), the soldiers disappeared. The tall white church at the head of the square looked out over the market. Larraínzar's market, in its current incarnation, provided a poor excuse for a visit. Today was market day, but most of the stalls were closed. Those that were open had no weaving for sale. A few stalls offered huge raw slabs of meat that had dripped black blood onto the plain wood they lay on. There were stalls selling plastic bowls and transparent plastic shopping bags, and a meagre selection of fruit. Empty wooden crates lay on the ground between the stalls. Skinny dogs were everywhere; occasionally somebody would kick a dog in the ribs or throw a rock at one to keep it away from the unhealthy-looking meat. The women were in traditional dress but, unusually, so were most of the men, who wore patterned red *chalecos*. The church incarnated a syncretic brew so pungent that it made the church in San Juan Chamula look like a conventional apostle of Rome. What was happening here, in fact, looked less like syncretism than the revival of traditional Mayan worship within the husk of a Catholic church. A line of about twenty men wearing fleecy black sleeveless vests filled the benches on either side of the church door. Five men and women stood on the steps, gazing into the church's smokey interior and chanting in Tzotzil. They reached the end of their chant and entered the church. I stepped forward and looked in the door. The altar appeared to have been removed – a common feature of syncretized churches – although it was difficult to know for certain because the smoke was so thick. The smell of wax and incense and the sound of Tzotzil chanting eddied past me and wafted into the square. The glimmer of candles pierced the smoke in hatched patterns of lighted points. The church had become a place of smokey cover from the presence of the army, a redoubt where Tzotzil was the language of power and Spanish did not enter, a hearth where the besieged Mayan culture renewed itself and spread out through the town.

This was not my place. To enter the church would be crass and insensitive, and possibly dangerous. I turned away from the steps and walked around the square. For a regional centre of 5000 people, Larraínzar barely seemed to have a functioning economy. A large banner draped across the building dominating the side of the square opposite the church addressed Mexico's outgoing

president: *Zedillo, respect our rights . . . !* A long exhortation followed, concluding with the words: *Army, get out of San Andrés
Sachm'chen!* Each of the many militant banners hanging on the
streets that were not patrolled by the Army referred to the town
by this Tzotzil name. The most outlandish banner I found was on
a side street. More than a metre in length, it explained in tiny
black print how citizens of different nations, including Mexico,
could apply to become official election observers for the upcom-
ing national elections. The banner was entirely in English.

   I walked down a long pitted street, a kind of prolongation of
the market, lined with more raw meat and scouted by more des-
perate-looking dogs. The street went down into a ravine, then up
again to a high crest from which I had a view out of town in both
directions. I sat down on the raised sidewalk, drank from my water
bottle and ate a pastry I had bought in San Cristóbal. I watched
children rolling a soccer ball up a steep incline then chasing it
down again. They scampered past my hiking boots without
acknowledging my presence. They did not compete for my attention in the coquettish way that village children often do, and they
did not beg like the urchins of tourist towns. In fact, they did not
see me. Their elders had behaved in the same way. The people in
the square, the people I passed on the street, simply looked
through me. It was not as though they were resentful of my intrusion or consciously avoiding me – I'd encountered this before: in
Bolivia, in Peru – but as though *I was not there*. The fact that I was
there meant that the Army had let me in, which was not a point in
my favour. I finished my pastry and walked up and down the
streets until it became obvious that no one was going to speak to
me. The fact that even five-year-olds were so raptly *trained* in their
behaviour towards outsiders gave a graphic indication of the level
of intimidation the town endured. Only the elders guarding the
church door had made the slightest acknowledgement of my presence: at one point I caught them – I thought – looking towards me
and sharing a laugh. But I couldn't be certain. When a culture is as
besieged, and as alien as Tzotzil culture was to me, the chances of

deciphering its reactions are almost non-existent. A few of the cavorting kids used more Spanish than Tzotzil when chatting among themselves, but that didn't mean I had any better chance of understanding them. They did not want to be understood by someone like me.

When, after an hour and a half, I gave up and walked towards the spot in the square where the *combis* to San Cristóbal were loading, I could feel the town release its collective breath. The silence broke. Men standing near the *combis* waved at me in welcome and began joking with me in Spanish. The van was packed, the atmosphere amiable, as we set off. When we reached the barricade the soldiers saw my face in the back row and ordered everybody out of the *combi*. A tall soldier stepped inside and slapped the ceiling. The soldiers surrounded me again; this time I was approached by a man in civilian clothes whose laminated photo I.D. linked him to the Immigration service. He wrote down my name and passport number on a sheet of paper. "And now you're on your way to San Cristóbal?" he asked.

"Yes," I said. San Cristóbal's name took on a comfortable sound: that was where I belonged; that was the place for tourists who would never understand what was happening in Chiapas.

The passengers returned to the *combi*. The affable mood had been squelched. For the next fifty minutes, until the van reached the outskirts of San Cristóbal and began to drop off passengers, no one uttered a word.

"Mexico Against Itself" includes sections from "Many Mexicos," Montreal *Gazette*, 25 November 2000, and "Here's Mexico's Best," Montreal *Gazette*, 2 June 2001.

3. MAYAN GUATEMALA REVISITED

"What we are engaged in is an anti-colonial struggle." Rigoberto Quemé Chay sits in the high-ceilinged corner office of the 19th-century city hall of Quetzaltenango, Guatemala's second-largest city. In this racially divided country, Quemé Chay, 60, is the first Maya to be elected mayor of a major city. Now his Xel-Jú movement, the most successful aboriginal political organization in the Americas, is making a bid for the impossible by running Quemé Chay as a candidate for Guatemala's presidency in the November 2003 elections.

Depending on how the question is asked, between 45 per cent and 70 per cent of the inhabitants of Central America's most populous country identify themselves as Maya. According to some studies, Guatemala's Maya, along with their cousins in the neighbouring Mexican states of Chiapas and Yucatán, are the most impoverished ethnic group in the Western hemisphere. The December 1996 peace accords that ended Guatemala's 36-year civil war were supposed to improve living conditions for the Maya. But post-1996 governments, regardless of party affiliation, have refused to implement the chapter of the peace accords dealing with indigenous rights.

"Implement that chapter and the country changes!" Héctor Rosada, the hard-headed sociologist who negotiated the peace accords by bringing together the military and left-wing guerrillas during the mid-1990s, fumes at the non-implementation of the aboriginal rights section. "That's the best part of the peace accords. If you don't implement it, nothing changes and twenty years from now we'll have another civil war."

Full implementation of the accords is a central plank of Quemé Chay's political platform. But so is pushing Guatemala's aboriginal majority into the country's political mainstream. "The candidacy has a symbolic element," he explains. "It's a step towards a broader democracy. We are proving that we have the ability to work within a political system that is not ours, and in so doing we are laying the groundwork for a multicultural society. By working within the system, we are breaking down the stereotype of the 'no-good Indian.'"

Racial prejudice in Guatemala runs so deep that many Maya have internalized it. Ricardo Cajas, head of Quetzaltenango city council, notes that one of the greatest obstacles faced by Xel-Jú has been persuading Maya voters that it is not shameful to vote for a Mayan candidate. Quemé Chay knows this shame well. As a young man he was a heavy drinker who rejected his Mayan identity and hated his non-Spanish surnames. He credits Xel-Jú, which began life as a Mayan community centre before evolving into a political movement, with giving him the self-confidence to stop drinking and build his career.

His 1996 election created political shock waves. When Quemé Chay was re-elected in 2000, the federal government cut off funding to the city, preventing him from taking office for six months. Even after seven years under a Mayan mayor, cool, mountainous, European-looking Quetzaltenango remains a city of unresolved tensions, where racist slogans are scrawled on walls and Mayan people are still banned from entering the city's posh tennis club. But with the most organized and educated Maya in Guatemala, the city is the natural base for the country's first Mayan presidential candidate. Quemé Chay knows that his chances of becoming president are slight. In the November elections he will face five well-funded right-wing candidates and a former guerrilla commander representing the left. His campaign speeches and television commercials promise "social revolution," yet his solutions to Guatemala's long-term problems are those of a moderate.

Asked about land reform, a defining issue in a country where three per cent of the population owns sixty-five per cent of the land, he shrugs off the postures of Mayan traditionalists such as Nobel Peace Prize laureate Rigoberta Menchú, who argue in favour of preserving Mayan culture by giving more land to the poor. "We've been out to the rural communities," Quemé Chay says, "and I can tell you that the children of Mayan peasants don't want to sow corn. The land issue has been politicized by both the left and the right. As we become more connected to global markets, productivity depends more on artisans, on a productive fringe of small and medium-sized businesses. In time, the land issue is going to become less important. The young people want education to bolster their citizenship by participating more in the economy.

"Participation," he repeats, in the voice of a man who has found his stride. "That's how you strengthen your culture."

* * *

Rigoberto Quemé Chay's presidential campaign didn't make it to election day. He ran out of money, his advertisements disappeared from television screens and his name was withdrawn from the ballot. Some said that he was brought down by the same failing as many earlier Guatemalan presidential candidates: that of being a regional leader without a national base; others interpreted this explanation as another way of saying that he was Maya. The November 2003 presidential elections were won by Oscar Berger, the very white descendant of German coffee barons from northeastern Guatemala. Incarnating the old-style charismatic Latin American strongman, Berger ditched his political party in mid-campaign and won as an individual. His victory gave Guatemala its third consecutive democratic election but left political institutions and the party system more tattered than before. Berger had a big landowner's view of the Maya. With his election, any chance that the aboriginal rights chapter of the 1996 peace accords, with its provisions for schooling in Mayan languages, might one day be implemented faded from sight.

I thought back to my meeting with Rigoberto Quemé Chay. The articulate, personable mayor of Quetzaltenango faltered only once during our interview. When I asked him whether he would campaign in the Quiché language of his community, Quemé Chay clasped his hands together. His face darkened.

"No. In the city we had to leave the language behind. That was the cost of educating ourselves."

This was the only point in the interview when he fell silent.

The pre-Columbian Mayan city-states dominated what is now southern Mexico, Belize, Honduras and eastern Guatemala. After classical Mayan civilization was destroyed by a combination of environmental and political factors around 900 AD, the lowland city-states were abandoned and the Maya relocated to Mexico's Yucatán peninsula and the highlands of western Guatemala, where they were conquered by the Spanish in the 16th century. Many Maya resisted assimilation into Hispanic culture, and today roughly six million people in Guatemala, southern Mexico and Belize continue to speak one of the thirty surviving Mayan languages. As a result of the 1996 peace accords, preliminary steps towards providing Mayan-language schooling, seen as the key to affording Mayan people greater social mobility, were taken in 1997; these efforts soon stagnated. Quemé Chay is a Quiché, the largest Mayan ethnicity in Guatemala. Of Guatemala's roughly 13 million people, about two million are Quiché. Nearly one million continue to speak the Quiché language, but Quemé Chay, like many urban Maya, speaks only Spanish. I was disappointed (though not surprised) to learn this, as I had been waiting to tell Quemé Chay: *Ren xintamaq Cakchiquel kaji' ik'*. For four months I studied Cakchiquel.

The third most widely spoken of Guatemala's twenty Mayan languages, Cakchiquel is understood by over 400,000 people. Mayan languages can differ drastically from one another, but Quiché and Cakchiquel are almost as close as German and Dutch. Cakchiquel is blessed with a larger population base than most Native American languages but is cursed by its location. Cakchiquel territory embraces the Westernized tourist towns of Antigua and Panajachel and most of the two-hour drive between them, a region of Guatemala where tourism, satellite television and the sweatshop economy have frayed traditional life. As I learned Cakchiquel, I found I was absorbing a language of which many Cakchiquels had grown ashamed.

I studied Cakchiquel in the colonial town of Antigua. Most of the surrounding villages are Cakchiquel-speaking, but many Cakchiquels prefer to speak Spanish when they go to town. The women fruit sellers in the raucous Antigua market are an exception, speaking in Cakchiquel on their cell phones to set prices for avocado or sapodilla fruit. Yet when I tried to bargain with these women in Cakchiquel, I received mumbled rebuffs. In their eyes, each word I uttered in their language was a slap at their "backwardness." Later, hiking in the hills above town, I ran into an elderly couple who were speaking Cakchiquel together. They asked me in Spanish where I came from. When I replied in Cakchiquel, the old man said in Spanish: "Don't talk like that. That won't do you any good in the world."

Maya who care about their languages consider the teaching in schools of the Mayan writing systems using the Latin alphabet, consolidated by Mayan intellectuals during the 1980s (the original hieroglyphic writing died out in the 16th century), as the only long-term hope for saving these languages spoken by nearly 30% of Guatemala's population. A written language, a language that appears in books and on billboards, they argue, is a language people want to pass on to their children. One night my Cakchiquel teacher, a woman in her thirties, was at home preparing my lesson. Her mother peered at her books. "If I'd known our language could be written," she said, "I would have taught it to you better."

To study a Mayan language is to bump your toes against the threshold of a universe that is local, specific, conservative yet ritualized. There are small, rewarding revelations. The fact that the same expression, *käk winaq,* describes both "foreigners" and "Spanish-speaking Guatemalans," exposes Mayan marginalization. A tortilla is *weij,* while bread is *kaxlen weij* – "white people's tortilla." There are sumptuous idioms such as *xepolpotijkï,* "they flipped out," used to describe people who have converted to born-again Christianity. Idealists seeking evidence of egalitarian pastoralism or New Age mysticism in Mayan culture are doomed to disappointment. Traditional Cakchiquel speech, rich in agricultural concerns, was also obsessed with social rank and possessions. Cakchiquel contains a surfeit of words for "boss" or "leader," and every noun is brutally possessed. One rarely says "the bread"; it is "my bread," "your bread," " her bread." A large lexicon referring to the Mayan calendar and its rituals survives among shamans; but, although Mayan spirituality is enjoying a revival, many Maya have lost this religious vocabulary.

The greatest challenge faced by the learner of a Mayan language is not the mouth-contorting pronunciation, but the degree of local variation. "Good morning" is *sakar* in my teacher's village, *sakariq* across the valley and *xsequer* farther north. Never having become state languages, the Mayan languages have not been standardized. Each new textbook I studied used unfamiliar vocabulary, or spelled familiar words in unrecognizable ways. Frustrated, I longed for a fixed set of words to learn. I felt I could not learn Cakchiquel because what constituted "Cakchiquel," unlike French or Spanish, changed shape even as I struggled to organize it in my mind. I almost gave up. Then I realized that Cakchiquel had a different lesson to teach me: the artificial nature of all language; the fact that systematizing speech and writing to make it generally comprehensible loosens the clasp between word and concept in which human speech originated. The language that serves the nation misrepresents the locality and distorts the intimate personal experience. In Cakchiquel's parochialism and fragmentation lay the roots of its value.

Ren ninjo yintamaq Cakchiquel jub'a chik. I want to study more Cakchiquel.

"Mayan Guatemala" is based on "Majority no longer silent" and "Maya once dominated Central America," Montreal *Gazette*, 17 June 2003, and "Cakchiquel Lessons," *Geist* No. 50 (Fall 2003).

4. NEW EUROPE GROWS OLD

When I first began travelling in Central and Eastern Europe in the late 1980s, the dividing lines on social questions were stark. Western Europeans supported the welfare state, Eastern Europeans craved the free market; Western Europeans defined themselves as anti-racist, Eastern Europeans expressed hostility towards ethnic minorities; Western Europeans saw feminism as a progressive force and often disapproved of pornography, Eastern Europeans considered feminism to be a communist conspiracy and viewed the spread of pornography as evidence of personal liberty. Above all, Western Europeans regarded the United States as a shallow culture promoting a foreign policy of dubious probity while Eastern Europeans worshipped America and all its works.

During the decade after the fall of the Berlin Wall these oppositions began to erode. Their erosion has been uneven and contradictory, yet undeniable. Beneath the divisions on economic policy, a growing convergence of cultural outlook between older and newer members of the European Union is taking shape. Donald Rumsfeld's January 2003 dismissal of France and Germany as "a problem," and his hopeful statement that "the centre of gravity is shifting to the East," laid the cornerstone for a U.S. policy of exploiting residual Cold War idealism about the United States in Eastern Europe to undermine Western European objections to the invasion of Iraq. In two speeches of breathtaking cynicism, in Bratislava, Slovakia on February 24, 2005 and Riga, Latvia on May 7, 2005, George W. Bush claimed the spirit of 1989 as the inspiration for the U.S. decision to invade Iraq, telling his Bratislava audience: "It is important to pass on the lessons of that period . . . . By your efforts in Afghanistan and Iraq and across the world, you are teaching young Slovaks important lessons." Yet Bush's desire that

Eastern Europeans, remaining forever mindful of their experiences under Soviet rule, will offer unquestioning support to any foreign adventure to which the U.S. attaches the "freedom" label, depends on a vision of Europe that is already outdated.

In 2002, after attending a conference in Athens, I hit the backpacker trail through Greece. My fellow backpackers, many of them young northern Europeans, spoke fluidly neutral Euro-English. They all disliked the United States, an issue that arose early in any conversation since I usually had to explain that I was not American but Canadian, at which point my fellow travellers relaxed and opened up. In that spring lull – post-September 11 but pre-Iraq invasion – disdain for the United States, in Europe as in other parts of the world, was muted by comparison with the virulence it would assume later, as the Bush doctrine slouched towards Baghdad to be born. I was surprised that when I reached Bulgaria, where I visited two Bulgarian friends who I had met on earlier travels, the attitudes of the Scandinavians and Germans who had crossed my path in Greece did not feel alien. The forces behind the repudiation of the United States were different, but the attitudes were similar. In Bulgaria, the turning point had been the 1999 bombing of former Yugoslavia, conducted by NATO but blamed on the United States.

One day I climbed Mount Vitosha, above Sofia, with my Bulgarian friend Tereza. We rode a ski lift up the mountainside then hiked through the trees into a rock-scarred landscape where spars of stale-looking snow resisted the tepid June warmth. Tereza was far more cosmopolitan than most citizens of introverted, mountain-ringed Bulgaria. The five languages she spoke included Turkish. Tereza's fluent Turkish made some of her friends uneasy: Bulgaria's Turkish minority, resented as a reminder of the centuries when the country was ruled by the Ottoman Empire, is treated with hostility by mainstream Bulgarians. During the 1980s Bulgaria tried to force its Turks to adopt Slavic names. Tereza's interest in Turkish culture originated in her long-term relationship with a Turkish man, as a result of which she continued to spend part of each year in Istanbul. Yet in spite of her appealing acceptance of Muslim culture, she had no sympathy for Bosnian Muslims or Kosovo Albanians. Tereza dismissed the atrocities committed by Serb forces during the war in former Yugoslavia as concoctions of the U.S. media, cooked up to provide a pretext for military intervention. Her hostility had deepened when, during the 1999 bombing campaign, one U.S. bomber, running off course, bombed Bulgaria by mistake. But the central issue was her identification with neighbouring Orthodox peoples. The bombing of former Yugoslavia alienated Orthodox opinion not only in Serbia and Macedonia, but throughout Greece, Bulgaria and Romania. Older people, who remembered tuning in to Radio Free Europe during the Cold War to hear news reports denied them by their own media, continued to idealize the United States. But for someone of Tereza's generation, the defining encounter with U.S. foreign policy was the bombing of Serbia, whose religion she shared and whose language was mutually intelligible with Bulgarian.

Dmitri, a friend of both mine and Tereza's, who I visited in a different region of Bulgaria, also mentioned the bombs dropped on Bulgarian soil. A bohemian with a mid-back ponytail and two university degrees who had learned fluent English at the American College of Sofia, Dmitri was earning his living as a hard-rock musician. Dmitri's political vision was in many ways more nuanced than Tereza's. In spite of his allegiance to Orthodox cultures, he acknowledged the reality of Serb war crimes and recognized that significant differences existed between the multiethnic political institutions that Serbian forces had fought to destroy in Bosnia and the intransigent ethnic insurgency of Albanian nationalists in Kosovo. Yet Tereza's choice of a Turkish boyfriend made him uncomfortable. The Turks had the potential to destroy Bulgaria. What if the Turkish minority regions began to fight for their independence and NATO bombers came in to support them?

Dmitri was considering applying for a scholarship to attend a foreign university. The thought of studying outside Bulgaria made him feel guilty; he was susceptible to the criticism that too many young people were leaving the country. One thing was certain: he would not be studying in the United States. His friends from the American College of Sofia had made that mistake. They had returned home after a year, disgusted by the closed-mindedness of American life, and transferred to universities in Western Europe. So where was he going? Dmitri mulled this over. Holland, perhaps. He wanted to live in an open society.

My friends' disaffection with the United States surprised me. It left me unprepared, however, for the violent hostility to all emanations of United States influence that I encountered during a trip through Romania and Hungary in March 2005. Donald Rumsfeld, it seemed, had highlighted the differences between Eastern and Western Europe just as these differences were fading away. Within the countries formerly dominated by the Soviet Union, a generational divide was opening up. After the death of former U.S. President Ronald Reagan, the Romanian magazine *Curierul Românesc* (*The Romanian Messenger)*, the international voice of the country's intellectual elite, ran a lead editorial under the headline (in English) "Thank You, Mr. President!" An editorial of embarrassing adjectival excess lauded Reagan as the bestower of "freedom" (not the way he will be remembered in Nicaragua, El Salvador, or Honduras). After reading this nonsense, I set off on my trip ready to wrestle with the diametrically opposed outlooks of a Europe divided between East and West.

Taking refuge from a blizzard in northeastern Romania in the home of a teacher with whom I was acquainted, I was introduced to her family, then to her fiancé. Romulus was a startling figure. A man in his mid-thirties, six-foot-four with black hair receding into a thinning widow's peak, his blue eyes bequeathed to his dark Romanian face by some Ukrainian ancestor, he had trained as an engineer and now worked in the non-profit sector. He was an enthusiastic and adventurous traveller. Romulus had toured the Balkans on bicycle, sleeping rough or in accommodation offered to him by people he met along the way. On a later trip he had hitch-hiked from northeastern Romania to Iraq, then back through the

Middle East as far as Libya. He retained many views typical of Orthodox society (NATO's bombing of Yugoslavia came up immediately), but it was his experience of other cultures, rather than provincial insularity, that had consolidated his hatred of the United States. Romulus had gauged the impact of U.S. influence on the wider world, and had reached dire conclusions. We retreated to an upstairs room to sit out the blizzard, and ate and talked for eight hours. My acquaintance the teacher became deferential in her fiancé's presence; in this way, as in the rounds of food with which the family supplied us, traditional values remained intact. During the Cold War those values had made young Romanians pro-American; in the era of globalization adherence to tradition contributed to a welling anti-Americanism.

Everything, in Romulus's eyes, was a U.S. conspiracy: not just the bombings and invasions, but even the European Union, at first glance a counterweight to the influence of the United States, was in fact doing the U.S.'s work, he claimed, by stripping Eastern Europe of competitive industry. Like Dmitri in Bulgaria, Romulus linked his anti-Americanism to a quest for a society that was "open." For a Romanian this implied a potentially disconcerting shift in values. A rambling, diverse country of 21 million people, Romania has always had large minority populations. Today there are more than two million Roma (or Gypsies), between one and a half and two million Hungarians, a few thousand Germans (the remnants of a community that once numbered 700,000) and, in the country's border regions, outposts of Serbs, Bulgarians, Ukrainians and Turks. There was a large Jewish population until it was destroyed by the Holocaust. Some Romanian rulers have governed by turning the majority against the minorities. The communist dictator Nicolae Ceauşescu owed his survival until the last week of the 1980s, in part, to his promotion of a nationalism that depended on the brutal oppression of ethnic Hungarians. In the post-communist era local politicians, most notoriously Gheorghe Funar, the ultranationalist two-term mayor of the city of Cluj-Napoca (which Hungarians call Kolosvár), who was defeated in June 2004, have appealed to similar instincts. Romanians are acutely aware that they will enter the European Union in 2007 with the largest minority populations of any recent E.U. member. (Slovakia, already an E.U. member, has substantial, though smaller, Hungarian and Roma minorities.) The E.U. has set adequate provision for minority rights as a condition for Romania's entry. The far-right Greater Romania Party, which opposes any accommodation of minorities, polled 12.7% of the vote in the 2004 presidential elections; yet the new centre-right government of President Traian Băsescu contains three ethnic Hungarian cabinet ministers. When I mentioned to my hosts in the snowstorm that I had heard people speaking Hungarian in the streets of their town, they nodded their heads. "This is normal. There have always been Hungarian people here. They have their churches, they have their lives . . . this is normal." The Romanian political commentator Christian Ghinea has written that in 1997, when President Constantinescu initiated collaboration with the main political party of the Hungarian minority population, "it was an utter shock for Romanians." The repercussions of this shock continued to be absorbed. I sensed the difficulty of the adjustment my friends were making to a society in which traditional expressions of interethnic animosity must be quelled.

The embattled equilibrium between traditional ethnic assertion and a greater openness perceived as integral to modernity is present in both Eastern and Western Europe, binding them closer together. Even liberal Holland has bred a successful far-right party and, in the aftermath of the assassinations of the party's leader, Pim Fortuyn, and of the filmmaker Theo van Gogh, has descended into ethnic strife of almost Eastern European intensity. The difference is that no one in Western Europe is trying to drive out traditional ethnic minorities: the hostility is directed at immigrants. The immigrant, by definition, is visible; the historical minority is often maintained in a state of invisibility. My literary companion during my travels in Romania was *Întoarcerea huliganului* (2003; *The Hooligan's Return)*, Norman Manea's ironic, beautifully digressive memoir of a Jewish-Romanian childhood and youth, capped by an account of his return visit to Romania in 1997 from long-term exile in New York. Manea's book is published by Polirom, the best Romanian publishing house; yet some Romanian intellectuals to whom I expressed my enthusiasm for Manea's writing grew tense or claimed not to have heard of him. At the same time, Manea's descriptions of the southern Bukovina of his childhood remain oddly myopic because, in his meticulous narration of the region's social dynamics, the Roma population disappears. It is impossible to travel in Bukovina without being aware of the thousands of Gypsies who inhabit the region, yet Manea pretends that they don't exist, even though they shared his own community's fate of being incarcerated, transported, starved and murdered during the Holocaust.

This refusal to see others who are different preoccupied me as I arrived in Hungary. Having had the mongrelized bulk of its territory sheared away by the Treaty of Trianon in 1920, modern Hungary is an ethnically uniform rump where, as in most of Western Europe, internal minority issues are cast primarily in terms of recent immigrants, in Hungary's case from China, Russia or Ukraine. Yet the fate of the Magyar minorities living outside Hungary, not only in Romania but in Slovakia, former Yugoslavia and Ukraine, continues to elicit strong emotions, culminating in Hungary's provocative decision to extend citizenship to Hungarians living outside Hungary. As the largest minority group, the Hungarians in Romania are the beneficiaries of much of the passion expended on this issue. When I first spent a month in Hungary in 1989, at a time when Romania's Hungarians were suffering persecution by the death-spasms of the Ceauşescu dictatorship, I found this rallying to the defence of a beleaguered culture uplifting; in the democratic context of the present, the violent hatred of Romania expressed by many Hungarians can feel like a retrogade obsession. Members of Romania's ethnic Hungarian minority, aware that they are economically better off than other Romanian citizens, are often more sanguine about the situation than people in

Hungary. Endre, an ethnic Hungarian professor from Cluj, told me: "Romanian law says that wherever Hungarians are 20% of the population we can have bilingual signs and government services in Hungarian. Personally, I would prefer a system more like that enjoyed by the Swedish minority in Finland: wherever you have 3000 Swedes, you get services. Here in Cluj there are 60,000 Hungarians, but because we are 18.9% of the population, we have no services. Still, in many smaller towns mayors have authorized services for Hungarians even in cases where we are 15% or less of the population."

My Budapest friends Pisti and Julcsi shared the vision of the Hungarians in Romania as one of continuing oppression. Julcsi and I have been friends and colleagues for fifteen years. Her husband Pisti and I disagree about politics. Having graduated from an experimental bilingual (English-Hungarian) school established in Budapest by UNESCO, Pisti speaks stunningly fluent English and grew up worshipping the United States. But, during my latest visit to Hungary, I discovered that raising his two young sons in the early 21st century was making it difficult for him to harmonize his nationalism with his idealistic vision of the U.S.A. Pisti's bookish older son Tibor, now aged ten, is already making speeches about the need to save the Hungarian minority in Romania; but father and son have different generational visions of the United States.

"For me," Pisti said, "learning English was a statement. It was about my freedom. It meant I could go into downtown hotels where they sold *Newsweek* and *Time* and get information my government didn't want me to have. Tibor's generation has English all around it. He knows he has to learn it but he's become indifferent."

"What about English as the language in which Europeans communicate with each other?" I asked, remembering my travels in Greece.

"The fact remains that the United States of America is the biggest source of English in the world today. When my son turns on the television and sees American soldiers going into somebody else's country and killing people, it doesn't exactly help the language." He hesitated, looking uncomfortable. "I don't want to say it, but learning English is a duty for him. I don't want to say it, but it's almost like Russian was before."

The European Union is not in the business of eradicating nationalism, but rather of containing nationalist impulses within a legislative framework. In both Eastern and Western Europe, closer formal associations with nearby countries have thrown national traits into starker relief. The rejection of the European constitution by France and Holland in May 2005, in the name of the preservation of national values, demonstrates that cultural nationalism in Europe is a broad-based force, not merely a bogeyman unleashed on Eastern Europe by the collapse of communism. Any clearly articulated nationalism, no matter how democratic, multi-ethnic and peace-loving the nation, will produce a dislike for the United States, whose current global quest for "freedom" mandates cultural homogenization on its own terms as the precondition for commercial efficiency. In Orthodox countries, such as Bulgaria and Romania, and countries with large Muslim populations, such as France, hostility to the U.S. has grown more swiftly than in relatively undiluted Catholic societies such as Hungary or Italy. Poland, with its fratricidal antagonism to Russian culture, will persist longer than other nations in seeking solace across the Atlantic. Yet this year, for the first time, I found I was able to criticize U.S. foreign policy in front of young Poles without provoking outrage. National differences will endure in Europe, however the future of the European Union unfolds; but the rift between "Eastern Europe" and "Western Europe," antiquated Cold War notions whose time is now past, is destined to fade away. To paraphrase Donald Rumsfeld, New Europe is growing Old.

"New Europe Grows Old" was published in slightly different form in *Guernica: A Magazine of Art & Politics*, June 2005.

5.   WATCHING THE G8 IN LUANDA

Fernando and I are watching the G8 on television. "Look at Bush and Blair pretending they want to help us," Fernando says. "They were happy to starve us until Africa started to do business with the Chinese."

The Chinese businessmen eat lunch at Nando's Chicken, Luanda's only fast-food restaurant. They pay USD$11 for a burger, fries and a Coke. The Chinese sit next to Texan oil men and Indian importers. The three groups ignore each other as they plot their next move. The streets outside are a chaos of construction hoardings. The oil companies are putting up thirty-storey towers next to the decaying white stucco mansions built during Angola's five centuries as a Portuguese colony. The Portuguese engineers who work on the buildings spurn Nando's Chicken. At lunch they follow their Angolan colleagues – black Angolans, brown Angolans, white Angolans – to unmarked restaurants down passageways where *feijoada* stew and *funje,* a glue-like paste made of cassava root, share the menu with Portuguese grilled cod. Having been expelled in 1975 by a Marxist independence movement, the Portuguese are creeping back, mingling with the locals as they did before, when Portuguese men dispatched to the colonies fathered the angry mixed-raced middle class that became the backbone of the leadership of the MPLA guerrillas. "Things are going badly in Portugal," the lugubrious young engineer who sat next to me on the flight from Lisbon said. "Our future is in Africa."

The Angolans are not sure they want the Portuguese back. They are tempted by the Chinese. At dusk on the Marginal, the magnificent boulevard that cuts around the vast bay in front of the pink palaces of the old colonial administration, the Texans and the Portuguese jog beneath the palm trees, and the Chinese jog after them. (Indian importers do not jog.) The Chinese are confident that Angola is entering the Chinese sphere of influence. In 1990 the MPLA government, formerly supported by Moscow and Havana and attacked by proxies of Washington and Beijing, renounced socialism. By the late 1990s the Angolans had learned to exploit the oil business to keep Washington's hawks at bay. But the MPLA still distrusts the West. The sons of cabinet ministers may study in Houston now (in contrast to the president, who earned his engineering degree in Moscow), but footsoldier cadres are sent on training courses in Cuba and the pro-government *Jornal de Angola* trumpets new deals with North Korea.

Above all, Angola distrusts the International Monetary Fund. In June 2005, in a rare breach of discipline, the IMF contravened its own regulations by posting on its website a working paper entitled, "In Angola the Only Institution is Corruption." Angola protested: the IMF took down the draft report. Angola continued to protest: the IMF issued a formal apology. Having humiliated the IMF, the Angolans told them to get lost; Angola did not need to negotiate a structural adjustment program. When you are on course to pass Nigeria to become Africa's largest oil producer, you can choose your friends. The 21st century belongs to China, and too many Chinese want to drive cars. The Angolan elite recognizes the Chinese model: unregulated capitalism presided over by unelected Stalinists. It is the same model that reigns in Angola.

When I arrived in Luanda, I got stuck at the airport and was rescued by a Lebanese businessman who advised me to enjoy the city during the day and avoid going out at night. Then I met Fernando, who wanted to meet after dark. "It is not advisable to walk around alone at night," he drawled, with the broad-vowelled precision that makes Angolan Portuguese easier to understand than that of Portugal or Brazil, "but you can walk with me."

Fernando is black and six feet three inches tall. An economist, trained in Goa, he supports the free market but despises the IMF. Fernando and I sit in one of the bars hidden down passageways. The crowd is foreigners and light-skinned Angolans: in some cases foreign men with Angolan women. A *semba* musician vanishes from the screen at the end of the room and Bush and Blair appear. "We want to be your partner," Blair says. The crowd at the bar jeers. No one hates a former social democrat as much as former socialists.

The city centre is deserted as Fernando and I hop bars. Luanda is like a ghost that only comes out at night. During the day the city is invisible. Construction gobbles up every block, scaffolding and cement-mixers and men pushing wheelbarrows elbow pedestrians and fruit-sellers into the middle of the street where the silver Prado jeeps ride bumper to bumper, snorting towards intersections innocent of traffic lights. The orange dust of the dry season, which Angolans call *cacimbo*, gusts up into the sunlight. The chaos disappears at night. The view clears: the contours of a 19th-century Portuguese city emerge. The colonial buildings display their beauty but also their fragility: the empty window frames, the crumbling red roof tiles, the shattered blue patterns of *azulejo* mosaics. I wonder how many of these buildings will be demolished to make way for the advancing office towers. For years Luanda was famous for enormous piles of garbage rotting in the streets. Then the government decided that garbage was a deterrent to foreign investment and overnight the fetid mounds disappeared. The country may suffer from a shortage of basic services – schools, highways, hospitals – but oil money can alter the landscape at will.

We are in another bar and angry Angolans are deriding the West's pets in Africa: Senegal, Ghana, Mozambique. All that those earnest corruption-fighters will gain by qualifying for Bush and Blair's debt relief is the privilege of handing over their social services to profit-making Western companies; that is the condition for G8 "aid." An old white Angolan in danger of toppling off his barstool tells me that under socialism Angola was producing 30,000 barrels of oil a day at $36 a barrel and everything was subsidized; now the country produces 1,000,000 barrels a day at $60 a barrel and people are starving. Only the Chinese can save the hungry. Angola and China have devised a barter exchange that bypasses money. It is not quite socialism, but in return for designated quantities of oil, the Chinese build Angola a highway, a housing development, a hospital; in return for long-term access to Angola's oil-rich continental shelf, Chinese engineers are going to revive the country's bombed-out railway network. There is no corruption because no money changes hands. "This isn't charity," the man says, "they need a market for their goods. The U.S. and Europe want to close them out." He shrugs. "If they want to raise our poor to a level where instead of starving they can afford to buy Chinese products, I won't complain."

As I walk home, it sounds like a fantasy. I pass the headquarters of U.S. oil companies. During the day each head office flies the MPLA flag: a yellow half tractor wheel, machete and star, in imitation of the Soviet hammer-and-sickle, on a red and black background. That, too, seems like a fantasy. Next morning I talk to a Western diplomat. "These infrastructure swaps with the Chinese are a good thing," the diplomat says. "Eventually even the IMF will have to admit that. Everyone else has rushed to join the neo-liberal world, but the Angolans are still suspicious. In the long run they may come out ahead."

That night Fernando and I are on Engels Street. Or maybe it is Marx or Lenin. Back at last night's bar, Bush and Blair are on television, talking about saving Africa. But we have put them behind us. We are on our way to listen to piano music in a bar without a television. The slender black barmaids wear short skirts and long, straightened hair that turns slick beneath the lights, and the crowd is a blend of wealthy Angolans and foreigners. I see Texans and Portuguese and even an Indian importer gloating over his mixed-raced female Angolan escort. There are no Chinese. They have more important things to do.

"Watching the G8 in Luanda" was published in slightly different form in *Matrix* No. 73 (Spring 2006).

6. TRAVEL, WRITING – AND THE UNEXPECTED LINKS BETWEEN THEM

Last summer, as I prepared to leave for a long trip through southern Mexico, my friends were certain they knew why I was going travelling. "You're going to get new material for your fiction!" they said.

No, I thought. I don't travel to get material: I travel because I need to travel. The writing and the travelling may spring from the same cluster of compulsions, but the relationship between them is not that simple. The next friend who greeted me with a comment about travelling to get material was treated to a quote from Evelyn Waugh: "One no more travels to get material than one falls in love to get material."

This was an effective retort, although, like many effective retorts, it sounds defensive. And it raises a question. Haven't some writers fallen in (or out of) love knowing they would one day write about the experience? Didn't Philip Roth, while divorcing his wives, know that he was destined to reimagine it all as fiction?

Writers will always be writers. Norman Mailer is said to have been planning *The Naked and the Dead* even as he enlisted for service in the Second World War. But this simple fact hides a more complex truth. The writer may have a clear conception of what the next book will be about, but that does not mean that the writer's imagination will go along with the idea. Heading off on a research trip can be one way of setting yourself up for an unexpected change of creative direction. Nothing disrupts a smoothly laid-out plot summary like the intrusion of experience. A long trip to an unfamiliar place, provided it includes a significant engagement with that place and its inhabitants, risks changing the writer as a human being. The individual who emerges from a transformative experience may no longer be capable of writing the story that has been promised to agents and publishers back home.

As a young writer in the 1950s, Anthony Burgess accepted a teaching job in Malaya (now Malaysia) after Roland Gant, Burgess's editor at Heinemann, advised him that he needed some creative distance from his obsession with Catholic guilt. The result of Burgess's five years in Malaya was not a fresh take on English Catholicism, but his decolonization trilogy, *The Long Day Wanes* (1956-59). Travel provided Burgess with new material, although not the material his editor had sought from him.

In our era, when literature is discussed largely as a commodity commanding multiple-digit advances and requiring elaborate publicity campaigns, many find it comforting to think that books, like the other merchandise for sale in our shopping malls, are produced according to consistent manufacturing processes. This, I think, is the source of the current cult of the research trip. Our materialistic age demands it. Knowing that the author went to Malaysia or Fiji, we believe that we can trust the author's vision – not just of Malaysia or Fiji, but of reality in general. The book is a good book, we proclaim, because it is based on facts!

Yet how many writers have piled up facts to no creative benefit? How many research-packed files lie untouched in writers' cupboards while imagination, like a wayward pony, has headed off over the horizon in pursuit of fresh sustenance? Most writers are familiar with the phenomenon of The Research Trip That Went Astray.

Three years ago I travelled to Yugoslavia determined to write something hard-hitting about the situation there. I questioned well-informed officials about the economy, corruption, language politics, ethnic tensions, splits in the regime. I travelled around, I had tea with opposition leaders. When I returned to my desk the piece that emerged, to my intense aggravation, was a fanciful novella about a mournful diplomat who is posted to Montenegro in 1912. The notebooks full of facts were interesting, but they had not stimulated my imagination. A visit to a Montenegrin moun-taintop, by contrast, had spun me into a creative whirl.

The 20th-century pioneer of fiction based on long stays in faraway places was Graham Greene. Critics used to refer to this sort of fiction as taking place in Greeneland. Yet Greene himself recognized that every Greeneland was not equally fertile for the novelist. In *Ways of Escape* (1980), the second volume of his autobi-ography, Greene wrote: "I wasn't seeking sources, I stumbled on them, though perhaps a writer's instinct was at work when I bought my ticket to Saigon or Port-au-Prince or Asunción . . . . Yet the Emergency in Malaya produced no novel, nor did the Mau Mau rebellion in Kenya. Not even a short story emerged from the occasion when I was deported by the American authorities from Puerto Rico or from my experience of the Communist takeover in Prague in 1948. Poland in the Stalinist 1950s left the novelist's imagination untouched . . . ."

Creativity cannot be induced because it depends on the unpre-dictable cross-pollination of external reality and half-buried, inces-santly evolving personal obsessions. Greene could not predict that Vietnam would give him *The Quiet American* and Haiti *The Come-dians*, while Malaya, Kenya, Prague and Poland left him creatively barren. Could anyone have predicted that Malaya during the polit-ical tension of the 1950s would give Burgess three novels and Greene none?

Bearing this in mind, I grow increasingly distrustful of writers who return from research trips planning to write the same book that was on the cards when they left. To me, this is a sign that they kept their eyes closed during their travels, or that the book is pre-programmed rather than nurtured by the writer's deepest emotional resources and most vital obsessions. Creativity depends in part on discipline, but it also depends on knowing when to rec-ognize when one creative plan has been outgrown and a new one is taking shape.

So it was with my trip to Mexico. I travelled widely, made a couple of new friends, met the usual quotient of odd characters on buses, and had one tense encounter with the Mexican Army in a Chiapas village sympathetic to the Zapatista rebels. Does all this add up to material for new fiction? Who knows? If I ever do write a piece of fiction based on my trip, I can be fairly certain that its subject will be something I had not thought of before leaving, and that, like most literature, it will take its author by surprise.

––––––––––––

"Travel, Writing – and the Unexpected Links Between Them" appeared in *Quill & Quire*, December 2000.

III:

WORDS IN THE WORLD

1.   THE TRANSLATION GAP

1.   Translation and the Writer

The writer's engagement with language is also an engagement with *languages*. The Western literary tradition begins with the crossing of languages that brought the literature of classical Greece to the Roman Empire. The transmission of the genres, motifs, styles, characters, themes of modern literature starts with this "translation," or carrying over. (The Germans, as always, make it explicit: *übersetzen*, to translate, is to "carry over.") Rome's assimilation of Greek literature is the catalyst for the next two thousand years of literary development. The national literatures of Europe, and the literatures written later in European languages displaced to the Americas, Africa, Asia, the Middle East and the Pacific Ocean, all descend from these early acts of translation. The pioneers of the idea of literature as a tradition – an idea without which there is no literature – were trilingual men of letters from southern Italy. "Translator-stylizers," Mikhail Bakhtin calls them. Bakhtin recounts that these men "had come to Rome from lower Italy, where the boundaries of three languages and cultures intersected with one another – Greek, Oscan and Roman."

If to know a second language is to possess a second soul, the men who filtered the Greek tradition they understood through the Oscan language that was native to them and into the classical Latin of the empire they served, had three souls. Western literature's yearning for perfect forms that are capable of expressing wholeness and completion originates in this harking back to Greece; but so does the Western tradition's fundamental rootlessness, its sense of perpetual expatriation, of being always at a one-step remove from the core of authentic experience. Not even the most provincial Western literature may pronounce from the sheltered bastion of a closed tradition (in contrast, say, to the classical literature of China). Behind the immemorial phrases of Shakespeare, the most English of Englishmen, glimmer the shadows of Italian Renaissance drama: its plot devices, its staging techniques, its settings, even, in translation, some of its phrasings. Shakespeare forges Englishness from a creative energy which dances on the cusp between English and Italian.

The monolingual writer is a postmodern, Anglo-American invention. In ages prior to ours, when all writers, by definition, were multilingual, literature's nature as an entity whose lustre was burnished by the fretting together of different linguistic strands was so obvious that it did not need to be stated. The mere existence of a spoof such as Jonathan Swift's "Battle of the Books," in which classical and modern literatures do battle like opposing armies, illustrates the tension that the past exerted on the present in eras when all writers of modern European languages read Classical languages and the guardian of a library, like Swift's protagonist, might sow discord if, "in replacing his *Books*, he was apt to mistake, and clap *Descartes* next to *Aristotle*."

In 19th-century Europe, two-souled readers, even if not proficient in Latin or Greek, read in French as well as – or instead of – in their own languages. Husbands in novels by Tolstoy and Dostoevsky complain about the influence of the salacious French novelist Paul de Kok on Russian women; later, in 1922, James Joyce's *Ulysses* trawls out the resonances of de Kok's surname with ironic gusto. More serious strains of French literature also had the delicious potential to corrupt: the diaries of Flaubert, for their vivid descriptions of syphilitic chancres contracted in Egyptian brothels; the novels of Émile Zola, for their explicit sex scenes, unthinkable in the work of writers across the Channel in Victorian England; the fiction of Remy de Gourmount or J.K. Huysmans, a Francophone Belgian, for its decadent and/or homoerotic sensibilities. In the 20th century, as the European bourgeoisie lost the habit of reading in other languages (a habit which the North American bourgeoisie never acquired and the South American bourgeoisie has never lost), translators became trend-setters. The vogue, in the English-language world, for Russian literature in the 1930s and 1940s, French existentialism in the 1950s and 1960s, and Latin American novels in the 1970s and 1980s, all depended on the prowess of translators. But the end of the Cold War and the onset of accelerated globalization have relegated translation to the back alleys of literature. In smaller cultures, translation remains a valued activity and respected writers may be, also, respected translators. But most of the world's larger cultures are averse to, even disdainful of, literature in translation. One of the cultural disasters of the present is that the world's two most internationalized cultures – the Anglo-American and the Muslim-Arabic – have the planet's lowest rates of translation activity. That these cultures have become obscurantist, belligerent, xenophobic and possessed of the bizarre belief that they alone hold the keys to truth is both a cause and a consequence of their disregard for translation.

Many literatures, however, take for granted that the writer is also a translator. In such societies, the writer blends a cosmopolitan grasp of literary technique with an earthy appreciation of local materials. In English-speaking Canada, where our better-known writers prefer the combination of exotic materials with provincialism of technique, novelist-translators are an alien phenomenon. The only exception to the rule in this country, and arguably anywhere in the North Atlantic Anglo-American world, is Montreal, where novelists as different as Jeffrey Moore, Robert Majzels and David Homel are also accomplished translators (as are Francophone writers such as Gaétan Soucy and Marie-Célie Agnant). In Canada, poets, whether traditionalists such as George Johnston or avant-gardists such as Erin Mouré, may be translators; but prose writers, by definition, are not. For writers in many other parts of the world, translation is an indispensable first step in the reconciliation of the local and the foreign which underlies the development of a literary style. The list of works translated by

Jorge Luis Borges, for example, is exhausting to contemplate. As a young man, Borges translated mainly from English, his masterpiece being a Spanish rendering of large sections of Thomas Browne's "Urn Burial"; in later life Borges published translations from German, French, Italian, Anglo-Saxon and Old Norse. The rhythms of Borges's prose in his essays and short fiction, which do not always feel natural to readers of Spanish, reveal the impact of his immersion in English and other Germanic languages. In turn, Borges's translations influenced younger writers. Mario Vargas Llosa has described how one of the most important days of his adolescence occurred when he discovered Borges's translation of William Faulkner's *The Wild Palms* and was unable to put it down. The structure of Vargas Llosa's novel, *The Green House*, with its debt to *The Wild Palms*, attests to the translation's influence. Borges's mother, Leonor Acevedo, was his collaborator in many of his longer translations; it is probably in deference to her sensibilities that the abortion scene in *The Wild Palms* is omitted from the Spanish translation.

A writer as different from Borges as Isabel Allende also owes the formation of her literary style to the experience of translation. Early in her life, Allende was employed translating romance novels from English to Spanish. Frustrated by the passivity of heroines who sought only to snare a good husband, Allende started to rewrite as she translated so that, in one notorious case, the heroine, who in the English original found happiness as a housewife, became in the Spanish translation a gun-runner in the Congo. The bleak precision of J.M. Coetzee's prose, while a reflection of his personality and his training as a computer programmer, was polished by his translation endeavours. Coetzee is a prolific translator of early Afrikaans writing and contemporary Dutch fiction into English. Haruki Murakami's invention of a modern, streamlined Japanese prose would have been much more difficult had he not had the experience of translating work by F. Scott Fitzgerald, Truman Capote, Raymond Carver and John Irving into Japanese. It is almost impossible, by contrast, to imagine Margaret Atwood or

Timothy Findley, Barbara Gowdy, Jane Urquhart, David Adams Richards, Wayne Johnston or Guy Vanderhaeghe, undertaking a literary translation. The very incongruousness of such an image helps to illuminate the definition of the novelist in English-speaking Canada: in a society such as ours, which is devoted to specialization, the novelist who also translated would be seen as less of a novelist. The legacy of 1960s literary nationalism, debased by mass consumerism, casts the English-Canadian writer as the representative of a certain ordinary, average Canadianness. Since ordinary, average Canadians don't speak other languages (or, if they do, know better than to advertise the fact), the writer-translator is ruled out of order in English-language Canadian literary culture. This fact helps to explain the lack of innovation in most Canadian prose.

2. For and Against Translation

Twice in my life I have taught in universities where the language and literature departments, recently amalgamated into a School, were based on the second floor of the Arts building, while the fourth floor was occupied by a large School of English and Drama renowned for its devotion to postcolonial studies. In both universities my colleagues and I in the language departments writhed at the ill-informed readings of Spanish American writers emanating from the postcolonialists. Whenever a student reported a glaring error to us we would snicker while, at the same time, feeling resentful that these caricatures were being communicated to larger numbers of students than we, who had been trained in this field, were able to attract. The rise of postcolonialism as the governing ideology of many English departments has served English professors as a licence to poach on language departments' terrain. English Departments now routinely agitate to close down the teaching of literature in language departments, aiming to reduce them to "Berlitz Schools" (the stated goal of one Chair of English

at the University of Guelph). The elimination of the teaching of
the literatures of France, Germany and Italy, English professors
allege, represents no loss since these literatures, having been written by "dead white males," are inherently reactionary. Literatures
seen to further the postcolonial agenda, such as those of Quebec
or Spanish America, are slated to be transferred to the English
curriculum, where they will be taught in translation, their language suppressed and the historical contexts that produced them
twisted into knots until they fit the postcolonial formula. Not for
nothing do my colleagues in languages refer to proudly postcolonial English professors as "the neo-colonialists."

The vehicle of this proposed restructuring is translation.
Contemporary university politics have converted translation
into the tool of a strand of professorial cant which, while claim-
ing to promote the concerns of a broadly conceived "Third
World," in fact enshrines the ideology of a corporate version of
globalization by teaching students that foreign cultures contain
nothing that cannot be expressed in English. Latin American
critics such as Hugo Achugar of Uruguay and Patricia
D'Allemand of Colombia have argued that supposedly left-wing
postcolonial English professors who try to shoehorn Latin
America into postcolonial theoretical models derived from the
history of the Commonwealth, in Achugar's words, "have not
abandoned certain habits . . . of the imperial history of the English language." (My translation.) The idiocies produced by these
tourists lost in foreign terrain and proposing to teach its literature and culture on the basis of a phrasebook acquaintance with
the language could fill volumes of satire. One of the unexpected
consequences of this dynamic can be to transform anyone who
works in a university and cares about literature or history (or the
Third World), into a visceral opponent of translation as a means
of teaching literature or understanding other cultures. In recent
years, acrimonious curriculum meetings where I'm forced to
argue against translation in order to justify teaching literature in
the original language have sharpened my awareness of the

limitations of literature read (and studied) in any language other than that in which it was written.

My first frustration with the teaching of literature in translation occurred when, as a graduate student, I was assigned to tutor an undergraduate on Gabriel García Márquez's novel *Cien años de soledad*. The student opened her paper by quoting José Arcadio Buendía's attempt to extract gold from "the bowels of the earth"; she went on to analyze digestive and fecal imagery in the novel. The problem is that the novel contains no such references: José Arcadio attempts to "desentrañar el oro de la tierra" ("to unravel gold from earth"). The verb "desentrañar," does, it is true, contain the root "entraña," or entrails. But writers of Spanish are not much more likely to associate unravelling gold from earth with images of bowels than are writers of English. The culprit here is García Márquez's devious translator Gregory Rabassa, who took a unilateral decision to make explicit the bowel-ish roots of the verb "to unravel." I realized that, rushed for time, the student had read the novel in translation. I could not teach her because we had read different books. *One Hundred Years of Solitude* is not *Cien años de soledad* just as, in Walter Benjamin's famous example, what a Frenchwoman understands by *pain* is not what a German understands by *Brot*. The difference between a long pale baguette and a heavy dark loaf represents only the beginning of the confusion sown by translation. A translation is an interpretation, so studying literature in translation is to interpret an interpretation: Rabassa extracts an image of bowels from García Márquez's unravelling; the student carries meaning one step farther from its point of origin by analyzing an image absent from the original text. Benjamin warns against this second level of diffusion in an often-quoted passage where he writes: "Translations [. . .] prove to be untranslatable [. . .] because of the looseness with which meaning attaches to them." Of course what Benjamin really wrote was: "Übersetzungen dagegen erweisen sich unübersetzbar nicht wegen der Schwere, sondern wegen der allzu grossen Flüchtigkeit, mit welcher der Sinn an ihnen haftet." In German the warning not to attach meaning to translations is more severe. "Looseness" is not a particularly good translation of *Flüchtigkeit*: "fleetingness" or "volatility" might be closer.

In moments when thoughts like these pass through my head I remind myself that if translation is an evil, it is a necessary and seductive one. At fifteen I fell in love with 19th-century Russian literature. To this day, I track down obscure Russian novels because no other literature communicates the same rich darkness. When, as a graduate student, I audited a course on the Russian novel in translation, taught by a professor who read the novels in the original, I realized how badly I had misread Nikolai Gogol's *Dead Souls*, mangling the terms in which the novel presents the themes of religion, serfdom and national destiny. My wariness was reinforced when one of my short stories was translated into Romanian. The story's title was "The Gentlewoman of Baku"; the translation emerged as "Femeia din Baku," or "The Woman from Baku." The ironic connotations of the word "gentlewoman" proved untranslatable; likewise, as Romanian usually translates the English "of" through a combined dative-genitive postpositioned particle that implies a tighter form of possession than is conveyed by "of" in English, the word "*din*" meaning "from," had to be used, giving the impression that my protagonist was a native of Azerbaijan, when in fact she was a foreigner resident in Baku. Undeterred, my indomitable translator, Irina Horia, decided to translate one of my Canadian short stories into Romanian. She came to a halt in a passage where a young boy dreams of growing up to be a relief pitcher in the Major Leagues. The boy imagines himself throwing "an unfathomable fork ball," a phrase which prompted a flurry of emails between Irina and me. My explanation that a fork ball was a curve that broke downwards out of the strike zone as it approached home plate set Irina a severe challenge in an Eastern European cultural context where baseball is unknown. Her translation of the unfathomable fork ball was to have the boy imagine himself defeating adversaries with "aruncările sale sub pragul bătăii," literally with "his throws below the thrashing threshold," a very inventive way to render the concept of a batter's strike zone in Romanian.

It is understandable that some authors wish to take control of their translations. Except in the cases of completely bilingual writers such as Samuel Beckett, Milan Kundera or Nancy Huston, such authorial lunges for total control almost always backfire. The Brazilian novelist João Ubaldo Ribeiro laboured to translate his masterpiece, *Viva o Povo Brasileiro*, into English by himself; the translation, *An Invincible Memory*, is a failure. But translation can also be an experience internal to the manuscript. The South African novelist André Brink, who publishes in both English and Afrikaans, writes his novels in drafts that alternate between the two languages. The Afrikaans third draft feeds off the changes necessitated in the second draft by virtue of its being in English; the English fourth draft draws on changes introduced in the Afrikaans third draft. Each language redirects the concerns of the other, yet the languages remain discrete and separate. When I translated a poem by the Nicaraguan poet Carlos Rigby from Spanish to English, Rigby was pleased and asked me to translate more of his work. This drew me into unexpected complications. Unlike most Nicaraguans, who are Spanish-speaking people of mixed Native American and Spanish ancestry, Rigby is a black West Indian poet from Nicaragua's isolated Atlantic Coast. He belongs to a culture where West Indian English is the language of the home, minority Native American languages such as Miskito and Rama are spoken in the surrounding bush, and education takes place in Spanish. Rigby, who now spends most of the year in Managua and is married to a woman from the north of Spain, writes in a Spanish prone to bilingual Spanish-English puns and interspersed with chant-like refrains in Native American languages. As his translator, I found myself with the bizarre task of restoring Rigby's poetry to his mother tongue, which, through a fluke of history, is not his literary language. Rigby and I speak to each other in Spanish. Occasionally he will ask me the English word for something related to computers or television. The modern part of Rigby's life has taken place in Spanish; English, for him, is the language of a rural, natural world, of parents and children in villages in the jungle. My translations must find a way to reflect the fact that for Rigby, in contrast to the experience of most people on this planet, English is a language that expresses what the world was like before technology.

Bilingual books are the most difficult to translate. I faced this hurdle in translating the young Angolan writer Ondjaki's novel *Good Morning Comrades* from Portuguese to English. The novel describes the relationship between Angolan schoolchildren of the 1980s and their teachers, who were Cuban. In the Portuguese original, the Cuban teachers speak in untranslated Spanish; a reader of Portuguese, even when unschooled in Spanish, will be able to follow most of what the teachers are saying. As large blocks of untranslated Spanish were not an option in a book published in English, I had to render the teachers' dialogue into English, but an English that suggested Spanish. I took advantage of Spanish words and expressions that are either cognates with English words (*la revolución*) or sufficiently familiar to English speakers that they could be left in the original (*¿qué pasa?*). The novel's humour, some of it depending on misunderstandings between teachers and students caused by words that look similar in Spanish and Portuguese but have different meanings in the two languages, was harder to capture. *Good Morning Comrades* was a challenge to translate because, among other themes, it is a novel about translation.

One response to the obstacle of translation, particularly for writers working in minority languages, is to publish in bilingual editions. The contemporary Maya-Quiché poet Humberto Ak'abal publishes his work in bilingual editions, with the Mayan and Spanish texts on facing pages. Yet not even this solves the problem. The Spanish translation of a line from Ak'abal's poem "Pa Ri Kitzijob'al" (literally "In their Voices") reads "su sueño está en las raíces," which translates into English as "their dream is in the roots." But the Quiché original reads: "ri kiwaram k'o chuxe' ri ulew." This means something like: "The dream of theirs is in, is going through, the earth." Neither Spanish nor English can contend with the way the Mayan "within" contains the idea of movement, nor, even more crucially, with the distinctive Maya cosmovision that signifies "earth" and "roots" with the same word, "*ulew*." Translation into any European language will crush this vital distinction, which is central to Ak'abal's vision. In a university committee meeting, I would be obliged to point out that interpretations of the poem in translation will produce superficial readings destined to assimilate Mayan cultural expression into pre-conditioned Western categories. In the wider universe, I would insist that translation, for all its deceptions, is as vital to us as water and that without it we are doomed to live barricaded against the world. In recognizing the limitations of translation we begin to understand how different other people are from ourselves.

3. The Insularity of English

Over dinner, I ask the Québécoise writer Sylvie Desrosiers, the successful author of novels for both adults and younger readers, whether any of her books have been translated into English. "*Non, pas en anglais*," she says. "I've been translated into Spanish, Greek, Arabic . . ." She lists three or four other languages, then shakes her head. "But not into English."

The month after Desrosiers's visit to Ontario, I am one of the hosts for the Ontario tour of the Salvadoran writer Horacio Castellanos Moya. The Salvadoran edition of Moya's novel *El Asco* (1997) – the title is roughly translatable as *Revulsion* – ran through six printings in a year and earned Moya so many death threats that he moved to Germany. Now in his late forties, Moya is the best-known Salvadoran writer of his generation. His novels come out in Spanish-language editions in San Salvador, Mexico City and

Barcelona; in France and Quebec he is considered a significant literary figure (he was the featured guest of the 2005 Salon du Livre in Montreal); his novels are also available in German and Italian. His work has not been translated into English.

The Peruvian writer Mario Vargas Llosa has declared that anyone who doesn't know English today is condemned to provincialism. This may be true, but it is necessary to add that anyone who reads only in English is also condemned to provincialism because in the last fifteen years the English-speaking world has turned its back on other literatures. Translation is an imperfect filter for literature; often it is a downright distortion. But when translation declines, literatures stagnate. Constance Garnett's translations, even though they are now acknowledged to be clumsy and deficient, brought Russian literature into the literate English-speaking consciousness in the early 20th century. Modernist prose benefited from this awareness. "I want to discuss Form, having been reading Turgenev," Virginia Woolf wrote in her diary on August 16, 1933. Across the English Channel, Woolf's near-contemporary André Gide devoted an entire book to trying to prove that Dostoevsky was a greater writer than Tolstoy. It is possible that early French translations of Russian literature were no more elegant than those of Garnett, but their publication reshaped literary debate.

The focus of literary translation changes with the political climate. Translations of Russian literature made the leap across the Atlantic in the early 1940s as the result of a U.S. government "amity program" that subsidized cultural exchange with Washington's Second World War ally, the Soviet Union. After 1945, the new ally was Japan: Washington funded the study of Japanese language and literature in U.S. universities. This stimulated the wide availability of translations of novels by Yukio Mishima, Yasunari Kawabata and Junichiro Tanizaki. These translations established a taste for Japanese fiction among readers of English, paving the way for the success in English translation of later writers such as Haruki Murakami and Banana Yoshimoto.

Political allegiances determined that we gained access to a broad spectrum of Japanese fiction but learned little of Chinese literature.

During the Cold War, series such as Writers from the Other Europe, edited for Penguin Books by Philip Roth, made us less provincial by ensuring that we could find novels by George Konrád, Bruno Schulz and Tadeusz Konwicki in our bookstores. The political imperative guaranteed that every word by the Soviet dissident Alexander Solzhenitsyn appeared in English, and assisted the careers of Milan Kundera and Ivan Klíma. Conversely, the Romanian dictator Nicolae Ceauşescu's policy of cultivating good relations with the West must take some of the blame for the fact that the great Romanian novelist Marin Preda was excluded from this wave of translation. The campus counterpoint to the promotion of dissident work from Eastern Europe took the form of acclaim for translations of Spanish American fiction. Personally, I hold those little shiny Avon paperbacks with the lush paintings on the covers responsible for driving me to master Spanish. The most popular edition of the emblematic Spanish American novel, *One Hundred Years of Solitude*, appeared in the Avon series, as did other pivotal works, such as Julio Cortázar's *Hopscotch* and Vargas Llosa's *The Green House*. Avon branched out into classics by older writers, such as the Cuban Alejo Carpentier, and began the task of remedying our ignorance of the riches of Brazilian literature.

The end of the Cold War brought this boom period for translation to a close. The widespread misconception that globalization means that the whole world speaks English has rendered translated fiction suspect. Where Avon used to flaunt the translating prowess of Gregory Rabassa or Thomas Colchie, publishers now try to keep the translator's name off the cover out of a belief that readers are reluctant to buy books that were not written in English. (Of the 100 bestselling paperbacks in the United Kingdom in 2004, only two were translations.) Every day we hear of the importance of China, yet we still know little about its literature. Brazil, India and contemporary Arabic writing remain enigmas. Now that Central and Eastern Europe no longer supply politically useful dissidents, we have ceased to translate the region's literature. No longer do English-Canadian undergraduates regard translations of Marie-Claire Blais novels as vital reading, as many did in the 1970s, nor do young English-speaking readers elsewhere receive substantial exposure to current French-language fiction from Europe, Africa or the Caribbean.

Even Spanish American writers, whose culture increasingly overlaps with that of the United States, struggle to find an outlet in English. In 2004 I watched the Miami-based Peruvian novelist and star talk-show host Jaime Bayly struggle with his frustrations during an onstage interview when a reader asked where she could find translations of his best-selling novels for her English-speaking friends. "I do not know why I am not translated into English," Bayly said.

The last five novels of the Nicaraguan writer Sergio Ramírez have won three major prizes in Europe, and have appeared on the bestseller lists of half-a-dozen countries, yet only one of these novels is forthcoming in English translation, from tiny Curbstone Press in Connecticut. The work of Roberto Bolaño, the central figure of post-1990 Latin American postmodernism, is only starting to filter into English. The era of Avon paperbacks is long gone. To walk into a good bookstore in France or Italy is to be arrested by unfamiliar names as one surveys local translations of writers from many countries whose work does not appear in English. And it is not only the Europeans who are ahead of us. The novels of Paulina Chiziane, a Portuguese-speaking Mozambican who is one of the most important woman writers in Africa, are not translated into English but may be enjoyed by readers in Bangkok through their translation into Thai.

At a time when everyone is asking why English-language fiction has stalled, why fewer readers buy novels, part of the answer must lie in the decline of translation. Alert readers of Spanish, French, German, Italian, Portuguese and other languages participate in an international aesthetic debate; readers and writers of English, condemned to silence by insular fantasies of global relevance, are missing out on the next wave of literature.

———————

"Translation and the Writer" was published in different form in *Quill & Quire*, April 2008, as "Prose of the World." "Translation and the Writer" and "For and Against Translation" were published in *Canadian Notes & Queries* No. 73 (Spring-Summer 2008) under the title "The Translation Gap." Sections of "Translation and the Writer" and "The Insularity of English" were included in a talk given at This Ain't the Rosedale Public Library, Toronto, 23 November 2007; the text of this talk was posted on-line on 3 December 2007. An earlier version of "For and Against Translation" was presented at the College of Arts Translation Colloquium, University of Guelph, 13 March 2004. "The Insularity of English" was published in *Geist* No. 61 (Summer 2006) and reprinted in *Sydney PEN Quarterly* (Australia) (October 2006). Since these essays appeared, one novel by Horacio Castellanos Moya has been published in English translation by New Directions in New York.

2. CARLOS FUENTES

When Kenneth Clark presented his lavish *Civilization* TV series in 1969, he omitted any reference to Spain or Spanish America. His, he said, was a history of civilization, not of intolerance. Clark's view of Hispanic culture, while unusual in its bluntness, typifies the blend of condescension, defensiveness and neglect with which many English-speaking commentators circle around the Hispanic world. *The Buried Mirror*, aired on Spanish, British, U.S. and Canadian television, is a calculated riposte, more than a dozen years in the making, to Kenneth Clark's disdain. Mexican novelist Carlos Fuentes, who hosted the series, wrote a coffee-table-sized book to accompany it.

The idea of Carlos Fuentes writing a coffee-table book may sound almost surreal to readers of his flamboyant fiction. But Fuentes has always been a writer of striking dualities. Best known for novels, such as *Terra Nostra* (1975) and *Christopher Unborn* (1988), which combine the sinuosity of Mexican baroque architecture with an insatiable hunger for the latest finds of the international avant-garde, Fuentes also enjoys a career as an interpreter of Latin America to the English-speaking world. In this strand of his work, such as his CBC Massey lectures, *Latin America at War with the Past* (1983), the exuberance of Fuentes's fiction yields to the more measured tones of the professional diplomat. *The Buried Mirror* (1992) describes the genesis of Hispanic civilization from prehistoric times to the present. Although the publication of this book during the 500th anniversary of Columbus's arrival in the New World can hardly have been a coincidence, the events of 1492 play a relatively minor role in Fuentes's narrative. His primary concern is the tension between the side of Hispanic culture that accepts, merges with and learns from outsiders – Romans, Jews and Moors in Spain, Indians and blacks in Spanish America – and the destructive quest for order and purity that gave birth to the Spanish Inquisition, General Francisco Franco and numerous doctrinaire Latin American strongmen.

Fuentes has been down this road before. The 800-page neo-Joycean outpouring of *Terra Nostra* – the most ambitious, infuriating, inconsistent and profound of his novels – projected its characters through the length and breadth of Hispanic history in search of the flaw that had condemned Spanish-speaking societies to poverty and stagnation. The blame seemed to fall on the recurrent impulse to exclude the other, the bearer of stimulating difference. In *The Buried Mirror*, Fuentes's analytical persona modifies the conclusion reached by its creative counterpart in *Terra Nostra*. His survey of Hispanic art, literature and cinema emphasizes that universality and engagement with the outside world. The question now becomes: why hasn't this cultural wealth been matched by comparable economic and political successes?

The root of the problem, Fuentes argues, lies in the circumstances attending the reconquest of Spain from Moorish occupation. (Fuentes's praise of the more than 700 years of Moorish rule as a time of fertile exchange among Muslims, Christians and Jews is one of the most intriguing aspects of this book.) In the heat of the reconquest, Spain acquired the first dim outlines of parliamentary government half a century before any other European nation. "Yet," Fuentes writes, "the same thing that made [civil rights] possible – a war against another religious and military force in Spain's national territory – prevented their flourishing. Once the war with Islam was over, the monarchy won a prestige it did not have in England or France . . . . The drive toward imperial conquest, the nature of Spanish colonization in the New World, and Spain's continuing role as defender of the Catholic faith . . . all derived from the experience of the reconquest."

The monarchy expelled the Muslims and Jews, impoverishing Spain both culturally and economically. The enlightened, proto-democratic legal framework remained on the books but was rarely observed. A similar rift between the legal nation and political reality has plagued the countries of Latin America. In a series of spirited sketches, Fuentes dramatizes the principal actors and events in their sad history; he devotes special attention to the importation of development models ill-suited to local needs. This book is enviably organized, lushly illustrated and very readable, if more demanding than most coffee-table fare. It might have benefited from tighter editing: Fuentes's English, though remarkably fluent, is not above the occasional syntactical gaffe. The English-speaking nations cannot afford to remain ignorant of Hispanic civilization, Fuentes tells us. Spain and Latin America have been contending for years with multiracial, multiethnic societies such as those taking shape in our cities. A case can be made that the Montreal or Toronto of today are in some ways reminiscent of Mexico City during the 16th and 17th centuries, in that they are sites of cultural and racial mixing destined to produce new fusions which, in the future, may be recognized as "typically Canadian." (The fact that our fusions often exclude our country's Native peoples is a significant difference, one that suggests Canadians may never achieve the rootedness in the soil of the nation that abides in Mexican culture. Our "typical Canadians" may always feel a little bit like immigrants.)

To understand ourselves we must learn from Hispanic failures and triumphs. Understanding Carlos Fuentes, however, may be a more difficult task. He is a public intellectual caught on the cusp of a Latin American culture evolving at blinding speed, leaving him stranded somewhere between the role of a sage and that of a rock star. The first public reading by Carlos Fuentes that I attended was in an independent bookstore in North Berkeley, California in 1986. Both Berkeley students and local Hispanic Americans thronged the nearby streets. The auditorium in the back of the bookstore filled long before I arrived; the bookstore filled up; finally the bookstore clerks placed loudspeakers on the

sidewalks. Two years earlier Fuentes, standing in for Lech
Wałesa, who was prevented from travelling by the Polish government, had given his televised Harvard University commencement address where, interrupted more than twenty times by
applause, he urged the United States – cleverly, if in vain – not to
conduct itself in Central America as the Soviet Union conducted
itself in Eastern Europe. Soon after, *The Old Gringo* (1985) became
the first Mexican novel to reach the U.S. bestseller lists. Fuentes's
standing in the United States had never been higher. That night in
North Berkeley, hundreds of us stood in the streets to listen to
him read in English from the punning opening pages of *Christopher Unborn*, at that time unpublished in either Spanish or English. After his reading, Fuentes emerged from the auditorium and
spent hours in the bookstore signing books and talking to people
in English, Spanish and French. Working-class Latin American
men, shuffling into the bookstore as though it were a country for
which they lacked visas, hoisted their children onto their shoulders to enable the youngsters to catch a glimpse of Fuentes.
"Mira, niña," I overheard one man say to his daughter. *"Mira al
mago."* ("Look, daughter. Look at the wizard.")

The second time I attended a Carlos Fuentes event, the Aztec
shaman had yielded some ground to the rock star. It was 1992, and
Fuentes had come to McGill University to speak about the 500th
anniversary of 1492: an anniversary of which, by way of *The Buried
Mirror* and the English translation of *Christopher Unborn*, Fuentes
became the living incarnation. Fuentes was sporting a deep sun-
tan. There was a sound-and-light show: slides and dramatic presentations of Latin American history before a huge auditorium.
The vision of Latin America offered by Fuentes was liberal, uncon-
troversial and tailored to the uninitiated. In a second lecture the
next morning Fuentes went into more detail. He signed my copy of
the Spanish edition of *Christopher Unborn*, but did not linger; he
seemed eager to escape chilly Montreal.

I saw Fuentes one more time, on a dreamy evening in London
in the late 1990s. I was wandering at dusk through Earl's Court

(where, I later learned, Fuentes maintains a rooftop flat) when I noticed a familiar figure in an expensive blue suit bending over the Barclay's banking machine. I stopped short, gaping. The sight was so incongruous that I could not prevent myself from staring. Fuentes, noticing that I had noticed him, gave me a courtly bow as he retrieved his money. He retreated to a large Bentley parked at the curb, got behind the wheel and, as he pulled away, dealt me an enormous wave.

The showman is never absent from either Fuentes's personality or his prose. His role as wizard, sage, secular priest assuming the prescriptive mantle borne in the Latin American past by medicine men and missionaries, coexists with something of the talk-show personality. The profundity of certain pages of his writing throws into relief the vulgarity of other pages. This side of Fuentes's creative persona enrages conservative Mexican intellectuals such as the late Octavio Paz who, after Fuentes's Harvard commencement address, became furious that his former protégé was receiving more attention in the United States than he was. The duality makes Fuentes, like D.H. Lawrence (an odd parallel, admittedly, but also a strangely appropriate one) a writer whose short novels, such as the classic *Aura* (1962) and *Distant Relations* (1980), display a kind of symmetrical perfection, while the longer novels, for all their force and exuberance, bog down in bouts of self-indulgence, overwriting, preaching and shameless borrowing from whatever is currently fashionable. *The Death of Artemio Cruz* (1962) comes closest to welding the symmetry of Fuentes's shorter novels to the power of his longer works. The ambitious early experimental novels *Where the Air Is Clear* (1958) and *A Change of Skin* (1967) don't completely cohere, but they breathe freshness and energy, and graft traditional Mexican culture to the modern world in original ways. *Terra Nostra*, in spite (or perhaps because) of its excess, may survive as one of the unbudgeable flawed monuments of Spanish-language literature. Fuentes's essay *The New Spanish American Novel* (1969) remains a milestone: a concise, incisive book that announced the arrival of the Latin

American novel on the world stage, and remains sharp and perceptive today. Like every work by Fuentes, it is a book of its era. Fuentes does not follow trends: he devours them. The British critic Gerald Martin once encapsulated Fuentes's career in the phrase "anything they can do, he can do better." The suspicion lingers that, by keeping up with trends so diligently, Fuentes may render his work dated. In recent years, most Mexican bestsellers have been written by women, such as Laura Esquivel (*Like Water for Chocolate*). At the same time, younger writers throughout Latin America have been muting the political themes that have traditionally dominated the region's literature and paying greater attention to private life. In his most recent major novel, *The Years with Laura Díaz* (1999), Fuentes demonstrates that he can write a women's novel about private life as well as anyone.

Born into a wealthy Mexican family in the early 20th century, Laura Díaz grows up among strong women barred by social convention from taking any public action beyond choosing the right husband. The execution of Laura's older brother at the outbreak of the Mexican Revolution in 1910 forges the revolutionary convictions that lead her into marriage with a radical union leader. As the years pass and the revolution grows corrupt, Laura realizes that the wife of a male left leader remains subject to the same restrictions as other wives. She leaves her husband and sons for the first of a series of lovers.

Like all of Fuentes's novels, *Laura Díaz* is at heart about the formation of Mexican culture. His earliest works, such as the short stories in *Los días enmascarados* (1954; The Masked Days), *Aura* and the novels *The Death of Artemio Cruz* and *A Change of Skin* exposed the Aztec, Mayan and African contribution to Mexican syncretism. In his recent fiction, Fuentes has emphasized the waves of immigration that created modern Mexico. He has drawn on the family of his paternal grandmother, German immigrants to the Gulf of Mexico port of Veracruz, to supply Laura Díaz's background. When Laura sets out into society she encounters further waves of immigrants: Trotskyites escaping from Joseph Stalin, Spanish intellectuals taking refuge from General Franco and later, American filmmakers who fled to Mexico in the wake of McCarthyism. Each of these groups influences Mexican culture and Laura's perception of the world. Yet for much of the novel Laura remains oddly passive, a bourgeois woman who, having claimed her freedom, does not know what she wants to do with it. She becomes a hanger-on to the famous painters Diego Rivera and Frida Kahlo, a peripheral figure among the brilliant Spanish exiles who enliven Mexico City in the 1940s, the lover of an expatriate Jewish-American filmmaker in the 1950s. Her lack of direction, psychologically credible on an individual level, reflects Mexico's long slumber under the 71-year reign of the Party of Revolutionary Institutions (PRI). Laura takes stock of herself as Mexico awakes. She discovers her métier in old age, becoming a photographer of the gruesome side of Mexican life just in time for the 1968 student revolts, whose violent suppression destroyed the PRI's credibility as a progressive force.

In spite of the parallel between her development and that of Mexico, Laura defies reduction to a symbol. Fuentes, the irrepressible linguistic innovator, has produced a novel of 19th-century sobriety, where individual and society are inextricably linked without either diminishing the other. No previous Fuentes novel has paid such close attention to the ways in which families cohere and disintegrate; it is hard to think of any novel that has evoked with such care Mexico City and its neighbourhoods. Fuentes's most readable novel since his 1985 bestseller *The Old Gringo*, *The Years With Laura Díaz* is the most controlled and disciplined of Fuentes's longer novels. The English translation accentuates the slight austerity of tone. Alfred Mac Adam, Fuentes's translator in recent years, is celebrated for his precision, not his imagination. In Mac Adam's hands, Fuentes's fluid Spanish emerges as cooler, clearer, less buoyant English. Yet there may be something appropriate in this. Fuentes's experimental intensity has waned as he has reached his seventies; this mainstream novel dramatizes his major themes in a more accessible form than ever before.

"Carlos Fuentes" draws on "The Wane of Spain," *The Globe and Mail*, 13 June 1992, and "Probing Mexico's Soul," Montreal *Gazette*, 3 February 2001.

3. JOÃO UBALDO RIBEIRO

In the state of Bahia, in northeastern Brazil, life is bolder and brighter than elsewhere on earth. Such, at least, is the view propagated by much of the region's output of traditional dance, popular music and fiction. The novelist Jorge Amado, author of more than twenty rollicking chronicles of Bahian life, was among those who identified João Ubaldo Ribeiro as the current standard-bearer of the Bahian tradition in fiction. Two of Ribeiro's earlier novels, *Sergeant Getúlio* (1986) and *An Invincible Memory* (1989), have appeared in English. *The Lizard's Smile*, which was originally published in Brazil in 1989, deserves a wide readership.

Bahia's raw essences – tropical squalor, Afro-Brazilian religion, political corruption, rich food and uninhibited sexuality – are the natural property of Amado (1912-2001). A writer of Ribeiro's generation (he was born in 1941) is inevitably both more conscious of the myths he is peddling and more aware of the outside world's erosion of the Bahia of folklore. In *The Lizard's Smile*, salty Bahian language faces challenges from other discourses. Dr. Lúcio Nemésio, director of the suspiciously modern clinic gracing the backward island off the Bahian coast where the novel is set, speaks in block-paragraphs of scientific jargon. His upwardly mobile young assistants affect Rio de Janeiro accents as a sign of status, while the local oligarchy sprinkles its conversation with English phrases. The characters often see themselves through a foreign lens: life in Bahia, one character remarks, is "like those English films about India."

Ribeiro also uses literary motifs. Ana Clara, the young second wife of the ambitious politician Angelo Marcos Barreto, expresses her sexual frustrations in a passage written as a parodic inversion of Molly Bloom's final monologue in *Ulysses*, ending with a

149

declamatory "No." Ana Clara's yearnings lead her into an all-consuming affair with João Pedroso, a biologist who has dropped out of modern life to work as a fishmonger. Through his attentive accounts of their lovemaking and of the dishes prepared by Ana Clara's cook, Ribeiro displays his fidelity to lustiness and rich regional cuisine, two staples of the Bahian novel since Amado united them in *Dona Flor and her Two Husbands* (1970). But the accent in *The Lizard's Smile* is on mutation. The decay of Bahian traditions is symptomatic of a larger disorder. Pedroso believes he has seen a lizard with two tails. Sightings of children who are neither human nor ape are reported in the island's jungle redoubts. Against the backdrop of sexual intrigue and Barreto's financial manipulations, Dr. Nemésio preaches the gospel of the brave new world to be ushered in by eugenics. The troubled priest Father Monteirinho and the *candomblé* healer Bará represent older faiths struggling to maintain their influence before the onslaught of science.

Ribeiro steers the novel's fast-flowing plot between the twin shoals of excessive melodrama and overt allegory. His characters, while not psychologically profound, remain vivid and credible. They sometimes talk too long, illustrating ideas that seem to belong to the author, yet most of their diatribes engage and entertain. Clifford E. Landers's translation catches the narrative's tone in fluid prose, its few tiny inelegancies stemming from an occasional tendency to carry over the Portuguese double negative into English.

What is at stake in this deceptively light-hearted novel is nothing less than the nature of humanity. At what point do the products of genetic engineering cease to be human? Of what moral consequence are the minor chromosonal differences separating humans from chimpanzees? Dr. Nemésio counters Father Monteirinho's humanist objections to eugenic experiments by arguing:

My humanism is because I'm a man, of course. If the dominant species were the gorilla and I were a gorilla, I would be a gorillist. Man is only a temporary species on a temporary planet in a temporary universe, and the least he can do for himself is utilize his intelligence to maintain his power over nature as long as possible.

Complementing Dr. Nemésio's ingenuous faith in science, Barreto embodies the cynical elite destined to preside over the implementation of new technologies. He frowns on drugs in public while abusing them in private, and rails against homosexuality, despite experiencing his greatest sexual pleasure from being sodomized by his hired assassin. Adorned with a high-tech Japanese wig to conceal hair loss from treatment for cancer, Barreto is himself a kind of eugenic creation, a marvel of modern science. Like the mutant children whose existence Dr. Nemésio finally confesses to Pedroso, Barreto is not fully human. In response to Barreto's cuckolding him and campaigning to expose Nemésio's experiments, Barreto destroys his wife and her lover without a tremor of remorse.

Pedroso's attempt to preserve traditional definitions of humanity is crushed by a traditional Bahian crime of passion carried out with technocratic efficiency. In spite of its ebullient tone, evil triumphs in *The Lizard's Smile*: technology, whose benefits have been debated since the novel's opening pages, consolidates the privileges of the powerful.

"João Ubaldo Ribeiro" was published in slightly different form as "Bahian Days," *Times Literary Supplement*, 5 May 1995.

4.   WOLE SOYINKA

In May 1994, four chiefs of the Ogoni tribe in eastern Nigeria were hacked to death during a rally organized to protest against the environmental desecration of their homeland. Ogoniland had been severely polluted by wanton oil extraction carried out by Shell Oil under a succession of military regimes. The president of the Ogoni movement, the writer Ken Saro-Wiwa, was prevented from attending the rally by a military roadblock. Saro-Wiwa's absence did not deter the military from charging him and eight of his colleagues with having murdered the chiefs.

Saro-Wiwa's trial was a terrifying farce. Uniformed soldiers machine-gunned the office of his defence lawyers. Witnesses changed their stories on command. Saro-Wiwa and his colleagues were convicted. As Commonwealth heads of state met in New Zealand to decide on a response, the Nigerian dictator Sani Abacha thumbed his nose at the world by hanging the nine men. The hangman was an amateur. It took him five attempts to kill Saro-Wiwa. "As he was led away from the scaffold the third or fourth time," the Nigerian Nobel laureate Wole Soyinka writes, "Ken Saro-Wiwa cried out, 'Why are you people doing this to me? What sort of nation is this?'"

No one, probably, is better qualified to discuss this question than Soyinka. The first African to win the Nobel Prize for litera- ture (mainly for his plays), Soyinka has been enmeshed in his country's cultural and political debates since the early years of in- dependence when Nigeria appeared to be one of the world's fu- ture superpowers. Indeed, in 1994 Soyinka himself narrowly escaped becoming one of Sani Abacha's victims, fleeing his home as the military came to arrest him. Friends smuggled Soyinka into nearby Ivory Coast, where he caught a flight to Paris. From there he began to roam the world on a UNESCO passport and denounce the Abacha dictatorship.

The Open Sore of a Continent (1996), assembled from Soyinka's lectures, probes far deeper than a mere polemical blast. In his characteristically offhand tone, Soyinka limits his references to his own predicament to a passing mention of "my 'Rambo' departure from the Nigerian nation space." A central concern of this book is to define and evaluate that peculiar space we call the nation, its existence increasingly problematic in an era of globalized culture and local ethnic assertion. Nigeria, its 100 million people evenly divided between Christians and Muslims and awkwardly split among three major ethnic groups and a host of minor ones, is particularly susceptible to these pressures.

What converts local identification into a full-blown secessionist movement, Soyinka contends, is a national fiction oppressively enforced. Examining a variety of cases in Africa and Europe, Soyinka urges his readers to abandon the language of "nonnegotiability": the doctrine that the nation must continue to exist at all costs. "At heart," he writes, "such language is subversive because it is designed to stop intelligent confrontation with the very issues whose resolution is essential to guarantee the emergence or continuity of such geographical spaces as true nations." The "true" nation is the space whose shared history over "an appreciable length of time" has reached a point where its identity as a nation "is contested neither from within nor without." But this sort of nation can emerge only from the bottom up, once people have contemplated the possibility of dissolution and decided that they prefer to lead their lives together. Constitutional tinkering by those in power, Soyinka warns, in a passage Canadian readers may find sobering, resolves nothing.

The Open Sore of a Continent is written in straightforward lecture-tour prose. Readers who were enchanted by *Aké: The Years of Childhood* (1981), Soyinka's miraculously vivid memoir of his upbringing in a Nigerian village, or those who recall *The Man Died* (1972), the densely rewarding reflections that emerged from

Soyinka's two-year imprisonment without trial during the Biafran War in the 1960s, will find only flashes of the eccentric original prose style of those books. But even in his talks, Soyinka's distinctive irascible tone occasionally cuffs aside the cultivated demeanour of the guest lecturer. Who else, in an address to Harvard University's august DuBois Institute, would describe a Nigerian government spokesman as "hurling imprecations on all opposition from a uniquely askew but cavernous orifice, an inundating spittle-launcher situated somewhere in his head"?

The pivotal date in Soyinka's account of Nigeria's decline is June 12, 1993. On that day Nigerians, acting as one people, turned a showcase election designed to rubber-stamp the military's grip on power into an exercise in democracy. In an election universally acclaimed for its orderly conduct, Nigerian voters repudiated their military rulers. The man they elected, M.K.O. Abiola, though no saint, offered a clear alternative to the generals. Blocked from taking office, Abiola ended up in a prison cell. The country's media was neutered, demonstrators were shot down in the street (Soyinka was present at one such massacre) and the economy went into free-fall as Sani Abacha and his cronies, shrugging off timid international criticism, continued to pocket much of the oil revenue. In 1994, twelve billion dollars vanished without trace from the national treasury.

If 12 June 1993 represented the culminating collective act of a unified Nigeria, Soyinka argues, then 10 November 1995, the date of Ken Saro-Wiwa's execution, may "have sounded the death-knell of the nation." Saro-Wiwa uttered his anguished final question – "What sort of nation is this?" – not as a Nigerian, but as an Ogoni. His challenge resonates not only through dictatorships like Nigeria's, but through all contemporary nations struggling to accommodate regional and ethnic differences.

"Wole Soyinka" was published in slightly different form as "Conscience of a Continent Speaks Out," Montreal *Gazette*, 23 November 1996.

5. JULIO CORTÁZAR

No writer played a more crucial part in the blossoming of Spanish American fiction during the 1960s and 1970s than Julio Cortázar. Carlos Fuentes and Mario Vargas Llosa credited Cortázar's novel *Hopscotch* (1963) with modernizing Spanish American literary language; Gabriel García Márquez inserted an allusion to it in *One Hundred Years of Solitude* (1967). In the aftermath of May 1968 in Paris, where Cortázar joined the students in the streets, he became not only a literary icon, but a political one. By the time of his death in 1984, his role as a spokesman for revolutionary causes nearly surpassed his literary reknown. The Sandinista government of Nicaragua awarded him a medal; François Mitterand underlined his disapproval of dictatorships of the left and right by granting French citizenship simultaneously to Milan Kundera and Cortázar (whose native Argentina had fallen under the heel of the generals in 1976). It was a curious transformation for a writer who had once personified the aesthetic school in Latin American letters. In the 1950s, accused by the Peruvian novelist José María Arguedas of turning his back on Latin America by moving to Paris to write avant-garde short stories, Cortázar defended the artist's right to pursue personal phantoms. Yet his final publications included polemical essays opposing U.S. intervention in Central America and a pamphlet denouncing multinational corporations.

The cornerstone of Cortázar's authority as cultural arbiter was the enormous reputation of *Hopscotch*. Radical in its form and uninhibited in its language, it shattered the residual naturalism of Spanish-American fiction. In the first, longest and most compelling of the novel's three sections, the hyperintellectual Argentinian Horacio Oliveira is enjoying a bohemian existence in the company of an international array of artistic expatriates, including his lover,

La Maga. The expatriates' brilliant multilingual conversations, exuberantly interweaving Latin American slang, bursts of English-language jazz lyrics and citations from French literature, create a dazzling linguistic landscape. Even Gregory Rabassa's excellent translation cannot capture all the wordplay; it inevitably mutes the original's contrasts between Spanish and English (the French is left intact). Immersed in literature and music, Oliveira pursues his quest for artistic transcendence: a search for a higher state (symbolized by the "heaven" of the hopscotch board) that is both existentially unattainable and linguistically inexpressible.

Oliveira's desire for La Maga (literally "the sorceress") incarnates his undefinable quest. Refusing to make dates, they drift around Saint-Germain-des-Prés until they run into each other. "Would I find La Maga?" is the novel's resonant opening sentence. La Maga, originally from Uruguay, possesses the liberation Oliveira seeks; but she has attained her heaven through her inability to intellectualize. Baffled by the avant-garde art that obsesses Oliveira, she reads the linear fictions of Honoré de Balzac and Benito Pérez Galdós. La Maga's "naturalness," however, is sometimes seen by Oliveira (and more troublingly, by the narrator) as undermining their shared aesthetic of liberation. Her conversion to motherhood after she regains custody of her infant son from an earlier relationship is depicted as a betrayal. Oliveira develops a confused belief that La Maga has had an affair with one of his friends. In the climactic scene of the opening section, a chaotic party with loud jazz music and irate neighbours, La Maga's sickly son dies, his death unnoticed amid the tumult. Showing Cortázar's narrative gift at its most gripping, this scene presages the disintegration of Oliveira's expatriate life. La Maga, grief-stricken, vanishes; deprived of an object, Oliveira's quest collapses into vagrancy, and he is deported to Argentina. On his return to Buenos Aires, he is greeted by his friend Traveler (who has never been anywhere) and Traveler's wife Talita. Cortázar's commentary on the provincialism of the Argentine middle class, in this second section, is acerbic and often as brutally obvious as the pun on

Traveler's name. Oliveira's escape into linguistic games and adult play flattens into a mechanistic response to an oppressive environment. Only the well-known scene in which Oliveira, Traveler and Talita join two buildings by extending planks of wood between facing windows retains something of the madcap verve of the Paris section. Once again drawn into a romantic triangle, Oliveira begins to hallucinate that Talita is La Maga. His search for transcendence thwarted by the limitations of the Argentine milieu, he commits suicide by hurling himself out of a window onto the "heaven" of a hopscotch board below.

Hopscotch's main claim to technical innovation lies in the third section. Many of these "dispensable chapters" discuss the literary theories of a writer named Morelli, who appears fleetingly in the Paris section. Perceptive yet pompous, Morelli wavers between being a mouthpiece for Cortázar's ideas about fiction and a parody of all literary theorizing. Cortázar's own insistence on the "active reader" is made clear by the novel's prefatory note, which invites the reader to choose between consuming *Hopscotch* in a linear manner or in an alternative pattern, beginning with Chapter 73 then leaping around, hopscotch-fashion. Each chapter ends with the number of the chapter that should be read next in the world of this "other" novel. When *Hopscotch* is read in this alternative sequence, the dispensable chapters slip inside the central story to provide a metatextual commentary on the unfolding structure. Yet no grand design is revealed; ultimately allergic to theories, Cortázar preaches only the pleasure of literary playfulness.

The novel's high place in the Latin American pantheon has slipped in recent years with accusations that it has grown dated. The dustjacket of the 1998 Harvill edition sees it as "anticipating the age of the web with a non-structure that allows readers to take the chapters in any order they wish." Yet, in whichever order it may be read, *Hopscotch* is a difficult book for the contemporary reader to finish. The vitality of the Paris section's depiction of a skein of expatriate friendships is not sustained in the more cerebral later parts. The claim of datedness, though, has itself become dated. Enough time has now passed to relieve *Hopscotch* of the burden of contemporaneity and put Cortázar in historical perspective as the last important male Latin American writer to live an expatriate life in Paris (today's Latin American intellectuals prefer U.S. university campuses). Like the French Surrealist works that influenced Cortázar, *Hopscotch* is best enjoyed as a quirky literary manifesto and an energetic document of a time now past.

The quality that renders *Hopscotch* most unfit for the web-surfing generation is its intense, allusive bookishness. Cortázar's short stories, more easygoing in this respect, remain far more accessible. Like his hermetic master Jorge Luis Borges, Cortázar has suffered in English translation from collections being dispersed so that stories written decades apart appear side by side. *Bestiary: Selected Stories* (1996), Alberto Manguel's scrupulous chronological arrangement of thirty-five stories written over more than thirty years, fills the longstanding need for a coherent English-language edition of Cortázar's shorter fiction. In his introduction, Manguel – like Mario Vargas Llosa in his introduction to the two-volume Spanish edition of Cortázar's stories published by Alfaguara in 1994 – verges on making an apology for the political engagement of Cortázar's later stories. Reading these fictions chronologically, however, suggests that Cortázar may not have changed as much as we think.

Prior to becoming known as a writer of fiction, Cortázar translated into Spanish the complete works of Edgar Allan Poe. His luminous early stories (such as "House Taken Over," in which an unknown force expels a brother and sister from a mansion, or "Circe," in which irrational powers intervene in a suburban courtship) mix supernatural occurrences with bitingly observed descriptions of pre-Second World War Argentine life. The reality shattered by the fantastic events that erupt in Cortázar's stories belongs to the realm of bourgeois illusion. The motorcycle rider in "The Night Face Up," gazing back on modern life from the Aztec human sacrifice into which an accident has hurtled him, perceives the absurdity of "an astonishing city, with green and red lights that burned without fire or smoke." Cortázar's injection of anarchy into the middle class's sacred routines (as in the comic "The Southern Thruway," where holiday makers returning to Paris are ensnared in an inexplicable traffic jam that lasts for days) may be read either as a trait of "uncanny tales" (Manguel's preference) or as profoundly political. The lacerating critiques of middle-class hypocrisy embedded in stories such as "Poisons" and "End of the Game," where naive child narrators see more than they realize, radiate a loathing of the ruling order. The stories of the last years sustain the same assault in more overtly ideological ways. Though the best political stories, such as "Apocalypse at Solentiname" and "Press Clippings" (both enlisting fantastic modes to denounce death-squad activity) are significant works, many of the later stories depend on unconvincing romanticized depictions of hippies and revolutionaries. Manguel chooses sparingly from the later volumes, tilting his selection towards the unfailingly taut earlier stories, where bourgeois life buckles before upheavals that are both startling and inevitable. The result is a glorious collection. *Bestiary* achieves a transcendence Horacio Oliveira would envy.

"Julio Cortázar" was published in slightly different form as "Lost Illusions," *Times Literary Supplement*, 7 August 1998. This essay provoked discussion in literary circles in Argentina, where it became the subject of the lead article in the weekend cultural supplement of *Clarín*, the country's widest-circulation newspaper. In the Latin American context, my approach to Cortázar's work was perceived as almost shockingly apolitical; critics worried, also, that by encouraging readers to "relieve Cortázar of the burden of contemporaneity" I was trying isolate his work from the broader Argentine tradition. My failure to discuss Cortázar's literary debt to Borges was pointed out. The critic Graciela Speranza concluded: "The view from abroad has its risks – errors of perspective, if you will – but it offers an autonomy that is unimaginable under the influence of local colour." Canadian readers would do well to approach foreign reviews of our books in the same spirit.

6. GÜNTER GRASS

When *Ein Weites Feld* was published in Germany in 1995, reaction was vitriolic. Germany's foremost literary critic, Marcel Reich-Ranicki, took the unusual step of appearing on television to warn that Günter Grass had written a bad novel that no one should read. The newspapers unleashed a maelstrom of denunciation. Grass's crime? His sour view of German reunification. By referring to West Germany's absorption of East Germany as *Anschluss*, the word usually reserved for Hitler's annexation of Austria, Grass had besmirched the German nation's most coveted achievement. When I mentioned the *Anschluss* controversy to an Eastern European friend who was visiting me at the time, he raged against Grass for half an hour, then began to cry.

Five years later, as *Too Far Afield* is published in English, it is difficult to recreate the mood which allowed this novel to make so many people furious. In the interim, Grass won the 1999 Nobel Prize for Literature, prompting the German media to stage a cautious rapprochement with the country's most notorious, difficult writer. Germans, meanwhile, have grown less defensive and more ironic about reunification. Derisive references to reunification as *Anschluss* crop up in daily conversation.

Grass, now in his seventies, has been a leftward-tilting thorn in the side of western German political orthodoxy for decades. Having grown up before the Second World War as part of the German-speaking minority in Eastern Europe – the people Adolf Hitler claimed to be "bringing back into the Reich" by invading his neighbours – Grass arrived in West Berlin as an outsider with a unique approach to German war guilt. His masterpiece, *The Tin Drum* (1959), fusing vivid descriptions of a minority reality with grotesque exaggeration, brutal wordplay and narrative innovation, was adopted as a model by younger writers attempting to breathe novelistic life into marginalized cultural backgrounds. In fact, one of Grass's most ardent disciples is Salman Rushdie. Grass's later novels about his East Prussian upbringing, *Cat and Mouse* (1961) and *Dog Years* (1963), also enjoyed substantial success. In recent decades, Grass's work has become increasingly cerebral. *Too Far Afield*, an extremely clever but ultimately rather ponderous book, perpetuates this tendency.

Opening in 1989, as the Berlin Wall crumbles, and closing in 1991 with the reunification of Germany, *Too Far Afield* follows the adventures of an aging East German intellectual and his ex-Secret Service "shadow." In good postmodern style, the two protagonists are both invented characters and self-conscious echoes of earlier literature. Theo Wuttke has survived the years of communist rule as a lecturer on cultural topics to East German community groups. His specialty is the work of Theodor Fontane, Germany's most important 19th-century novelist. Wuttke's knowledge of Fontane's life and work is so detailed that friends call him "Fonty."

This, for the English-speaking reader, is where the problems begin. The words "Theodor Fontane" do not appear in the novel. While Wuttke is referred to as Fonty, Fontane is called the Immortal. Each page contains some sort of allusion to Fontane's life or work: the reader who is unaware of Fontane will be plunged into a welter of untraceable references. Krishna Winston's translation is so painstaking that it is surprising she did not include a preface explaining Fontane's importance to German culture. (The novel's title is a quote from Fontane that would be instantly recognizable to most literate Germans.) Fontane's great adultery novel, *Effi Briest*, can stand comparison with Flaubert's *Madame Bovary*, but where Julian Barnes can confidently title a novel *Flaubert's Parrot*, a work of fiction that places Fontane at its core is likely to bewilder readers of English because classical German literature is not read in English-speaking countries.

Lacing together Fonty and the Immortal enables Grass to draw intricate parallels between Germany's recent reunification and the first attempt at forging a single German state in the late 19th century. As Fonty plods through a changing Berlin, the reader is tugged, often in mid-paragraph or even mid-sentence, back into the Germany of Theodor Fontane. Through this interpenetration of past and present, Grass develops dozens of tiny, sardonic links between contemporary Germany and the Germany of Kaiser Wilhelm that eventually lunged into the First World War. Fonty's secret service shadow is referred to alternately as Hoftaller and Tallhover. *Tallhover* is the title of a spy novel by the East German writer Hans Joachim Shädlich. Grass, who smuggled Shädlich's first manuscript out of East Berlin in the 1970s, here appropriates Shädlich's character for his own novel. Wuttke/ Fonty and Hoftaller/Tallhover are employed by the Handover Trust, a former archive that is now a privatization ministry. Deviously though Grass deploys them, his Fontane allusions become a padding that distances the visceral realities of a society undergoing dramatic change. The reader receives glimpses of German reunification: souvenir-hunters chip at the Wall, bargain-seekers flood East Berlin furniture stores, street corner money-changers ply their trade. There is the ritual first meal at a McDonald's restaurant, the influx of Western television, a glance at the environmentally ravaged East German countryside and meetings with Eastern fishing families fearful of the Western developers determined to convert their seaside village into a pricey tourist resort. Yet in a novel that manages to be both elaborately abstract and grindingly particular without ever becoming fully evocative, these scenes are not developed.

Grass makes only cursory gestures towards exploiting the satirical potential of his protagonists' privatization work. He gives fuller play to allegorical set pieces such as the marriage between a reticent East German spinster and a grasping West German developer that serves as a symbol of reunification. (The marriage ends in divorce.) The arrival of Fonty's illegitimate French granddaughter, now a graduate student researching the work of the Immortal, breathes some human life into the book. In the closing fifty pages,

Fonty and Hoftaller break free of their postmodern armour to emerge as sad old men for whom the reader feels compassion. But the best of this novel – its provocativeness, its ingenious use of literary allusion, its rumbling humour and mainly unrecoverable punning – has become muted in translation.

"Günter Grass" was published in slightly different form as "Germans Hated It," Montreal *Gazette*, 18 November 2000, and was reprinted in the Edmonton *Journal*, 10 December 2000. In August 2006, Günter Grass recovered his unpopularity by confessing that as a teenager he had served briefly in the Waffen-SS in East Prussia. The long-term impact of this admission on his literary reputation remains to be seen.

7.   HARUKI MURAKAMI

On March 20, 1995, at the height of the morning rush hour, the Tokyo subway system was attacked with poisoned gas. Aum Shrinriyko, a religious cult that inspired mesmerized devotion in its thousands of followers, orchestrated the simultaneous release of sarin, a gas twenty-six times more lethal than cyanide, on five lines of the vast underground network. Five thousand commuters and subway staff were hospitalized; in a near miracle, only twelve died. The poisoned gas attack, occurring a few weeks after the lethal Kobe earthquake, signalled the close of the postwar era of Japanese stability and economic success. In the minds of many Japanese, the attack ushered in a period of uncertainty about Japan's destiny and core values. The novelist Haruki Murakami, who had been living in Europe and the United States, returned to Japan a few months after the attack. In the two books of interviews combined in English as *Underground: The Tokyo Gas Attack and the Japanese Psyche* (2001), Murakami attempts to understand the tragedy through the voices of commuters and cult members.

Aum appears to have lacked any concrete strategic objective. Motivated by a conviction that consumer society was doomed to collapse, spurred on by the growing megalomania of the cult's leader, Shoko Asahara, facilitated by the cult members' disdain for the "unenlightened" citizens of secular society, the attack remains a brutal enigma. Those who released the gas included graduates of Japan's top universities: members of the Japanese "superelite." Aum theology contained a sufficient grounding in Buddhist precepts to attract those seeking traditionalist solutions to contemporary alienation, mingled with oddball elements, such as a belief in the prophecies of the Provençal seer Nostradamus and a hatred of Freemasons.

The first half of *Underground* contains interviews with sixty victims of the gas attack. Japanese modesty made it difficult to find victims – particularly female victims – willing to discuss their experiences. Murakami treats his interviewees with painful solicitude, introducing them in flattering terms, refraining from challenging contradictory testimonies and thanking his subjects lavishly. Readers familiar with Murakami's novels, particularly his more outlandish incursions into semi-science fiction, such as *A Wild Sheep Chase* (1989), may be disconcerted by the curbing of his customary imaginative boldness.

Culturally necessary as his approach may be, the result is that few of the interviews are individually memorable. The tough old man who slipped into a coma, then revived after doctors had given up on him, the Irish jockey caught in the crowd, a wrenching interview with a man whose timid sister was reduced to a near-vegetative state, an interview with a young widow: these stand out. But overall the picture that emerges, intriguing in its way, is a mass portrait of a cautious, worried population, in which every commuter is aware that Japan's economic "bubble" has burst. A certain bleakness, a fear that consumer society has become inescapable yet failed to fulfill its promise, creeps over Murakami's considerate encounters with decent people, preparing the ground for the compelling second part of the book, where Murakami interrogates those who fled consumerism in search of the "enlightenment" promised by Aum.

Palpably disturbed by his meetings with the victims, Murakami is less polite to the cult members. He questions their searches for meaning, their willingness to abandon their families, their feelings towards cult leader Asahara and their often grudging admissions of Aum responsibility for the attack. The most striking characteristic shared by Aum devotees is a humourless empiricism. Murakami spars with them, telling one cult member, "Since I'm a novelist I'm the opposite of you – I believe that what's most important is what *cannot* be measured."

Murakami's fascination with the attack is accentuated by the fact that it took place underground. As he points out, images of subterranean life shadowing surface reality dominate his major novels. In his masterpiece, *The Wind-Up Bird Chronicle* (1998), scenes set in wells generate an alternative reality that evokes both the tranquillity of the traditional society buried by industrialization and the suppressed nightmares of history, such as Japan's ruthless occupation of Manchuria during the 1930s. *The Wind-Up Bird Chronicle* was such a climactic statement of Japanese life and consciousness that it isn't surprising that his subsequent novels have been more limited in scope. The central character of *Sputnik Sweetheart* (2001), Sumire, is a young woman novelist whom the narrator chides for her grandiose ambitions: "Sumire was dead set on creating a massive 19th-century-style Total Novel, the kind of portmanteau packed with every possible phenomenon in order to capture the soul and human destiny."

Murakami himself used to write this sort of novel, but now his voice is more laconic, his narratives more compressed. Sumire's story is told by the male friend who is her confidante. He is in love with her, but she has feelings only for her art. When her creativity falters, she accepts a job working for Miu, a successful female entrepreneur. Sumire falls in love with Miu, who tries to reciprocate but cannot overcome the frigidity caused by a trauma experienced in her youth. The two women are sharing a house on a Greek island when Sumire vanishes. From this simple design, Murakami forges a deeply felt, delicately understated chain of resonances and dualities. Rather than descending into a well, Sumire's spirit hovers over her friends like a satellite. The lives of Miu and the narrator feel empty, yet their emptiness is haunted by an obscured reality promising an intangible fulfillment. In this touching novel, Murakami's underground world has migrated into outer space.

In his next book, *After the Quake* (2002), a collection of six precisely shaped short stories, Murakami dramatizes the emotional uncertainty that prevailed in the aftermath of the other disaster to strike Japan in 1995, the Kobe earthquake. The book opens and closes with images of the quake, yet none of the stories is set in Kobe. These often wildly imaginative mood pieces strive to capture an indefinable feeling of spiritual emptiness. In "UFO in Kushiro," Komura's wife abandons him after watching the quake on television. In a note she writes that "living with you is like living with a chunk of air." A friend at the office gives Komura an introduction to his sister, on the condition that Komura bring the sister a package. The contents of the package, which may be empty, are never divulged. Once Komura has handed it over, his sense of loss drives him to the brink of violence.

Murakami specializes in exploring the angst of Japanese twentysomethings. "Landscape with Flatiron," though the least deftly resolved of the stories, provides an evocative glimpse of young dropouts in a beach town. In "All God's Children Can Dance," Yoshiya's relationship with his girlfriend is stunted by his Oedipal subservience to his ultra-religious mother. "Honey Pie" follows an emotionally cool young writer through fifteen years of a romantic triangle. Junpei's career advances, but his belated realization that he has failed to act upon his feelings for the woman he loves diminishes his achievement. Writing stories for his beloved's infant daughter, who is tormented by nightmares about "the Earthquake Man," salves his pain.

In "Thailand," the only story with a central character belonging to Muakami's own generation, emotional emptiness congeals into a "hard white stone." Satsuki, a successful thyroid doctor going through menopause, decides to take advantage of a conference in Bangkok to relax at a luxury resort. The exotic setting and her conversations with her Thai driver help her to confront suppressed childhood traumas. In its outlines, this is a familiar story, but Murakami's faultless clustering of images invests the tale with a resonant strangeness.

Murakami uses the measured repetition of images to knit the collection together. The empty box in "UFO in Kushiro" returns to close the book in "Honey Pie." In "All God's Children Can Dance," Yoshiya's girlfriend tells him that when he dances he resembles "a

Super-Frog." This prepares the ground for "Super-Frog Saves Tokyo," the most weirdly imaginative of the stories. Mr. Katagiri, an overworked Japanese everyman, comes home to discover a six-foot-tall frog in his kitchen. Quoting Nietzsche and Conrad, the frog explains that together they must fight a subterranean monster called Worm, who is planning to attack Tokyo by setting off an earthquake even more devastating than the one in Kobe. A stunned Katagiri consents. Before he can assist Super-Frog, he is shot in a business dispute. As he recovers in hospital, different levels of reality collide in a scene of surreal repulsiveness. "Super-Frog Saves Tokyo," all the more ambiguous for its tongue-in-cheek tone, shows Murakami's writing at its most inimitable.

"The short story is on the way out. Like the slide rule," Junpei comments. Murakami's adoption of this "doomed" form illustrates the dilemma he has faced since 1995. A writer who used to pack all of Japan into his novels, Murakami has lost his faith in an integrated Japan. This has shaken his commitment to the novel. The oral history of *Underground* and the slightness of *Sputnik Sweetheart* represent two attempts to capture Japanese reality in forms that diverge from the "total novel." In *After the Quake* he turns to the short story, searching for a form capable of embodying the fragmentation he perceives around him, and culling startling images from the void that appears when "the earth cracks open with a roar."

"Haruki Murakami" is based on "Murakami goes subterranean," *The Globe and Mail*, 19 May 2001, and "Earthquake rocks Japan – and writer's faith," *The Globe and Mail*, 23 November 2002.

8. MARIO VARGAS LLOSA

Rafael Trujillo, ruler of the Dominican Republic from 1930 to 1961, was the most enduring of the Latin American dictators who came to power during the interwar years. Ascetic, disciplined and sexually ravenous, Trujillo was a slavish imitator of the United States who developed into one of America's worst enemies. *The Feast of the Goat*, Mario Vargas Llosa's novel about Trujillo's assassination, has been acclaimed as one of the author's most important works. The Spanish edition has sold more than a million copies since its publication in 2000; critics are already debating the novel's place in the Spanish American canon.

Vargas Llosa's portrait of the assassination and the political manipulations in the aftermath of the tyrant's death is controversial. Joaquín Balaguer, the president who succeeded Trujillo, though in his mid-nineties at the time of the novel's publication, remained an influential figure in the Dominican Republic. Vargas Llosa allowed Balaguer to read the manuscript (or have it read to him, as Balaguer had gone blind) before he published the novel. Balaguer appears in the book as an opportunist whose ambition produces a democratic culture that he did not foresee.

In Europe and Spanish America, *The Feast of the Goat* has been praised as a soaring return to form for Latin America's most respected novelist. Isabel Allende may sell more books and Gabriel García Márquez may be better known worldwide, but, novel for novel, no Latin American writer can match Vargas Llosa's achievement over the last forty years. In the 1960s, while still in his twenties and an ardent admirer of Fidel Castro's Cuba, Vargas Llosa published three structurally complex novels. *The Time of the Hero* (1962), *The Green House* (1965) and *Conversation in The Cathedral* (1969) combined avant-garde narrative techniques with a wide-screen 19th-century realism and a seething anger at social injustice to create novels that have become classics in the Spanish-speaking world. During the 1970s, Vargas Llosa lost his faith in Castro, drifting into an ironic mode that produced the popular comic novel *Aunt Julia and the Scriptwriter* (1977). By the end of the decade, influenced by European thinkers such as Jean-François Revel and Friedrich Hayek, Vargas Llosa reconstituted himself as a neo-liberal. His best-known novel of the 1980s, the sombre epic *The War of the End of the World* (1981), worked out his new vision through an account of a rebellion in late-19th-century Brazil.

Literature took a back seat to politics in the late 1980s as Vargas Llosa launched his exhausting campaign for the presidency of his native Peru. Running on a platform imitative of the ideas of Margaret Thatcher, he was defeated in the 1990 elections by Alberto Fujimori. After his defeat, Vargas Llosa moved to Europe, vowing to ignore politics and devote himself to literature. He spent the 1990s in Berlin, London and Madrid. The novels he published were elegant but slight. His best book of the decade was *A Fish in the Water* (1993), his irascible memoir of his presidential campaign.

The Feast of the Goat is a startling comeback. The intricate orchestration of multiple storylines combines with a dramatic narrative tone; a current of anger snarls beneath the surface. The suffocation of a small country dominated by a fanatically disciplined military man is evoked through an attention to detail as meticulous as that with which the dictator rules his nation. With voyeuristic gusto, Vargas Llosa dramatizes the connections between the aging Trujillo's machismo, his lust for power and his faltering sexual potency with the teenage girls procured for him by his henchmen. The pivotal character of this novel about machismo is a woman. Urania Cabral, the daughter of one of Trujillo's senators, is hustled out of the country as an adolescent, shortly before the dictator's assassination. In the late 1990s, now in her late forties, Urania returns to the Dominican Republic to confront her family with their collaboration with the dictatorship. Urania's challenge to her family alternates with an almost minute-by-minute account of the assassination. Vargas Llosa's unusual gift for integrating complex structures with headlong storytelling enables him to narrate Trujillo's death three times, from different points of view, without breaking the forward flow of the action.

The Feast of the Goat owes its popular success in large part to its resemblance to Vargas Llosa's major early novels, *The Green House* and *Conversation in The Cathedral*. The broad canvas, the political and military themes, the fast-moving narrative often enfolding different time frames within a single scene, all conspire to make it fulfill the Spanish-speaking public's image of a Vargas Llosa novel more thoroughly than any of his other recent works. As the novel's two central narrative threads converge, Urania's determination to confront her family with their collaboration with the dictatorship dovetails with the story of the assassination in a gory rape scene that has contributed to the novel's notoriety.

The tendency of a corrupt government to implicate an entire society in its moral decay is a theme Vargas Llosa has developed before, most notably in *Conversation in The Cathedral*. Two important differences appear in the theme's treatment here. The earlier novel, written during Vargas Llosa's existentialist phase, lamented the ways in which pervasive corruption deprived citizens of the capacity for meaningful action. In *The Feast of the Goat*, the cost of corruption is described not in terms of a lack of existential authenticity, but as a loss of liberty. Reflecting Vargas Llosa's current neo-liberal preoccupations, all-engulfing corruption becomes the enemy of free will: "In this country, in one way or another, everyone had been, was, or would be part of the regime . . . . [Trujillo] had taken from the people the sacred attribute given to them by God: their free will."

The second striking difference lies in the emphasis given to the figure of Trujillo. In *Conversation in The Cathedral*, the dictator, General Odría, never appears. By contrast, Trujillo's personal quirks, from his failure to perspire to his sexual exploitation of adolescent girls, are described in loving detail. Fascinated by power, Vargas

Llosa reserves his closest scrutiny for the hangers-on who have advanced in Trujillo's shadow. The most intriguing characters are Urania's father, the cerebral senator who sacrifices his family in order to retain his privileges, Johnny Abbes, Trujillo's sadistic yet subservient chief of secret police, and, above all, Balaguer, Trujillo's puppet president, an ascetic, unctuous man who is a gifted poet in private and a cipher in public. Balaguer's awakening into a Machiavellian strategist during the crisis provoked by Trujillo's death makes for gripping reading. The tension between the sexually predatory soldier Trujillo and the introverted, asexual writer Balaguer, embodying the poles of male identity between which Vargas Llosa's protagonists have always oscillated, provides this novel with many of its most engrossing moments. Balaguer's eventual triumph is not only the victory of democracy, but also of literature over politics, and even of a code of civilized male ambition over violence and barbarism. A writer by vocation, Balaguer rewrites the history of the Trujillo regime into a fiction justifying his own rise to power.

Vargas Llosa also rewrites the Dominican Republic's history. His depiction of a brisk transition to democracy overlooks much of the country's recent past. Only four years after Trujillo's death, 20,000 U.S. Marines stormed ashore to suppress a rebellion against a right-wing coup that had overthrown the country's elected left-of-centre president, Juan Bosch (who, inevitably, was also a talented short story writer). Balaguer won his next "democratic" election with the help of paramilitary thugs who kept Bosch confined to his house so that he couldn't campaign. In 1971, when Balaguer became president for the third time, his secret police murdered two hundred opposition politicians on the way to polling day. Urania, returning to modern Santo Domingo, has forgotten that history did not end with Balaguer's 1961 "democratic coup." Sitting in her hotel room and getting her news from CNN, she remains oblivious to the country's reversion to its early Trujillo-era role as an American lapdog whose economy depends on sex tourism (a field in which the Dominican Republic's specialty is the prostitution of infants) and the virtual enslavement of economic migrants from neighbouring Haiti.

Edith Grossman's translation opts for a literal approach, a valid strategy with a work whose complexity resides in its elaborate narrative structures rather than in allusive language. Yet some scenes, particularly those couched in the subtle Spanish American lexicon of racial difference, would have benefited from a more interventionist translation. When Vargas Llosa writes that the face of one of Trujillo's generals shows "inconfundibles reminiscencias raciales," it is clear to the Spanish-speaking reader that the general's face is more African-looking than those of most officers of his rank. The English reader is unlikely to know what to make of Grossman's excessively literal translation, "a complexion with unmistakable racial reminiscences." Similarly, Grossman's decision to render the Spanish "negro" as "nigger" produces a translation harsher than the original. But her approach is effective in conveying the headlong energy of this remarkable novel, whose reimagining of the history of a time and a nation remains unputdownable even when it is not always reliable.

"Mario Vargas Llosa" draws on "Vargas Llosa Returns to Form in Novel," Montreal *Gazette*, 3 November 2001 and "Death of a Dictator," *Times Literary Supplement*, 12 April 2002.

9. CUBAN WRITING BEYOND
INSIDE AND OUT

For the last thirteen years of his life, Alejo Carpentier (1904-1980), Cuba's greatest 20th-century novelist, lived in Paris, where he served as his country's permanent cultural attaché in France. By living outside Cuba yet remaining inside Fidel Castro's regime, Carpentier broke the rigid dualism that has seen Cuban writers since the early 1960s divide into "adentro" and "afuera": inside and outside, with the regime or against it. The extent to which the work of writers living inside and outside Cuba has developed, at least in the eyes of some, into two mutually exclusive literatures can be seen in books such as Carlos Espinosa Domínguez's voluminous study of Cuban literature in exile, *El peregrino en comarca ajena* (2001; The Pilgrim in an Alien Village). Espinosa Domínguez treats diaspora writing as a phenomenon uncoupled from the historical trajectory of Cuban literature. Aside from fleeting references to major figures such as Carpentier, José Lezama Lima and Virgilio Piñera, Cuban writers who are not exiles do not appear, nor does the author acknowledge the evident transmission of literary influence between writers inside and outside Cuba. In discussing certain writers, Espinosa Domínguez has air-brushed important influences out of the portrait. It is astonishing that in a book which sets out to assess the work of every single Cuban poet in exile, the name of Nicolás Guillén (1902-1989), the most widely read Cuban poet of the 20th century, does not appear at all. But of course Guillén remained loyal to Castro's regime: he was the first president of the Writers' Union of Cuba after the Revolution, an unimaginable position for a man of mixed race to have held prior to 1959. His small, mahogany-floored office, into which I was

179

ushered by an excited housekeeper during a visit to Havana, has
been preserved as a shrine since his death. It is axiomatic, therefore, to Espinosa Domínguez and many others, that Guillén could
not possibly exercise any influence on Cuban poets in exile.

This willful truncation of a literary tradition owes much to
ideology and a fair amount to racism, a subject that the Cuban
diaspora refuses to address. Cubans living outside Cuba are over-
whelmingly white while the majority of Cubans living inside Cuba
are mixed race or black; racial stereotypes contribute significantly
to Miami's despisal of Havana. The globalization of the post-1990
world has had the unexpected consequence of making this rigidly
dualistic outlook more difficult to sustain. Cuba, like other nations,
now produces writers who direct their work almost entirely at the
international market, presenting national material in ways that
would be unacceptable within Cuba but which play on foreign fascination with the country. The collapse of the Soviet Union, reducing Cuba to selling its tropical charms on the open market, has
created a third category of Cuban writer: those who live "inside"
but publish "outside." Like the notorious *jinetera* prostitutes who
cater to foreign tourists, recent Cuban fiction has thrived in the sex
trade. The shamelessly self-promoting exiled writer Zoé Valdés, a
former member of the Cuban elite, was the first to exploit this market niche. Valdés's novel *Yocandra in the Paradise of Nada* (1995)
enjoyed international success by fashioning a cocktail of anti-
Castro ideology and explicit sex. But it is writers who continue to
live in Cuba who are the masters in this field. Valdés looks like a
genteel amateur by comparison with Pedro Juan Gutiérrez.

Dirty Havana Trilogy (2001) follows its male protagonist from
the worst days of Cuba's economic depression in 1994 to 1997,
when the economy once again began to improve. The book is
divided into three sections, each containing more than twenty
short, stark stories. Natasha Wimmer's translation, though appro-
priately hard-boiled, confuses the historical context by removing
the dates that appear at the end of each section of the Spanish edition. The first-person narrator shares the author's name and

elements of his biography. A journalist in his forties, he has lived in Europe and travelled widely. But as socialist society crumbles, so does his life. His wife leaves him and moves to New York. Dismissed from his job at a radio station, he must fend for himself in a small rooftop apartment in the slums of Central Havana.

The narrator's decision to skirt the issue of his expulsion from his job is typical of an aesthetic that concentrates on the harsh details of daily survival. Gutiérrez displays little interest in formal politics. His reticence may be due to his continuing employment as a journalist in Havana, but it also reflects a ferocious misanthropy hostile to human society in any form. His bile is more effective for being delivered in a conversational tone. Gutiérrez's frank confessions coexist with a striking tendency towards vagueness. Characters' ages alter from story to story. The narrator's offhand references to passing time add up to at least twice the purported three-year span of the book's action. At first he is living with a teenage son; later, the son vanishes, and he introduces a younger son from a different relationship; later still, he says he has "no children." He drops hints and does not pursue them: "I was back from Málaga and I was sleeping around a lot. Málaga was a great blow to my heart, but I'd rather not discuss it. Not yet. It'll be a few years before I can talk about what really happened to me in Málaga." This coyness, which is both affecting and irritating, contrasts with the book's brutal naturalism. The gaps and inconsistencies mimic the disconnectedness of Cuban society after the disintegration of socialism. Although Gutiérrez's stories are very short, they often change direction without warning or run together apparently unrelated vignettes. Attention-getting opening sentences – "Last night, in the middle of the music, the drunken uproar and the usual Saturday racket, Carmencita cut off her husband's penis" – turn out to be peripheral to the stories they introduce.

The narrator, Pedro Juan, scrutinizes the squalor of his neighbours' lives. But he is scarcely better off himself. Like others, he buys and sells and steals and works degrading jobs. He is robbed, beaten and imprisoned a number of times. In one story he is bitten

in the stomach by a rat and must seduce a nurse he finds physically
repellent in order to acquire a scarce rabies vaccine. Increasingly
isolated, Pedro Juan relates to others mainly through exuberantly
heartless sex. His preferred sexual activity is anal penetration of
black and mulatta women – an act, he assures the reader, that
helps to show a woman "who's boss." He hits women who anger
him, and sometimes also those who please him. As disturbing as
these scenes may be, they illustrate the resurgence of Cuba's racial
divides. Pedro Juan is of distant African ancestry and believes in
aspects of Afro-Cuban religion, yet he grows increasingly aware of
the anomaly of his white skin. Hearing drums pounding at night,
"I remembered those movies about explorers on the Congo. 'Oh
no, we're surrounded by cannibals.'" For a while he is fortunate
enough to live with a mulatta *jinetera* who supports him with the
dollars she earns having sex with tourists. Pedro Juan sits at home
and writes stories whose philosophy reflects that of the book: "Not
a single lie. I only change the names. That's my profession:
shitraker . . . Only an angry, obscene, violent art can show us the
other side of the world, the side we never see or try not to see so as
to avoid troubling our consciences."

Pedro Juan's elemental anger contains an unexpected strain of
tenderness. One of the attractions of this grotesquely readable, if
unevenly written, book lies in the narrator's candid observation of
the coarsening of his own physical being. It is difficult to think of
another heterosexual male writer so attentive to the body. The fascination with which Pedro Juan gauges the copiousness of his ejac-
ulations against the aging of his flesh and the days that have
elapsed since his last sexual encounter has the paradoxical effect of
humanizing Gutiérrez's sketches of damned souls. The book's
final third, where the first-person narration is interspersed with
less immediate third-person stories about neighbourhood characters, is much less readable than the first two sections. *Dirty Havana
Trilogy* goes on too long, but it is easy to see why this novel has
been more popular "outside" Cuba than any other recent work by
a writer "inside."

By contrast *Thine is the Kingdom* by Abilio Estévez, a poet and figure on the Havana theatre scene, is an important work of Latin American fiction that has been ignored in English. The most accomplished Cuban novel since Alejo Carpentier's *Reasons of State* (1974), and possibly since José Lezama Lima's divine *Paradiso* (1968) – familiar to non-aficionados of Cuban literature through the "Lezama Lima dinner" scene in Tomás Gutiérrez Alea's film *Strawberry and Chocolate* – *Thine is the Kingdom* is a gloriously Proustian account of past time recaptured. The characters inhabit a small, overgrown estate on the edge of Havana known as La Isla, a microcosm of Cuba itself, which is bracing for a tropical storm. There is little forward action, other than the ominous appearance of a bleeding, arrow-pierced character known as the Wounded Boy, who resembles St. Sebastian. The novel consists of a succession of interior monologues in which the energy and richness of the literary and philosophical speculation make temporal stagnation into an absorbing reading experience. David Frye's excellent English version, free flowing in its rhythms but faithful to the original, deserved, but did not receive, a wide readership.

The characters are extravagant creations: a barefoot countess, a former opera singer called Casta Diva, a Jamaican English teacher named Professor Kingston, a gay bookseller known as Uncle Rolo. Their literariness, which might be a weakness in a less self-conscious novel, contributes to the narrator's promotion of literature as a superior form of life. One character says: "God, what I wouldn't give to be a character in a novel! It's the only way to have a truly intense life, full of vicissitudes, an imaginary life, I dreamed of being the character of a great book." The same character later imagines herself "escaping, confronting the horizon on a raft." The horizon, a point one moves towards without ever reaching it, is Estévez's metaphor for the work's other major theme: death. An extended meditation on death precedes the denouement; the narrator lauds literature's ability to "abolish time, or rather, give it a different meaning, jumble the three known tenses into a fourth

tense that covers them all and induces what could be called
simultaneity."

Estévez's invocation of the simultaneity of literature as a bulwark against death and the passing of time comes wrapped in exu-
berant prose and hundreds of literary allusions. The translation
includes useful notes on the references to Cuban poetry and history, but Estévez casts his net far wider. Decadent writers of the
turn of the last century, such as J. K. Huysmans and Oscar Wilde,
and playwrights such as August Strindberg and Maurice
Maeterlinck, are crucial to the novel's imagery. As the storm pres-
aging "the end of the world" draws closer and the woods of La Isla
appear to "advance" in the wind, allusions to *Macbeth* thread
through the prose. The novel's vitality emerges from the tension
between Estévez's yearning to recreate a specific past – the pre-
revolutionary suburban Havana of his childhood – and his belief
that all literature evokes not "reality," but other literature.

Estévez both embraces and spurns Cuban history. Landmarks
in the country's embattled quest for independence are woven into
the novel's fabric, but most are mentioned in passing. A subplot set
in the 19th century reveals that La Isla, in a parodic wink at Gabriel
García Márquez's fictional town of Macondo, has its origins in
incest. Having related this tale with tropical, quasi-magic realist
lushness, the narrator interrupts: "Did you like it? No, it's a fake
story, too melodramatic, too graphic, sounds like it was told by a
southern writer from the United States. Then I'll just have to tell
you the story of Consuelo, you'll like that one."

The almost taunting tone of the narrative interventions
reaches a climax in the epilogue. The narrator argues against
Flaubert's conception of the writer as an omnipresent yet invisible
deity, militating for a more overtly intrusive approach on the
grounds that, "God isn't even invisible. We see him every day, in
the most unlikely forms." By this point, La Isla has burned to the
ground and the narrator decides: "it's time to reveal that at that
exact moment the President of the Republic, Fulgencio Batista, was
fleeing by plane to the Dominican Republic . . . . and the Rebels,

with their long, impetuous beards, were taking charge of the situation." The English edition pre-empts this long-deferred reference to politics with a cover blurb which tells us that *"Thine is the Kingdom* takes place in the months immediately prior to the Cuban Revolution of 1959." As the remainder of the epilogue, an impassioned disquisition on the centrality of literature to human existence, demonstrates, Estévez dislikes this sort of political allegory. It is no coincidence that the novel's story ends the instant politics becomes inescapable.

The popular success of this demanding novel in Spain, Germany and France (where it was awarded the 2000 Prix du Meilleur Livre Étranger) has not been equalled in the United States, where response has been sparse, restrained and, in Miami, often hostile. Dedicated to the late gay Cuban writer Virgilio Piñera, *Thine is the Kingdom*, a novel celebrating gay themes written by a gay writer who lives comfortably with his partner in Havana, had the great misfortune of being published in English just as *Before Night Falls*, Julian Schnabel's romanticized film biography of the life of Reinaldo Arenas, arrived in the cinemas. *Before Night Falls* was a gift to the U.S. media machine, which has always used the oppression of gays in Cuba as a wedge to alienate liberal sympathies from Castro's regime. The orgy of mindless Cuba-bashing set off by Schnabel's film dictated that, in the realm of media-fabricated public perception, a writer such as Estévez and a book such as *Thine is the Kingdom* could not exist. And so they did not. Yet Arenas, portrayed in the film as a rebel to the cause of "freedom," was capable of carrying off very young boys to have sex with them, a habit that provoked complaints from parents. The attacks on Cuba's treatment of gays prompted by the release of *Before Night Falls* led mainstream U.S. news organizations to condone, and even champion, pedophilia, something that would have been unthinkable had the pedophilia taken place in New Jersey or Ohio. The media frenzy deliberately blurred the line between the film's setting in the 1960s and 1970s, when gays were brutally oppressed everywhere in Latin America, but more systematically in Cuba than elsewhere, and the present, when gay life in Cuba is not appreciably harsher than that in other smaller Latin American countries. (The film *Strawberry and Chocolate* played an important role in this social shift by initiating a nation-wide discussion inside Cuba about attitudes towards homosexuality. In 1993, the year of the film's release, Fidel Castro recanted the homophobic statements he had made in the 1960s and early 1970s.)

The existence of writers such as Gutiérrez and Estévez – one might add to the list the polished, literate detective novelist Leonardo Padura Fuentes, who also lives in Havana and has large audiences both in Cuba and abroad – complicates the dynamics of Cuban literature in healthy ways, breaking down the rigid dualism between "inside" and "outside." That dualism is disintegrating in other ways, as gay writers once banned by the regime, such as Virgilio Piñera and Severo Sarduy, are once again being published in Havana. Few countries in the world have produced as much good writing per capita as Cuba; the false division between "inside" and "outside" only obscures a strength and diversity that should be evident to readers everywhere.

"Cuban Writing Beyond Inside and Out" includes sections from "Flesh of the Damned," *Times Literary Supplement*, 16 March 2001, "Storm over La Isla," *Times Literary Supplement*, 13 July 2001, and my review of Carlos Espinosa Domínguez, *El peregrino en comarca ajena: panorama crítico de la literatura cubana del exilio*, "Reviews of Books," *Bulletin of Spanish Studies*, Volume LXXX, No. 5 (2003).

10. GABRIEL GARCÍA MÁRQUEZ

Gabriel García Márquez's fiction owes its fascination to a tension between intimacy and remoteness. The narrative worlds of *One Hundred Years of Solitude* (1967) and *Love in the Time of Cholera* (1985) are intensely personal without being obviously autobiographical. The sculpted narrative voice, with its old-storyteller self-assurance, rebuffs elementary attempts to peer into the author's psyche. Never having written a novel as overtly confessional as Mario Vargas Llosa's *Aunt Julia and the Scriptwriter* (1977) or Carlos Fuentes's *Diana, the Goddess Who Hunts Alone* (1996), García Márquez, by comparison with his Spanish American contemporaries, exerts the appeal of a familiar enigma.

García Márquez was in his thirties when he perfected his old storyteller voice. Now in his mid-seventies, he has allowed the voice to grow more relaxed and confiding as he turns to the first volume of his memoirs, *Living to Tell the Tale* (2002). The respected translator Edith Grossman has rarely been challenged as she has here. She resorts to footnotes to explain regionalisms and puns; in spite of a good general rendering, Grossman does not quite capture the intimate quality of the original. The anecdotal directness of this memoir is recognizable from García Márquez's journalism, yet above all the tone recalls his fiction. The enthusiasm with which this book has been read throughout the Americas in its Spanish-language edition owes much to its unmasking of the autobiographical sources of the novels. The dramatic opening, where the author's mother, Luisa Márquez, hunts down the impoverished aspiring writer in a café in Barranquilla and asks him to accompany her into the jungles of his childhood to sell the family home, begins a process of exposing the prototypes for the fiction, giving the reader the illusion of breaking through the carapace of the García Márquez narrative voice to understand the genesis of his novels.

Some of the prototypes are obvious, such as Colonel Nicolás Márquez, the author's maternal grandfather, with whom García Márquez lived for his first eight years, and who would become the model for Colonel Aureliano Buendía in *One Hundred Years of Solitude* and the stoic veteran of Colombia's civil wars waiting for a pension that never arrives in *No One Writes to the Colonel* (1961). Colonel Márquez revered the memory of Simón Bolívar, "the greatest man ever born in the history of the world." A painting of Bolívar's corpse hung in the family living room. When the infant García Márquez asks his grandfather if Bolívar is greater than Jesus Christ, the reader sees the first glimmerings of *The General in His Labyrinth* (1989) taking shape. In similar fashion, Macondo turns out to be a decayed banana plantation on the edge of García Márquez's native town of Aracataca. He had used the name in three books before he learned that it was a tropical tree.

The most engrossing points of connection with the novels are those on which García Márquez does not comment. The oldest of his family's eleven children (his father had five other children by extra-marital liaisons), García Márquez spent much of his early childhood separated from his mother, whose defining role in his life is evident in his dramatic claim that her death in June 2002, at the age of ninety-seven, coincided to the hour with his completion of this memoir. One of their reunions was arranged to celebrate the birth of his younger sister, Margot. As an infant the little girl refused food, eating the damp earth of the garden like Rebeca Buendía; in *One Hundred Years of Solitude*, the infant's taste for earth is transferred to an adolescent. The images of a mother entering a silent town to reclaim the body of a son shot trying to commit burglary, of the Colonel's illegitimate sons visiting him once a year, and of a priest who is reputed to levitate during Mass, contribute to the illusion of understanding the novels' origins. But this is an illusion. García Márquez insists that, "Life is not what one lived, but . . . how one remembers it in order to recount it." Doubt has been cast on whether García Márquez actually made the return trip up the Magdalena River with his mother with which the memoirs open. In a sense it doesn't matter whether what we discover beneath the fiction is simply another fiction, as long as the reader believes he has found a truth.

The illusion of understanding the novels' origins is most persuasive in the case of a Belgian refugee from the First World War, a chess companion of Colonel Márquez, who committed suicide by inhaling a cyanide solution. After observing the body, the infant García Márquez utters the *bon mot*, "The Belgian won't be playing chess anymore." The phrase is repeated by the women of the family to the point where the author looks back on it as "my first literary success." The scene illustrates how the novelist's imagination parses images from life as fictional creations: the Belgian becomes the model for Gaston, the Belgian who brings a debased version of Western technology to Macondo in the final pages of *One Hundred Years of Solitude*, while his suicide evolves into the opening scene of *Love in the Time of Cholera*, where Dr. Urbino examines the body of his chess partner, the West Indian refugee Jeremiah de Saint-Amour, who has committed suicide by inhaling a cyanide solution.

Colonel Márquez's death expelled his grandson from the decaying jungle town into the chaos of a very large, very poor family. Having reunited the family on the Caribbean coast, García Márquez's father, a mercurial man, invested his savings in a pharmacy. When the business failed, he took off up the Magdalena River, naming his eleven-year-old son head of a swarming household that lacked financial support. García Márquez's school years were marked by ugly poverty: head lice, rickets, hunger. The features typical of a writer's upbringing – the perpetual reading, the occasional teacher who recognized his abilities – are lent a distinctively Caribbean flavour by the predominance of oral culture. The future writer read the poets of the Spanish Golden Age in order to memorize and recite them; as an adolescent he entered singing contests. It was for one of these that his mother, his accomplice in keeping the family clothed and fed, requested he register not only with his paternal surname, García, but also with the maternal Márquez. In his father's absence, the young Gabriel José García was evolving into Gabriel García Márquez.

He won a scholarship to a good secondary school, but at fifteen he became embroiled in a dangerous affair with a married woman whose husband had a reputation for violence. A move was necessary, and he reluctantly consented to go to Bogotá, "a remote, lugubrious city where an insomniac rain had been falling since the beginning of the sixteenth century." His pilgrimage by riverboat to the chilly Andean capital in search of a scholarship led him to a boarding school that transformed him from a Caribbean regionalist into a man with a vision of a varied but unified Colombian nation. García Márquez belongs to a relatively fortunate generation of Colombians who grew up between the end of the civil wars at the beginning of the twentieth century and the outbreak of *La Violencia*, when war again became the country's daily reality. The destruction of this period of peace dominates the second half of the memoir and inspires some of its most gripping passages.

The assassination of the maverick Liberal presidential candidate Jorge Eliécer Gaitán, on April 9, 1948, is the crucial watershed in twentieth-century Colombian history: the moment when reform failed. After Gaitán's death, the old political parties, the Liberals and the Conservatives, locked themselves into a brutal struggle which over the next decades would corrode civil society, allowing the parallel powers of guerrilla armies, death squads and drug traffickers to dominate public life. In 1948 García Márquez was a first-year law student who had published three short stories. He arrived on the scene a few minutes after the assassination. His vivid description of a suspicious, well-dressed man urging the outraged crowd to kill the supposed assassin is a startling addition to to debates about the events of that day, which exerts an influence on Colombians similar to that of the assassination of John F. Kennedy on Americans. As fighting between Liberal and Conservative supporters in the weeks after the assassination left most of Bogotá in smouldering ruins, García Márquez escaped to the Caribbean coast. In Barranquilla and Cartagena, he slept in parks, on beaches and in brothels, earned pocket money by writing a newspaper column, argued about books, abandoned a first attempt at a novel and began the agonizing composition of the Faulknerian novella *Leaf Storm* (1955).

García Márquez's assessment of his personality during these years is bleak. "My poverty was absolute, and I had the timidity of a quail, which I tried to counteract with insufferable arrogance and brutal frankness. I felt I did not belong anywhere, and even certain acquaintances made me aware of this." Yet his torrential activity tells a more complicated story. The memoir reveals glimpses of a man of supernatural vitality, great social gifts and workaholic determination. The reader sees the distinctive García Márquez style, characterized by the elimination of adverbs and the compression of dialogue into single declarative statements, emerging from the meshing of his journalistic apprenticeship and his memories of his grandparents' house. On visits to the Magdalena River town of Sucre, where his parents had settled, he met Mercedes Barcha. Following the custom of the time, he remained emotionally loyal to her during their long courtship while continuing to frequent the brothels. In this book's last line of dialogue, García Márquez tells an acquaintance that he still does not know who he is. Yet with the publication of *Leaf Storm* he had begun the process of mythologizing his past in a way that would give birth to the confident voice of the old storyteller.

By his late twenties García Márquez was a professional journalist. He worked for the Bogotá newspaper *El Espectador* during its days as one of Latin America's great institutions of investigative reporting. Non-aficionados may find the final chapter of this book, with its detailed account of Colombian journalism during the 1950s, less riveting than the rest. But this suggestive, impassioned, surprisingly vulnerable memoir is certain to stand as one of García Márquez's most important books.

I was assigned "Gabriel García Márquez" in October 2003 by an editor at the *Times Literary Supplement* whom I had not worked with before. The piece was accepted, edited and sent to me in proof. It failed to run in the issue for which it had been scheduled, then was delayed for weeks; a senior editor finally spiked it. A younger editor offered compensation by inviting me out to dinner at a Turkish restaurant near Victoria Station in London, making this the only piece of unpublished writing for which I have been paid in food.

11. PÉTER ESTERHÁZY

In the late 1980s, when I was preparing to visit Hungary for the first time, I found that the only contemporary Hungarian writer whose work was widely available in English translation was the dissident George Konrád. When I reached Budapest and told my new Hungarian friends of my admiration for Konrád's novel *The Loser* (1980), I discovered that they had not heard of the book; it could not be published in its author's homeland. Yet, in contrast to the Western stereotype, Hungarian readers did not divide writers into heroic dissidents and lackeys of the regime. Most good fiction emerged from a literary middle ground between these political extremes.

In those days prior to the birth of mass tourism in Central Europe, travellers were expected to display a strong interest in the cultures of the countries they visited. To satisfy this expectation, the Budapest publisher Corvina produced fiction anthologies in English translation for the local market. It was while broadening my acquaintance with Hungarian writers whose work was unavailable in the West that I discovered in one such Corvina anthology the fiction of Péter Esterházy. The first Esterházy story I read was called "No Title; This Isn't It Either." Its whimsical absurdism intrigued yet baffled me. I had similarly mixed reactions to other Esterházy short stories, as I did to his *Helping Verbs of the Heart*, a poignant yet puzzling novel that appeared in English in 1991.

No such reservations are possible with regard to Esterházy's *Celestial Harmonies* (2004). Less a novel in a traditional sense than a display of supernatural literary virtuosity hitched to a tormented obsession with heritage, fatherhood and history, *Celestial Harmonies* is a powerful, challenging work destined to unsettle readers in many countries.

The book is divided into two parts. The first 400 pages contain 371 numbered paragraphs that ring an inexhaustible variety of changes on the lives of fathers. There are no named characters: the central male character in each paragraph is called "my father" and the central female character "my mother." Nor does anything so mundane as a plot put in an appearance. Each paragraph spins off its predecessor in the way that a capricious symphony might pick up a motif from an earlier movement. Many of these subtle links are rooted in the novel's language and wordplay. It is a compliment to the translation, by Corvina's Judith Sollosy, that, in spite of rough patches and a few clumsy renderings of puns, the first half of the novel sustains a feeling of coherence and direction. Esterházy's prose retains its playfulness but gains a vivid muscularity that has not been evident before in English. The energetically recounted vignettes shuttle back and forth through Hungarian history: in one paragraph the Holocaust is taking place, in the next it is 1526 and the Turks are invading, then we are plunged into the pomp of the Austro-Hungarian Empire. Readers unfamiliar with the chronology of Central European history may find this shifting narrative landscape, for all its vividness, difficult to bring into focus. The true chronological motion of this half of the novel is found in the lives of fathers. The early paragraphs are about fathers as youths, the next group is about fathers meeting mothers, then there are fathers fathering children, fathers conducting careers and affairs, fathers growing old and finally fathers ascending to "the heavenly spheres." Stubbornly, this book remains a novel, even though the first half resembles a poem and the second half reads like a dissident memoir.

Whereas the first part of *Celestial Harmonies* is vacant of names, the second part is haunted by a single name: Esterházy. The author descends from Hungary's most famous aristocratic family, whose vast estates in Transdanubia, the country's wealthiest region, elevated them to commanding roles in monarchies and empires, then brought them into the sights of the communists after 1945 as "class enemies" of the socialist state. Péter Esterházy, born in 1950, spent his childhood in the countryside to which his family had been exiled as manual labourers after being stripped of their castles and servants. The novel's second half opens with the declaration that "the Communists are here," then splits into a dual narration charting both the short-lived Hungarian Communist revolution of 1919 and the more enduring regime imposed by the Soviets after 1945. The diaries of older Esterházys occupying government posts lead to the memories of the little boy in the countryside who feels seven centuries of privilege bearing down on him each time he utters his name. The child vomits in fear as his father, a young man raised to be an aristocrat, is beaten and arrested in the village square. In a gruelling scene, the father spits on his six-year-old son for signing a confession to get him out of jail. Esterházy's emotional frankness would be wrenching on its own. Informed by the novel's poetic first half, many of these tortuous passages acquire complex resonances that challenge the reader's understanding of paternity and inheritance.

Grateful as I was to be able to read this magnificent novel in English, I couldn't help wondering: has Esterházy finally broken through the screen of translation because, like Konrád fifteen years earlier, he is now peddling anti-communism, the English-speaking world's accepted theme for writers from Central Europe? Yet sometimes the right book is translated for some of the wrong reasons. The appearance of this novel in English enlarges our humanity.

"Péter Esterházy" was published as "Hungarian Rhapsody" in *The Globe and Mail*, 17 April 2004. My friend Mária Palla, of Kodolányi College in Székesfehérvár, Hungary, later wrote to me to point out that, after the Hungarian publication of *Celestial Harmonies*, Esterházy discovered that his heroic father had been an informer for the secret police; this, it turned out, was why the family was eventually allowed to return to Budapest from its rural exile. Esterházy reacted with a second book of reflections on fatherhood that took into account this new information. This book, to no one's surprise, has not been published in English.

12. JOSÉ SARAMAGO

"It's only after the age of seventy that you will become wise," an elderly woman tells the protagonist of José Saramago's novel *All the Names* (1997), "but then your wisdom will be of no use, either to you or to anyone else." For Saramago's fiction, wisdom has meant a steady migration towards parable. The social realism of early novels such as *Levantado do Chão* (1980) yielded to playful historical tales and allegories of Iberian history in *Baltasar and Blimunda* (1982), *The Year of the Death of Ricardo Reis* (1984), *The Stone Raft* (1988) and *History of the Seige of Lisbon* (1989). In 1992, when Saramago turned seventy, he published *The Gospel According to Jesus Christ*, his first novel set outside Portugal or Spain. The controversy ignited by this novel prompted Saramago to leave Portugal and settle in the Canary Islands. The novels that have appeared since that time – *Blindness* (1995), *All the Names* and *The Cave* (2000) – have plumbed the ominous universality of mainly nameless figures enduring ordeals visited on them by forces they do not understand. The city in which *Blindness* takes place betrays no culturally distinctive features. If the cramped bureaucratic world of *All the Names* recalls the Portugal of the Salazar dictatorship, the connection is never made explicit. While the displaced rural artisans of the Platonic *The Cave* have names that could be Portuguese, their uprooting at the whim of market forces is emblematic of the extinction of artisan cultures around the world. Enhancing this broader perspective is Saramago's growing preoccupation with the ultimate futility of all human effort. Both tendencies suggest that the individual matters less in Saramago's current fiction than in past works; yet individual characters, whether or not they have names, are as warmly conceived and their struggles are often as gripping as in the early fiction.

The Double was published in Portugal in 2002, the year of Saramago's eightieth birthday. It feels like the summing-up of a writer who cannot lay pen to paper without being reminded of the canonical status of his achievements. The first printing of 80,000 copies in a country of eleven million people indicates the gigantic shadow Saramago casts not only over other Portuguese writers, but over himself. The protagonist of *The Double*, who stumbles upon a more successful public incarnation of himself, suffers from an analogous dilemma. Tertuliano Máximo Afonso is a divorced history teacher who spends his evenings reading about ancient Semitic cultures (the detail appears to be an admonishing wink at conservatives in the United States who have ascribed Saramago's pro-Palestinian polemics to anti-Semitism). Tertuliano extends Saramago's repertoire of obscure protagonists projected into circumstances that intensify their isolation. Introducing Tertuliano, the narrator writes:

> What one mostly sees, indeed it hardly comes as a surprise any more, are people patiently submitting to solitude's meticulous scrutiny, recent public examples, though not particularly well known and two of whom even met with a happy ending, being the portrait painter who we only ever knew by his first initial, the GP who returned from exile to die in the arms of the beloved fatherland, the proofreader who drove out a truth in order to plant a lie in its place, the lowly clerk in the Central Registry Office who made off with certain death certificates, all of these, either by chance or coincidence, were members of the male sex, but none of them had the misfortune to be called Tertuliano, and this was doubtless an advantage to them in their relations with other people.

Readers of earlier Saramago novels will recognize the allusions to the protagonists of *The Manual of Painting and Calligraphy* (1977), *The Year of the Death of Ricardo Reis, History of the Seige of Lisbon* and *All the Names*. The sentence exemplifies the distinctive

Saramago style, blending the leisurely tone of the traditional story-teller with sly postmodern commentary. A Saramago sentence may begin with an account of events, incorporate an exchange of dialogue, branch off into a digression and conclude with a deflating jab at the digression's assumptions. Controlling the rhythms of his long sentences through the distribution of commas, Saramago creates a voice of rolling inevitability. The humour springs from the sudden interjections of dialogue or observation that divert a sentence from its expected course. In this way, the startling events that dominate Saramago's recent fiction generate comic effects even as they disturb. Tertuliano, who rarely watches films, rents a video on the recommendation of a mathematics teacher at his school. He falls asleep and misses most of the action. When he awakes, feeling overcome by apprehension, he rewinds the video and spots a minor character whose appearance is identical to his own but for the fact that the actor wears a moustache. This provokes a sardonic digression about moustaches, in which the avoidance of Tertuliano's crisis of identity heightens the reader's anxiety.

Tertuliano becomes a patron of his local video shop. In chronological order, he rents the productions of the company responsible for the film in which his double appears. At first the actor plays minor roles; his characters are not identified by name in the credits. By following the actor's career, Tertuliano learns his screen name, Daniel Santa-Clara. In order to discover Santa-Clara's real name, Tertuliano writes him a fan letter, which he signs with the name and address of his lover, Maria da Paz, a bank clerk who is desperate to get married and whom he is on the verge of dumping.

As Tertuliano's quest proceeds, the contradictions of the novel's setting become more perplexing. Tertuliano is aware of computers, yet writes his letters on a manual typewriter. There are video machines, but no mention of the internet. The characters have Portuguese names, there are references to *fado* and Catholicism, yet the metropolis where Tertuliano lives is not Lisbon. The narrator intervenes to clarify matters:

The moment has come to inform those readers who, given the, so far, rather scant urban descriptions, have created in their mind the idea that this is all taking place in a medium-sized city, one, that is, of fewer than a million inhabitants, but the moment has come, as we were saying, to inform them that, on the contrary, this teacher, Tertuliano Máximo Afonso, is one of the just over five million human beings who, with major differences in standard of living and other differences that defy all comparison, inhabit the vast metropolis that extends over what were, long ago, hills, valleys and plains, and which is now a continuous labyrinthine duplication both horizontally and vertically, initially made more complicated by components we will term diagonals, but which, meanwhile, with the passing of time, have brought some measure of equilibrium to the chaotic urban mesh, for they established frontier lines which, paradoxically, instead of driving things apart, brought them closer together.

The "duplication" represented by the city (the Portuguese reads "sucesiva duplicação horizontal e vertical de um labirinto") brings "things" together (the "things" is a necessary invention of the highly accomplished translator, Margaret Jull Costa, to bridge the gulf separating the syntax of Portuguese and English; in the original it is the diagonals that are brought closer together). This sketch of the city reveals the kernel of the novel's themes. Saramago has suggested in interviews that The Double closes his "trilogy of identity." All the Names dealt with the impact of bureaucracy on identity and The Cave with community identity besieged by globalized industry. The Double can be read as an exploration of the distorting effect of the visual media on individual identity: of how the media transform human traits into products that can be endlessly duplicated. It is unfortunate that the duplication motif has disappeared from the English title of O Homem Duplicado (The Duplicated Man). By harnessing his allegory to a setting which is imaginary yet familiar, neither too close nor too far removed from recognizable social reality, Saramago induces readers to consider the fragility of individual identity amid the commerce of images that defines our culture. The actor shields his private life behind the screen name, yet the film company, in its reply to Maria's fan letter, reveals that his real name is António Claro. By phoning Claro at home Tertuliano brings "things" closer together, fusing the actor's public and private selves, while himself drawing closer to his identical other.

The paradox that duplication, rather than multiplying human possibility, erodes diversity, is acted out through the two men's inexorable attraction. Claro rebuffs Tertuliano's suggestion that they meet. The mere knowledge of the possible existence of a man identical to himself unsettles his relationship with his wife, Helena. Having resigned himself to not meeting Claro, Tertuliano receives a phone call in which Claro announces his intention to send Tertuliano directions to a dilapidated farmhouse. In a comic scene, Tertuliano drives to the farmhouse wearing a false beard. The two men close the door and strip naked. Having examined one another in vain for signs of physical difference, they promise that, "We'll stay away from each other." Fearing that the media will exploit them as "circus freaks," they strive, without success, to disentangle the skein of their lives.

As the plot grows more complicated, images of duplication proliferate. Claro shuttles between his private life and his public identity as Daniel Santa-Clara. Tertuliano, whose name recalls both the 3rd-century Christian convert Tertullian and the Portuguese noun *tertúlia*, meaning a small gathering of people, begins to suffer from a split personality. He engages in page-long dialogues with "common sense," a voice of reason that tries to rein in his erratic behaviour. The bank clerk Maria da Paz is duplicated by a second Maria, a clerk at the company that produces Claro's films. These elements remain sufficiently mobile and autonomous that any attempt at a schematic deciphering of the novel's meaning is doomed to frustration. A second paradox emerges: as the two protagonists lose control of their identities, their fate comes to rest

more and more firmly on the particularities of individual character. This reliance on character has kept Saramago's fiction readable
as the sometimes murky fog of allegory has swallowed place,
names and temporal setting.

In his search for security, Tertuliano finally offers to marry
Maria da Paz. Claro, having discovered that the fan letter which
caused the production company to divulge his real name was
signed by Maria, resolves in his anger that he will seduce her by
pretending to be Tertuliano. Two ingenious plot twists bring the
story to an eerily satisfying conclusion. While *The Double* probably
will not rank as one of Saramago's major achievements, it is readable, thought-provoking, scrupulously constructed and, in the
main, narrated with buoyant high spirits. The digressions, longer
than in the past, sometimes grow ponderous. The narrator occasionally fusses over his characters for too long before releasing
them to act out their destinies. The other quality that is absent from
this novel is the projection of individual lives against a broad historical canvas that contributed to making Saramago such a popular novelist, particularly on the Left. The love story in *Baltasar and
Blimunda* takes place against the background of the construction of
the Mafra Convent. The death of Ricardo Reis coincides with the
fascist takeover of Portugal. An impatience with the limitations of
allegory, occasionally perceptible in *The Double*, appears to have
influenced Saramago's most recent novel. *Ensaio sobre a Lucidez*
(2004; *Seeing*), echoes the Portuguese title of *Blindness* (*Ensaio sobre
a Cegueira*). Set in another nameless city, where nameless characters participate in a spoiled-ballot campaign so successful that it
destroys liberal democracy, the novel features caricatures of prominent Portuguese politicians. The author parlayed the themes of
Seeing into a public call for Portuguese voters to spoil their ballots
in the 2004 European Elections (oddly, since Saramago himself was
standing as a candidate on the Communist Party slate). Regardless
of whether such actions are wise, there is little denying their use-
fulness as long as they continue to enable Saramago to produce
good fiction.

"José Saramago" was published in slightly different form as "The Man Who Met Himself," *Times Literary Supplement*, 6 August 2004.

13. ROBERTO BOLAÑO

Between 1996 and his death at the age of fifty in 2003, Roberto Bolaño, previously a little-known poet, published eleven novels that brought him fame and commercial success even as his health collapsed. His death in the midst of a period of torrential productivity has complicated assessment of a figure whose place in Spanish American letters was already difficult to define. A Mexican-reared Chilean who returned to the Chile of Salvador Allende only to be forced into exile at the age of twenty after General Augusto Pinochet's 1973 military coup, Bolaño lived most of his adult life in Mexico and Spain. Many of his novels have the outward form of detective stories. His central work, a 609-page literary pastiche called *Los detectives salvajes* (1998; *The Savage Detectives*), won two of the Hispanic world's major literary awards, the Herralde Novel Prize in Barcelona and, more importantly, the Rómulo Gallegos Prize in Venezuela. Not yet available in English, *Los detectives salvajes* is one of the major works of Spanish American postmodernism.

Bolaño's understanding of postmodernism was shaped by his experience of exile. Behind his recycling of popular forms and ironic manipulation of grand cultural currents lies a lament for lost wholeness. Unlike the great Latin American novelists of the 1960s, who tried to "totalize" the national life of Colombia, Mexico or Peru, Bolaño, a self-defined "Chilean-Mexican-Spaniard," straddled cultures and versions of the Spanish language, exploiting the contradictory strains in his own cultural make-up. Bolaño's melancholy awareness of vanished social cohesion lends his novels a humanity that enables them to delve far deeper than their clever pop-culture surfaces might lead a reader to expect.

Bolaño's great subject is the dispersal of social groups and the individual's relegation to a void dominated by randomness and solitude. In *Distant Star* (1996) the dispersal is caused by political calamity that dispatches the characters into exile. *Los detectives salvajes*, by contrast, opens in 1976 as an artistic *Bildungsroman* narrated by a 17-year-old aspiring Mexico City poet named Juan García Madero. Compelled by his uncle and aunt to study law when in fact he yearns to be a writer, García Madero frequents poetry workshops where he meets members of a movement known as "los real visceralistas" – the Visceral Realists. The epicentre of Visceral Realist activity is the home of the Font family, whose alluring daughters, María and Angélica, are accomplished poets. García Madero adopts the rebellious attitude of the Visceral Realists, who are described as existing somewhere between Surrealism and Marxism; he writes poems, neglects his studies and has sex with various young women, including María Font.

Living hand-to-mouth, the Visceral Realists satirize the great Spanish American poets. As is statutory in recent novels about Mexico City intellectual life, Octavio Paz is subjected to relentless ridicule: his formalism, his clothes, his Cadillac, his wife, and even his name, become the butt of jokes. In spite of these satiric elements, *Los detectives salvajes* appears to be on course to narrate the story of a young artist's coming-of-age. It is a surprise then, when, 140 pages into the novel, Bolaño derails this plan.

The seamy side of Mexico City life catches up with the Visceral Realists in a series of violent encounters with thugs. Quim Font, the father of María and Angélica, succumbs to mental illness. When two of the young Visceral Realists, Ulises Lima and Arturo Belano, leave the capital on a mysterious quest through northern Mexico, the group begins to break up. The narrative structure mimics this fragmentation: García Madero's voice is supplanted by a succession of more than thirty different narrators, who relate their encounters with former members of the Visceral Realist movement in half a dozen countries between 1976 and 1996. Through the eyes of both Visceral Realists and strangers, the reader watches a generation of idealistic young people losing their way. The dispersal of the Visceral Realist group becomes a meta-phor for the dissolution of a Spanish American literary culture that laid claim to continental unity and the ability to make statements that resonated beyond the literary world. One character, parody-ing the old Mexican song "La vida no vale nada" ("Life is worth nothing"), chants "La literatura no vale nada" ("Literature is worth nothing"). Bolaño's characters, here as in his other novels, are compulsive readers, matching each experience to a literary ref-erence. Yet in *Los detectives salvajes* the fabric of allusions shared by literate Spanish Americans is shredding; far from altering percep-tions of the world, the Visceral Realists' antics become meaning-less. To some extent, this is the view of a former poet looking back on poetry circles from the presumptuous vantage point of the novel. It is telling that the major Spanish American novelists escape Bolaño's satire. The Chilean novelist José Donoso (1924-1996), against whose baroque modernism Bolaño's taut post-modernism is reacting, makes a walk-on appearance, but not even Donoso is identified by name.

Ulises Lima and Arturo Belano carry their quest from Spanish America to Europe and the Middle East. At the outset, they claim to be looking for information about the life of Cesárea Tinajero, a Mexican avant-garde poet of the 1920s. Tinajero also belonged to a movement known as Visceral Realism, a fact that reinforces the futility of the young poets' efforts to create an art that is new. Ulises Lima, in a parodic debasement of the Ulysses story, becomes a traveller without a destination; his odyssey grows meaningless. On a trip to Israel in search of a former girlfriend, he befriends a large Austrian, fails to realize that the man is a neo-Nazi spy, and ends up in jail. During the 1980s, accompanying a group of Mexi-can writers to Nicaragua to show solidarity with the revolution, Lima misses his plane home and takes two years to find his way back to Mexico City. By the end of the novel he barely speaks or acts. Arturo Belano, who came to Mexico as a refugee from south-ern Chile, has a surname which resembles that of his creator. Like

Bolaño, he settles in Barcelona and enjoys success as a novelist until he is struck by a fatal illness. Throwing himself into reporting African wars, Belano is last seen on a Liberian battlefield. The final section, returning to García Madero's narration of events in 1976, pulls the rug out from under Lima and Belano's quest for Cesárea, concluding with an image of emptiness that abandons language altogether. In spite of the extreme bleakness of Bolaño's vision, the reader carries out of this profound novel a mass of vivid incident recounted by a supple voice effortlessly at home in half a dozen countries and equally persuasive in writing from the points of view of characters who are Mexican, Spanish or Chilean, female or male, gay or straight, Catholic or Jewish.

After *Los detectives salvajes*, Bolaño's shorter novels feel like elegant slivers. *Distant Star* is the second of Bolaño's novels to appear in English. The translation by Chris Andrews, who translated Bolaño's *Nocturno de Chile* (2000) as *By Night in Chile* (2003), is both inventive and precise. The story opens in 1972 in the southern Chilean city of Concepción, where an aspiring writer named Alberto Ruiz-Tagle joins a poetry workshop. Salvador Allende is President of Chile. The young poets' literary passions blend with their political enthusiasms. Ruiz-Tagle, by contrast, does not discuss politics. In 1973, after the Pinochet coup, the members of the workshop scatter. They leave for exile in Europe or join revolutionary movements elsewhere in Latin America. Those who remain in Chile are imprisoned, tortured or murdered. The narrator, Arturo, who may be Arturo Belano, tries to understand the fate of his old friends. His claims to truth limited by lack of information, he says, "From here on, my story is mainly conjecture." Arturo believes Ruiz-Tagle to be responsible for the deaths of two beautiful poetry-writing sisters, who presage the Font sisters in the later novel. When Arturo himself is imprisoned, a plane flies over the prison camp writing poems in the sky. The pilot, Carlos Wieder, becomes one of the cultural heroes of the Pinochet regime. Wieder flies to Antarctica and writes "Antarctica is Chile" in the sky. Newspaper photographs reveal Wieder and Ruiz-Tagle to be the same man. Released into exile in Europe, Arturo and his friend Bibiano O'Ryan try to reconstruct Wieder's artistic trajectory.

Much of the humour in the novel's early sections arises from in-jokes about Chilean poets. These sardonic moments pave the way for an investigation into the ominous paradox of the fascist artist. An introduction presents *Distant Star* as a coda to another Bolaño title, *La literatura nazi en América* (1996). The final section of the earlier work dealt with Lieutenant Ramírez Hoffman of the Chilean Air Force. *Distant Star* was written as "a longer story that, rather than mirroring or exploding others, was, in itself, a mirror and an explosion." The mirror does not reflect a great artist corrupted by fascism, as in Thomas Mann's *Doctor Faustus*, but rather what passes for art under a fascist regime, and the cost to the individual of producing this soulless kitsch. While the scattered former poets of *Los detectives salvajes* mourn the loss of literature's spiritual power, Wieder and his stunts, vacant from the outset, are mere simulacra of the artist and artistic creation.

A coarse miscalculation deprives Wieder of his position as the darling of the Pinochet elite. He holds an exhibition of photographs of the faces of women murdered by the regime, shown during torture or after death. Wieder's celebration of these images unsettles the guardians of "Christian civilization." He drops out of sight and his career spins into a nether world. Wieder may be the creator of a patriotic war game that catechizes young Chileans about the victory of "the Chilean race" over Peru and Bolivia in the War of the Pacific (1879-1883). Escaping to Europe as democracy returns to Chile and investigations into the past implicate him in human rights abuses, Wieder publishes derivative poems under pseudonyms in far-right fringe journals, works as a camera man on pornographic films, and finally adheres to a Parisian cult whose mission is to deface great works of literature with bodily fluids.

Like Jorge Luis Borges's short story, "Tlön, Uqbar, Orbis Tertius," which can also be read as an anti-fascist fable, *Distant Star* seeks to understand malevolent forces through the decipherment of obscure texts. Arturo and Bibiano resemble Borges and his friend Adolfo Bioy Casares in undertaking their sleuthing from a sedentary position. In the final chapters, Bolaño introduces an exiled Chilean detective to do the legwork to locate Wieder. The narrative's light touch and witty tone make harsh material uncomfortably easy to digest. Floating above the ideological fray, *Distant Star* achieves a poignant, disconcerting account of a man made rudderless by the loss of his humanity. Bolaño's response to extremism is to express compassion for the extremist. This imaginative sympathy enables his fiction to evoke meaninglessness in a way that is deeply human.

"Roberto Bolaño" was published in slightly different form as "The Visceral Realists Strike Again," *Times Literary Supplement*, 5 November 2004. I wrote this piece just prior to becoming aware of the Spanish publication of Bolaño's posthumous magum opus, the 1119-page novel *2666* (2004). In this exhausting book, left incomplete at the author's death, the son of a great European writer is implicated in the mass murder of women in the border towns of northern Mexico. The speed at which Bolaño must have been writing as death closed in on him is terrifying to imagine, but the high literary level he maintained is equally daunting to contemplate. In a stroke of serendipity, Bolaño's final months of life coincided with his appearance as a character in Javier Cercas's novel *Soldiers of Salamina* (2001), which sold more than a million copies in Spanish. Cercas's novel helped spread the Bolaño cult, already growing in Latin America, into Europe. The *Times Literary Supplement* followed up my piece with other articles on Bolaño. A few weeks later Farrar, Straus and Giroux in New York bought English translation rights to *Los detectives salvajes* and *2666*, and stories about Bolaño began to filter into the U.S. press. (The three short books by Bolaño translated by Chris Andrews, an Australian whose literary contacts are mainly British, were published by Harvill in the U.K.) It is ironic that the push to translate the major works of the dominant Latin American novelist of the post-1990 era originated not in the United States, the route by which Latin American writing used to enter the English-speaking world, but in London. The fact that an Australian translator, a British publishing house and a British literary journal were central to this push suggests that literary intellectuals in the United States no longer scrutinize Latin American literature – or, arguably, any non-English-language literature – as closely as they once did. Having begun to absorb Latin America as a Free Trade Area, the United States has ceased to respect the region as a culture. The era when García Márquez, Vargas Llosa, Borges, Fuentes and Cortázar were inescapable reference points in U.S. literary debate is slipping away. The deadening effect of a vision of globalization that shrinks world culture to that which is available in English makes Americans of all nations less intellectually alert, including those who live for literature.

14. THE ANGOLAN NOVEL

The Portuguese language is spoken more widely, and in a more standard form, in Angola than in any other former Portuguese colony in Africa. In Mozambique, where English is also important, Portuguese has spread more slowly. Creolized dialects rule street-life in Guinea Bissau and the two-island republic of São Tomé and Príncipe. In the Cape Verde Islands, Creole is gaining ground in public contexts, including literature. Angola owes its distinctness to two calamities: slavery and civil war. As the source of Portugal's slave trade to Brazil between the 16th and 19th centuries, Angola developed a class of African middlemen – known, confusingly, as "Creoles" – who managed the trade for their colonial masters. The Creoles adopted Portuguese-speaking, Catholic culture and often intermarried with European traders. In the early 20th century, when large-scale European settlement of Angola began, the Portuguese government's attempts to marginalize the Creoles in order to strengthen the settlers failed to stem mixing across racial lines. The syncretized culture of the capital, Luanda, gave birth to the MPLA (Popular Movement for the Liberation of Angola), the Marxist guerrilla force that went to war against Portuguese colonialism in 1961, took power in 1975, and, under a more opaque ideological banner, remains in power today. For most of the country's history, the MPLA has been at war with rival guerrilla factions, South Africa or Zaire. In the 1990s, when Mozambique was settling its civil war, Angola returned to the battlefield. The worst fighting in the country's history drove millions of people out of rural areas into the crowded *musseques* of zinc-roofed cinderblock houses on the outskirts of Luanda. Here African languages are in retreat; most urban young people speak only Portuguese.

Reliable figures are scarce, yet with four million inhabitants, Luanda is probably – after São Paulo, Rio de Janeiro and Belo Horizonte in Brazil – the world's fourth-largest Portuguese-speaking city.

Angola's first president, Agostinho Neto, was both a poet and a Creole married to a white woman: the father of the nation was also the father of three mixed-raced children. Today, while the MPLA has abandoned Marxism (even though the streets of downtown Luanda continue to bear the names of Marx, Engels and Lenin), the governing party's multicultural legacy lives on. Current Angolan fiction, like the revolutionary leadership in the 1970s, is monopolized by men of mixed race. The dominant writer of the 1960s and 1970s, José Luandino Vieira, a working class white man who wrote his books during a twelve-year incarceration in the colonial government's concentration camps, twisted the Portuguese language in search of an instrument to express Angolan reality. Vieira lapsed into creative silence after independence (he now lives as a recluse in Portugal), but the quest for *Angolanidade* ("Angolanness") persists.

Angola's best-known writer, Pepetela, is closely identified with this quest. "Pepetela" became the guerrilla codename, and later the pen-name, of Artur Pestana, a sixth-generation Angolan of predominantly European ancestry born in Benguela, in the country's southern coastal region, in 1941. Trained as a sociologist and MPLA operative in Algeria during the 1960s, Pepetela fought as a guerrilla for seven years, rising to the position of a regional commander during the defence of Angola against the first South African invasion in 1975. From 1976 to 1982 he was Deputy Minister of Education. Pepetela's 15 books have earned him large audiences in Portugal, Brazil and some European countries. He owes his international reputation to *Mayombe* (1980), a tightly observed novel about the ethnic and ideological splits and sexual tensions afflicting a group of MPLA guerrillas. *Mayombe* was so controversial that President Neto himself had to approve its publication in Angola.

In Pepetela's later fiction the transition from insurgency to nation-building turns *Mayombe*'s portrait of ethnic strife on its head in the search for cultural fusions capable of reconciling Angola's diversity into syncretic unity. In *Yaka* (1984) (which, like *Mayombe*, is available in English), a Bakongo statue initiates a white settler family into engagement with the Angolan nation. *Lueji, o Nascimento de um Império* (1989; Lueji, the Birth of an Empire) shuttles between a retelling of the rise of the Lunda people of northeastern Angola to imperial grandeur in the 16th century and a modern story about a mixed-race Luanda dancer, who shares the queen's name and struggles to put on a ballet celebrating the historical Lueji's accomplishments.

The MPLA's abandonment of socialism in 1990, combined with the return to war in 1992, undermined the construction of *Angolanidade. A Geração da Utopia* (1992; The Utopian Generation), Pepetela's most popular novel after *Mayombe*, follows the lives of four Angolan revolutionaries from their student days in Lisbon through the struggles of the 1970s to total disillusionment by the early 1990s. *Párabola do Cágado Velho* (1996; The Old Turtle's Parable) abandons the Creolized makers of modern Angola to tell the story of the war in the countryside from the perspective of the African poor. *A Gloriosa Família* (1997; The Glorious Family) returns to the 17th century to trace the first glimmerings of *Angolanidade*, as it emerged in opposition to the Dutch occupation of Luanda between 1641 and 1648. The Van Dum family (whose name echoes that of the Van Dúnems, the most powerful of Luanda's Creole dynasties) define the culture they defend in terms of Catholicism, the Portuguese language and their mixed racial identity. These values, which are presented as positive, are undermined by the Van Dums' brutal reliance on the slave trade. Narrated by a Van Dum slave, the novel insists on the corruption that attended the Creole class from its inception.

A Gloriosa Família marks the end of a cycle in Pepetela's work in which the Creoles serve as a model for the nation. His two recent novels about the Luanda detective Jaime Bunda ("James Bum"), an overweight descendant of the great Creole families, turn to satire. Pepetela is an ambitious writer, but he is rarely subtle. He has a compelling narrative gift and a deep emotional investment in his characters. He writes in efficient standard Portuguese, seasoned with a very mild sprinkling of African words. His weakness is narrators who spell out for the reader insights amply demonstrated by the action. The sardonic tone of the Jaime Bunda novels parlays this editorializing tendency into a conduit for acerbic commentary on contemporary corruption. The first novel, *Jaime Bunda, Agente Secreto* (2001) opens with the murder of a young girl on Angolan independence day; it ends with a criminal mastermind, who is a high government official, congratulating detectives on national television for arresting someone else for crimes he has committed.

In *Jaime Bunda e a morte do americano* (2003; Jaime Bunda and the Death of the American) Pepetela pokes fun at the Luanda-centrism of younger urban Angolans by forcing Jaime to leave the capital to solve the murder of an American engineer in Benguela. The government fears that unless the murderer is arrested, the United States will declare Angola a terrorist nation. The narrator warns that many Angolans continue to resent the U.S. for its support of apartheid-era South Africa, although few will say so, "preferindo hoje blandiciosas globalizações mais pós-modernistas" ("preferring today appeasing globalizations more in the spirit of postmodernism"). The novel itself partakes of the postmodern spirit in being modelled on the case of a Portuguese engineer who was murdered in Benguela in 1950. The imperial mantle having passed from Portugal to the United States, Washington sends an FBI agent to Benguela to shadow Jaime's investigation. Besotted with U.S. popular culture, Jaime looks forward to meeting a real FBI agent, only to have his expectations upstaged when the agent turns out to be a light-skinned African-American woman who bears a suspicious resemblance to Condoleeza Rice. Jaime's blundering attempts to seduce the agent are rebuffed as she opts for an affair with the winner of the Miss Benguela contest. Behind this comic plot, which shreds the Creole elite's last pretensions to patriarchal authority, a tragedy unfolds. Júlio Fininho, a young man demobilized from the army to face unemployment, falls in love with Maria Antónia, a mixed-race woman forced to support herself through prostitution. Trapped by the manipulations surrounding the murder investigation, they see their future – and by implication that of Angola – destroyed. The only glimmer of hope, ironically, lies in the postmodern device of multiple narrators who suggest competing solutions, the second less grim than the first, to the mystery of the American's death.

Manuel Rui, also born in 1941, has followed a trajectory similar to that of Pepetela. A native of Huambo, in Angola's cool central highlands, Rui is of mixed Portuguese and Ovimbundu parentage. He practised law in Portugal while beginning his literary career. Returning to Angola in 1974, Rui served as the MPLA's Director of Information and Propaganda, wrote the country's national anthem and composed an Angolan version of "The Internationale." A collection of short fiction from this phase of his career was published in English under the title *Yes, Comrade!*(1993), but it is Rui's later, more comic and disenchanted work that has secured his reputation. Rui is best known for a short novel, *Quem Me Dera Ser Onda* (1982; If Only I Were A Wave on the Sea). Told with rippling lightheartedness, this satire on socialist housing policies recounts the story of a man who is accused of "capitalist speculation" when he begins to raise a pig in the bathroom of his flat. In comic scenes, the man's young sons, motivated purely by the desire to save the pig's life, play havoc with the state bureaucracy.

Rui's latest short novel, *Um Anel na Areia* (2002; A Ring in the Sand), was published just as Angola's 41 years of civil war ended. Maritime imagery emphasizes the characters' rudderlessness, as, one by one, African religion, Catholicism, Marxism and consumerism are discarded as moral guides in a society where war has pulverized all systems of belief. Marina, a young secretary, receives a gold ring from her boyfriend Lau the first time they make love on the beach. Her response is to toss into the ocean, as an offering to the goddess Kianda, the inferior rings she inherited from her late mother. Marina's colloquial interior monologues dramatize her regret at having jettisoned her inheritance. In spite of her successful career – fluent in English and adept with computers, she and Lau are Angola's potential new middle class – Marina is stymied by the fear that the war may not end quickly enough to prevent Lau from being conscripted. Her paralysis is inseparable from the crisis of values that crystallizes when she loses his ring in the sand. Neither her status-conscious aunt nor her depressed best friend can offer reliable counsel as to how she should live her life. The tale ends with a rhetorical question asking who is in charge and a tentative suggestion that the family is the only institution worth saving.

José Eduardo Agualusa, also from Huambo, belongs to a different generation. Born in 1960 to a Brazilian father and a white Angolan mother, Agualusa was imprisoned by the MPLA in adolescence for his membership in a far-left splinter party. Profoundly marked by the events of 1977, when a violent internal coup attempt sparked savage repression that left thousands dead, Agualusa roamed the world for years as a kind of "loyal dissident," often speaking on Angola abroad but refusing to live in the country (he has only recently moved back to Luanda). Agualusa's pared-down fiction extols the cultural incongruities characteristic of Creolized societies; he has cited Bruce Chatwin as an influence. His first novel, *A conjura* (1989; The Conspiracy) reconstructs a 1911 uprising against Portuguese colonial policies that were designed to curb intercultural mingling; his epistolary historical novel *Nação Crioula* (1997) was translated into English as *Creole* (2003). *Estação das Chuvas* (1996; Rainy Season), his most powerful work, breaks down the emotional distance that sometimes accompanies Agualusa's stylistic elegance, by making explicit the narrator's engagement in historical events.

Agualusa's most recent novel *O Vendedor de Passados* (2004; *The Book of Chameleons*) is narrated by a gecko clinging to the wall of the home of Félix Ventura, a Luanda antiquarian book dealer. As an albino, Ventura is often mistaken for a white man. Taking advantage of his access to old books and photographs, he constructs fictionalized genealogies, complete with memorabilia, for *nouveau-riche* members of the Luanda elite, "proving" their Creole ancestry. The client known as José Buchmann poses a particular challenge because he is white. Ventura provides Buchmann with a genealogy attesting to his origins in a white settler community in southern Angola. Accustomed to indulging the snobbish fantasies of the new black business class, Ventura is alarmed when figures from Buchmann's fabricated past come to life. The gecko, meanwhile, relates his memories of a previous life in which he was a man: not just any man, but Jorge Luis Borges. The parallels between Buchmann and Borges the "book-man," fuelling Agualusa's insights into the ways in which history is created by books but cannot be contained by them, are ingenious. Told in short, ironic scenes, *O Vendedor de Passados* is consistently taut and witty. Unfortunately, the novel's violent conclusion, which re-enacts the gruesome fate of the couple who staged the 1977 coup attempt, does not emerge organically from events in Ventura's bookshop; the story's final twists feel imposed.

Both history and earlier Portuguese-language African literature influence the work of Ondjaki, the first significant writer to emerge from the generation that grew up with the revolution. Born Ndalu de Almeida in a mixed-race family in Luanda in 1977, Ondjaki is the author of nine books. Some of his early work is slight, but his autobiographical novel *Bom dia camaradas* (2001; *Good Morning Comrades*), a bittersweet memoir of the relationship between Angolan pupils of the 1980s and their Cuban schoolteachers, is honest and affecting. Ondjaki's most recent novel, *Quantas Madrugadas Tem a Noite* (2004; How Many Dawns Has the Night), marks a large step forward. Narrated in a rough-edged Luanda slang twisted with knotty wordplay and many literary allusions, the novel recounts the attempts to bury the deceased Adolfo Dido (the name is an obscene pun) in the face of obstacles posed by bureaucratic obtuseness and a tropical downpour. Adolfo claimed to have fought in the civil war (in a province bypassed by the war); two women, each maintaining that she is his spouse, aspire to the pension due to his "state widow." Yet, as one character remarks, in order to have widows, the state must be dead. Denied a decent burial, Adolfo has no choice but to come back to life and reveal himself as the tale's narrator. At one level, this novel is about Angola's inability to bury the corpse of the Marxist state. But it is also a celebration of the Portuguese language in Africa; the Lisbon edition contains a glossary of three closely printed pages. Ondjaki's voice recalls the stories of Luandino Vieira; there are allusions to the Mozambican writer Mia Couto, to Pepetela, to Brazilian novels. In its boundless energy, *Quantas Madrugadas Tem a Noite* illustrates that contemporary Angolan fiction is responding not only to history, but to an evolving literary tradition.

"The Angolan Novel" was published as "The Quest for *Angolanidade*," *Times Literary Supplement*, 23 September 2005. I was hoping that this article would contribute to stimulating interest in Angolan fiction among readers of English. Within two years, three of the novels discussed here – Pepetela's *Jaime Bunda, Secret Agent*, Ondjaki's *Good Morning Comrades* and Agualusa's *The Book of Chameleons* – had been translated into English in Great Britain or Canada. Agualusa's novel won the 2007 Independent Foreign Fiction Prize, the award which introduced José Saramago to readers of English. There is now some hope, at least, that more translations of Portuguese African literature may follow.

IV:

WORDS FOR OUR WORLD

1. YES, TORONTO, I DO OWN
A BLACK TURTLENECK

In his *Globe and Mail* column of March 16, 2002, the journalist and writer Russell Smith attacked a pre-publication excerpt from my book *When Words Deny the World*, which was due to appear the next month. Though I had been expecting disagreement with my ideas, I was surprised by the emotional tone of Smith's response. It's not every day that one is called a "smarmy prig" in *The Globe and Mail*.

Smith's anger suggested that I had struck a raw nerve. In my book, I argue that the increasing centralization of the media in Toronto has coincided with Toronto's integration into the global book market. A Toronto media culture of personality and image holds sway over literary Canada. This has instilled a parochialism in Toronto writers, who acknowledge as writers people whom they know, or whose photographs they recognize. Finding out about other writers by reading, I mischieviously insinuated, was un-Torontonian.

The interpretation of my argument presented in *The Globe* was probably best summed up by the column's headline, "The myth of the black turtleneck conspiracy." In fact, I was deriding neither black turtlenecks (I own one myself) nor conspirators. I was trying to describe some of the ways in which, in my view, globalization has fragmented the idea of a national Canadian culture. I was pointing out evidence of the widening cultural and financial chasm between writers who live in Toronto and those who live elsewhere in the country, particularly as reflected in the increasing disparity between the amounts of media coverage received by these groups.

The mere fact of my article's having provoked a strong response seemed to confirm this geographical bias. Excerpts from my book have been published in the past. But when I published them as a resident of Montreal, the Ottawa Valley or London, England, no one in Toronto considered me worth refuting. By virtue of having moved to southern Ontario, I have become significant enough to be condemned.

Smith's column reaffirmed this hierarchy through its non-mention of another writer. Smith mentions "a furious Newfoundland writer" who published an article criticizing Toronto. The writer (who is Kenneth J. Harvey) is not identified. He is simply an outraged Newfie – a familiar Toronto stereotype. Not living in southern Ontario, he is not worth rebutting by name.

While suppressing the "regional" writer's identity, the column excoriates Harvey for attacking three Toronto writers "never having met or read any of them." Notice the order of the verbs: met comes before read. The Torontonian emphasis on image gives priority to personal contact; for Smith, reading a writer's work is of secondary importance.

This order of priorities returns when Smith describes me as being "very angry that no one's ever heard of him and [he] blames it all on Toronto." In fact, I wrote that I was known as a writer elsewhere in Canada but not in Toronto. This is not the only place where my points are misrepresented. Smith also writes: "Henighan . . . scorns me . . . for not being well-known outside Toronto." This is incorrect. In fact, I wrote that due to his access to the Toronto media, Smith's fiction was better known nationally than that of a similar writer would be if that writer lived in Winnipeg.

Smith parlays this confusion into a "contradiction" in my argument. He claims that I, not he, am in the privileged position. This leads to the assertion that "media culture" is impotent; misguided provincials may confer a "mythical power" on the media, but in fact, the column argues, media attention does not boost writers' careers.

This kind of backflip logic, where powerful institutions are portrayed as beleaguered, betrays the Toronto writer's ambivalence about his own position.

I do not know of any writer or publisher who regards media attention as irrelevant. Yet Smith tries to persuade us that none of this matters. Perhaps it is not surprising that the column concludes with two short paragraphs that contradict each other.

Smith first announces that I am "the establishment." Then my views are dismissed as "sour grapes." The two conclusions are incompatible: someone whose views are "sour grapes" is, by definition, excluded from the establishment.

As always in the culture of personality, the contradiction belongs to the author. When it comes to the Toronto media's myopic vision of Canadian literature, Smith, who can see that the emperor has no clothes, wants to keep wearing his black turtleneck.

"Yes, Toronto, I do own a black turtleneck," was published in slightly different form in *The Globe and Mail*, 6 April 2002.

2. COURT JESTER

One of the indispensable figures of contemporary journalism is the cutting-edge cultural commentator. The columnist who offers sardonic insights into trends, fashions, television shows and publishing personalities has become an institution. Like most readers, I have scanned the irony-drenched ruminations of these pundits in newspapers and magazines, but until recently, I gave little thought to the contradictions inherent in their position. This changed when the publication of *When Words Deny the World* landed me on panels with outspoken cultural observers.

Accustomed to book promotion as an exercise in slipping into university radio studios to attempt the impossible by talking about short stories or a novel in a way that might persuade a listener to hunt down a small press book and buy it, I discovered that the pleasure of promoting a non-fiction book was the directness with which one could speak to an audience about the book's subject matter. The pain, though it was enlightening pain, came from the fact that participating in the discussion were anointed cultural critics.

On a Toronto television show I faced Hal – not the robot (though the analogy is not entirely misplaced), but a commentator of particularly rampant contradictions. Hal had been described to me as a "scenester," a figure who brought a whiff of the underground to mainstream broadcasts and publications. He wrote for a magazine that had once been a bastion of the political left; he and I shared the distinction of having attacked the Giller Prize. Yet contrary to what you might expect from a critic with these credentials, Hal was no anti-globalization campaigner. When issues of corporate control came up, he leapt into line with the CEOs. Unnerved by this contradiction, I began to wonder whose side the pop culture commentator is on.

At the host's prodding, the conversation had turned to the disappearance of place from the Canadian novel: the outpouring of
novels set in undefined locales, the peculiar state of Canadian
commercial publishing, which allows explicitly Canadian cities
and details to grace our historical novels but rarely those set in the
present. We turned a jaundiced eye on Michael Ondaatje's *Anil's
Ghost*, Anne Michaels's *Fugitive Pieces*, Barbara Gowdy's *The White
Bone*, Rohinton Mistry's *A Fine Balance*, Margaret Atwood's *Alias
Grace*. We underlined the paradox that in spite of being one of the
world's most urbanized countries (more than 80 percent of our
population lives in cities), Canada produces few urban novels. Hal
made no objection to this point; indeed, he claimed to have pio-
neered it himself. But when I invoked the homogenizing forces of
globalization and commercialization as being at the root of the
problem, I made a surprising discovery: Hal loved homogenization. "Place is irrelevant to a novel. A few years from now you'll go
to Sri Lanka and say, 'I drank coffee at the Sri Lanka Starbucks, I ate
at the Sri Lanka McDonald's.' It won't matter where you are
because everywhere will be the same."

As the gods of editing were merciful to Hal, consigning this
section of the show to the cutting-room floor, I can't verify that
these were his precise words. But the thrust of the diatribe was
unmistakable. Like the transnational marketing executive flattening regional cultures in order to sell the same burger to everyone,
Hal had fixed his sights on diversity as the enemy. In a fever, he
began to speak of his upbringing in a faceless U.S. suburb: "There's
nothing there – nothing!" Today U.S. and Canadian shopping
malls were indistinguishable. Soon, he said with breathless antici-
pation, everywhere would be the same!

Was this an example of fashionable irony? Was Hal kidding
us? Alas, he was not.

A friend who plays tennis informs me that the sporting goods
chains in U.S. and Canadian shopping malls offer surprisingly different mixes of equipment for sale. One peculiarity of globalization
is that all societies are inundated with similar products but not all

products get equally good receptions everywhere. Even within the ersatz world of transnational consumerism, differing product mixes offer a stubborn, if diminished, index of local specificity. Recent Canadian novels, for all their no-name pandering to the international market, retain their dominance in Canadian book-stores because Canadian readers accept them as products of a particular local literary environment. But what struck me most forcefully was not the inaccuracy of some of Hal's claims. It was his eagerness, when challenged by a call for diversity, attention to history, a sense of place, to enlist in the corporate campaign to enforce sameness in order to feed interchangeable products to identical imaginations everywhere; his insistence that art would be better once cultural difference had been erased.

The pop culture commentator is the court jester of the corporate fiefdom. His job is to use irony to keep consumers talking about a dumbed-down, commercialized simulacrum of cultural engagement. But, as I learned from Hal, the whisper of an alternative vision causes him to leap to the king's defence. As with court jesters everywhere, his humour stops short at the point where it questions the sovereign's right to rule.

"Court Jester" was published in slightly different form in *Geist* No. 48 (Spring 2003).

3. TOTALITARIAN DEMOCRACY

In 1982 I had my first argument with an American about Saddam Hussein. As an undergraduate at a liberal arts college in the United States where everyone read *The New York Times*, I supplemented my reading by browsing the British papers. In one of them I discovered an exposé on Iraq. According to the article, Hussein's regime was "more repressive than that of East Germany."

Armed with this information, I waded into the suppertime discussion of Middle East politics. The demonization of Iran was in full flow when I sat down in the dining hall. "Iraq's no better," I said. "Hussein's regime is more repressive than East Germany."

My classmates were outraged. "Saddam Hussein is a loyal American ally," Peter, from Pennsylvania, said. "He's a bulwark against Iran!"

"He's a dictator!"

"You're a communist!"

In recent weeks I have wondered whether Peter remembers calling me a communist for criticizing Saddam Hussein. While our exchange hardly represents the summit of refined political debate, it does highlight the historical amnesia that is a defining characteristic of the United States. In his pilgrimage from loyal ally (remember which country rewarded Hussein for his use of chemical weapons on Kurdish peasants by issuing him new agricultural credits and vetoing a U.N. Security Council resolution that would have condemned his acts?) to invasion target, Hussein has trodden the path of Manuel Noriega of Panama, the mujahadeen of Afghanistan, and Jonas Savimbi of Angola (whom the U.S. helped to assassinate in 2002, after having funded him for many years). Once CNN drenches these figures in its Manichean imagery, the history of how they acquired their power evaporates. The panic of the present annihilates memory.

In George Orwell's *1984*, Winston Smith's society exists in a state of perpetual war. Sometimes the war is against Eurasia, with Eastasia as an ally, and sometimes the pattern is reversed. The population believes that the enemy of the moment has always been the enemy. For Orwell, this historical amnesia is a defining trait of totalitarianism. Pope John Paul II has called the United States an "imperial democracy." Its enforcement of historical amnesia makes the oxymoronic "totalitarian democracy" more accurate. In a totalitarian democracy 200,000 New Yorkers can march against war without making a political impact because U.S. networks will not report the event; while the past is obliterated, the present is brutally censored.

I am writing this in Guatemala, where newspapers now punningly refer to the United States ("Estados Unidos," in Spanish) as "Estamos Hundidos," a double-edged phrase that means both "We're bogged down," and "We've collapsed." Here, surrounded by eighteen centuries of visible history, including the ruins of both the greatest civilization of pre-Columbian America, that of the Classic Maya, and the greatest empire of early Renaissance Europe, that of Spain, it is impossible not to ponder imperial decay. As a Canadian, one has to think about how we plan to survive next to a belligerent empire whose decadence has reached the stage of "totalitarian democracy."

Our prognosis is not good. Few small countries bordering empires have outlasted those empires' death throes. Prime Minister Chrétien's policy of not sending the Canadian Armed Forces to Iraq was initially popular, but as CNN intensified its propaganda assault, many Canadians changed their minds. Did we lose our nerve, lose touch with our history of participation in multilateral institutions, lose our grip on global public opinion, or lose our ability to think? We need to think with minds attuned to a wider range of experience than watching CNN. We will not survive alongside a totalitarian democracy by shackling our brains to the sinking galleon. Relying on the U.S. for 86 percent of our export markets replicates the single-crop penury of many Third World countries; it encourages a mental dependence that robs us not only of our particular Canadian history but of access to any historical perspective on the present.

We must diversify or die. The most positive moment of the Iraq crisis was the conference in Mexico City among the Prime Minister of Canada and the Presidents of Mexico and (by telephone) Chile on how to confront the hemisphere's wayward juggernaut. The sloganeers who dominate the opinion columns of our two anti-national newspapers proclaim "integration" with the U.S. as "natural." Yet nothing could be more unnatural than the notion that the outcome of globalization is not to join the world, but to join the neighbours. Thinking diachronically rather than spatially, it is far more "natural" for us to strengthen our links with our near-neighbours in Latin America, who share our historical experience of contending with the elephant in the backyard. By the same logic, Western Canada has natural ties to Asia, while Atlantic Canada, Quebec, and parts of Ontario, have natural ties to Europe (though not exclusively to these places). Forging counterweights to the U.S. would make us not only more economically resilient, but less susceptible to the historical amnesia that turns democracy into an oxymoron.

"Totalitarian Democracy" was published in slightly different form in *Geist* No. 49 (Summer 2003).

4. BAD SPELLERS

Mordecai Richler, in a withering put-down, once dismissed the novelist Frederick Philip Grove as "a good speller." In the summer of 2003, grinding through 160 Canadian books as a jury member for the Governor General's Literary Award for Fiction in English, I learned that for many contemporary Canadian writers Grove's level of dubious distinction remains out of reach.

It may sound perverse to become fixated on spelling while reading for a literary prize. But serving as a juror for the Governor General's Awards is like a gruelling road trip. You try to read a book every day and usually fail. When you succeed, while each town does not look identical, there are, in most cases, distinct similarities: coming-of-age rites, failing relationships, cultural alienation. Like a child in the back seat longing to ask, "Are we there yet? Can I go back to reading for fun?", you count the passing fenceposts and giggle at the funny names on the mailboxes.

Standard Canadian spelling follows British spelling in many, though not all, cases. (The British drive on "tyres," use "aluminium" siding and "realise" that they can be sent to "gaol.") Like other aspects of Canadian culture, our spelling, in spite of its second-hand appearance, is unique. Part of our inheritance is a system for distinguishing between related nouns and verbs. The laminated card that authorizes you to get behind the wheel of a car is a "licence," but the bar from which you take a cab home is "licensed." Your son "practises" a sport, but you drive him to "practice."

My students at the University of Guelph – not to mention the vast majority of my colleagues – are unable to master this system. Many of them write "colour" and "favour" and sometimes "centre," as a basic declaration of identity, but after that they throw up their hands. Their confusions mirror the inconsistencies of the signs we see around us, where dissonant spellings mingle. Our newspapers offer little guidance. For years Canadian newspapers used U.S. spelling. In the early 1990s *The Globe and Mail*, in theory, changed to Canadian spelling. Major Southam papers, such as the Montreal *Gazette*, switched to an impoverished version of Canadian spelling, adopting "centre" but not "colour"; under Conrad Black's ownership of the former Southam newspapers, the "-our" forms came into use, though some American spellings ("traveler," "two-story house") were retained. *Quill & Quire*, another editing anomaly, brandishes a house style that juxtaposes the Canadian "offence" with the U.S. "defense."

On the basis of my Governor General's reading I concluded that this half-eroded Canadian spelling is becoming the new norm. Older writers, whichever usage they preferred, were consistent. Margaret Atwood and Robertson Davies, edited in Toronto, used Canadian spelling. Mavis Gallant and Alice Munro, their stories edited at *The New Yorker*, conformed to U.S. usage. Some younger Canadian writers with large U.S. audiences, such as Douglas Coupland and Naomi Klein, also employ straight U.S. spelling. Coupland's choice of spelling matches his obsession with U.S. popular culture; with Klein, whose work defends local cultures, the spelling feels like a contradiction.

Most younger Canadian writers, even the best ones, spell inconsistently. Michael Redhill, in *Fidelity*, shuffles between "moulded" and "molded"; Ann-Marie MacDonald, in *The Way the Crow Flies*, alternates the U.S. "crenelated" with the Canadian "panelled." While these writers' lapses are rare, in many who are less accomplished the inconsistencies run rampant. Almost no Canadian writer, not even Leo McKay, Jr., who is a high school teacher in Truro, Nova Scotia and one of the few Canadian authors who continues to write "snowplough" rather than "snowplow," can resist the insidious spread of "license" as a noun. Any spelling adopted by high school teachers in Truro, Nova Scotia has become the Canadian standard.

The case of "licence/license" and "practice/practise" shows how inconsistency (also exemplified by hyper-corrections such as a "licenced" bar or an "honourary" consul) is the hallmark of cultural erosion. In the Ottawa Valley village where I grew up grade four girls from families with modest formal schooling would chant, "'Ice' is a noun so when 'practice' is a noun you write it with 'ice.'" This dictum enabled them to disentangle "licence" from "license" and spell "defence" correctly. Such seemingly trivial ditties are the bricks and mortar of a culture.

It is tempting to shrug off the scattershot spelling of current authors, attributing it to an uphill struggle against U.S. spellchecks (although most computer programs now offer a Canadian spell-check option), or seeing in the inconsistencies a typical Canadian compromise between American and British customs. But this won't wash because current spelling is too irregular to fit neat definitions. A conscious move away from British spelling towards American forms might be interpreted as an ideological statement in favour of integration into U.S. culture – and to some extent the promotion of U.S. spelling in Alberta and British Columbia may be seen this way. (Hence the unusual spelling career of B.C./Alberta novelist Gail Anderson-Dargatz. Her first novel used U.S. spelling; after acquiring a national audience she switched to Canadian spelling.)

To state the spelling question in terms of British versus American is to misunderstand it. Canadian writers long ago forged distinctive spelling conventions. The question is why – without any of the passion that swirls around spelling wars in countries like Germany, Portugal or Romania – these conventions are fraying even as they have been consolidated by the publication of volumes such as the *Oxford Canadian Dictionary* (1998). My summer reading turned up a "theatre" here, an "odour" there, with other spellings intermittently Americanized; where the authors stumbled, the editors failed to pick up the slack. This is not a conscious decision, nor is it trivial: it is evidence in microcosm of a culture that is being forgotten.

"Bad Spellers," was published in *Geist* No. 51 (Winter 2003).

5. IN PRAISE OF BORDERS

The train crossed the border while I slept. I woke in another country. This time there was no midnight inspection, no bullying border guard. I remembered past ordeals: the official in Vermont who squeezed out my toothpaste tube on the train from Montreal to Philadelphia, another who hauled me off a bus for a forty-five-minute interrogation that culminated in his shouting that the friend I was visiting in Boston could not be American if she had a Hispanic name.

A French border guard in the Pyrenees had stuffed a sniffer-dog's snout into my backpack so hard that the creature whimpered, and a Czech official, eager to record the Czech names in my address book, had pulled me back after I had crossed into Poland. Moldovan guards removed most of my clothes searching for dollars; a Peruvian soldier stranded me for hours on a strip of hot sand by refusing to stamp me into Peru after I had been stamped out of Ecuador.

These experiences evaporated into the morning light as the train rolled into the capital. The southernmost region of the country where I got off the train was called "the Borders." Daily parlance insisted on the boundary's significance. Scotland had defied nearly three centuries of political union by retaining a different legal system than England, different religious traditions, a different school and university curriculum, different banknotes, different names and accents.

Most intangibly and tellingly, Scotland felt different. I remembered how, in my teens, when I briefly attended a Scottish school, the sense of entering an unfamiliar atmosphere enveloped me the moment I stepped out of Waverley Station to the sight of the bulging cliffs falling away below the sheer stone ramparts of

Edinburgh Castle. The feeling returned on the morning of my arrival from London in December 2003. Postmodern stylization had made the restaurant food more palatable and given the tourist attractions a slick veneer. Scots had embraced the new era as an opportunity to consolidate their borders. Cranes and scaffolding were visible everywhere as the Scottish Parliament and its attendant institutions took shape. Eons from Braveheart, Rob Roy or Bonnie Prince Charlie, today's Scots have modelled themselves less on warrior chieftains than on the self-assured distinctness of small, efficient European welfare states.

We do not need tyrannical or racist border guards, but we do need borders. The current cant about "the borderless world" overlooks the obvious: there can be no internationalism without nationalism, no interdependence without independence. As Mark Abley wrote in his recent book *Spoken Here*: "No one has yet figured out how to be a citizen of the world and only the world." International experience – all experience, in fact – rings hollow if the planet is undifferentiated and no exertion, adaption or personal growth is required to stretch oneself between cultures. Besides, the differences that borders foster can be delicious.

In August 2001 I used the last day of my Eurail Pass to board a train that crossed "borderless" Western Europe from Amsterdam to central Switzerland. South of Frankfurt, the castles of the Rhine paraded past. At the Swiss border the train left the European Union without an immigration inspection. We passed through Basel and Zurich and rode along the edge of the Zürichsee, where swimmers frolicked in the water at fenced-in resorts. The mountains seemed to bleed greenness until, at the end of the lake, they grew taller, stretching into huge, fractured-looking boulders. At seven o'clock in the evening the train reached the end of the line at Chur, in international jet-set country. Local trains departed for expensive resorts like Davos and St. Moritz.

I had stepped out of my price bracket. Hotel rooms in Chur started at around $250 a night; I could find no pensions or bed-and-breakfasts. In search of a place to sleep, I returned to the station and hopped the next train back to Zurich and Basel. Night was falling. The waters of the lake, now emptying of swimmers, had absorbed the greenness of the mountains. The train emptied in Basel at ten o'clock at night. Basel's hotels, too, proved to be beyond my battered budget. Even the sleazy place over the strip joint cost $150 a night. I returned to the train station, approached three young backpackers and asked them how they could afford to stay in this expensive city.

"You have to cross the border," they said.

Basel (Bâle, in French) lay at the junction of Switzerland, France and Germany. The train station was divided between Switzerland and France. By moving to the French end of the station, travellers left regimented Switzerland for a more expressive culture that accepted sleeping in train stations. I watched as American and Asian backpackers showered in immaculate Swiss bathrooms, locked their packs in vault-like Swiss lockers, then walked to the end of the platform, showed their passports to the official seated beneath the blue sign that said "France," and disappeared through the double doors of the border to bed down on the tables and benches of the French end of the station.

I was so charmed by this solution that I nearly adopted it myself. In the end I chose a third option, boarding the last train of the night to Freiburg, Germany, where I found a pleasant, affordable pension. As I fell asleep, I murmured praises to cultural multiplicity and the borders that enabled it to flourish.

"In Praise of Borders" was published in *Geist* No. 52 (Spring 2004).

6. WRITING THE CITY

As Canada is one of the world's most urbanized countries, a reader knowing nothing of contemporary Canadian writing might expect to find a surfeit of urban novels in our bookstores. Yet novels explicitly set in Canadian cities form a mere sliver of our novelistic production. Literary dynamics are always evolving, but there is little denying that among the Canadian novels that have received the most critical and commercial attention during the last fifteen years, most are set in other countries, in the Canadian past, or in parts of Atlantic Canada where the present can be made to feel like the past. *A Fine Balance*, *The English Patient*, *Fugitive Pieces*, *The White Bone*, *Fall on Your Knees*, *Away*, *Alias Grace*, *The Colony of Unrequited Dreams*, *No Great Mischief*, *The Englishman's Boy*, *Anil's Ghost*, *The Stone Carvers*, *Testament*, *Crow Lake*, *The Last Crossing*, *The Polished Hoe*, *Mercy Among the Children*: this roll-call bypasses engagement with the cities where we live.

Not long ago, a young Toronto journalist interviewed me about my novel *The Streets of Winter*, which is set in Montreal. As our conversation proceeded, I detected a certain reductive dualism in his way of framing his questions. For this interviewer everything urban was good and everything rural was bad. This, I suggested to him, was the wrong reason to promote urban novels. We are only occasionally interested in urban fiction for its urbanity, let alone as a way of snubbing rural communities or asserting that our cities finally have become "world-class." We read the urban novel because urban life is the dominant dimension of our present. The neglect of urban novels is part of the broader disparagement of the Canadian present.

During the 1990s and arguably until Jean Chrétien made us feel good about ourselves again by remaining aloof from George W. Bush's sordid colonization of Iraq, Canadian self-deprecation plunged to a deep nadir. Bludgeoned into sacrificing our public culture to the malevolent deity of competitiveness, many Canadians retreated into local, ethnic or commercialized cultures, sparking a rise in regionalism, identity politics and bland no-name art. This mood combined with structural changes in the publishing industry to promote the historical romance as the novelistic form best adapted to the international market. When large publishers ceased to maintain slush piles, relying instead on literary agents to pre-select the raw material for their lists, the urban novel was sidelined.

I observed this tendency first-hand when I sent the manuscript of *The Streets of Winter* to an agent.

"All the scenes in this novel," the agent said, "are about people talking to people! I want scenes that are big – big in every way . . . !" The message was clear: think film rights. A writer friend told me that after he submitted a section of his new novel to his agent, the first question was: "Who do you see playing the lead?" Jane Austen wouldn't have stood a chance under this interdiction against scenes blemished by "people talking to people" (even though, as period characters, Austen's clever conversationalists have morphed into pleasing screen presences); the aesthetic of the "big scene" would rule out of order the great urban novels of Charles Dickens, Honoré de Balzac, Henry James, James Joyce, Robert Musil. Would Mordecai Richler find a major publisher if he were starting to write about St. Urbain Street today? It is telling that some significant Canadian writers who used to practise the urban novel, such as Margaret Atwood and M.G. Vassanji, no longer do so. In the race to capture the attention of an increasingly visual world, the urban novel is at a disadvantage because, unlike the historical romance, it does not feature the epic battles, gory massacres, blizzards or ships trapped in ice that whet the appetites of film producers.

This bias is compounded by a fear that detailed references to the Canadian present will not travel. Zadie Smith, Monica Ali and Andrea Levy may write about multicultural neighbourhoods in London, but, we are told, if you try to do the same with Toronto, Montreal, Vancouver or, God forbid, Edmonton or Ottawa, no agent will take you on because you'll never sell foreign rights. I don't think this is necessarily true; but the belief that it is so, among agents and publishers, contributes to making the Canadian urban novel predominantly a small-press form. In the spring 2004 publishing season, unusually, a handful of urban novels did appear; since none of them became bestsellers, the current dynamics are unlikely to change.

Our novels' focus on foreign locations and the 19th century means that the denizens of the modern city get short shrift in our fiction: immigrants, people of colour, gay men and lesbians, service employees, single adults, the homeless. By eliding the importance of city life, the novels promoted by our larger publishers propagate a Canada that is white, straight, settled and a few generations behind the Canada most of us live in. In every country the largest cities are attended by myths, many of them elaborated by literature. The feebleness of the Canadian urban novel means that we rarely mythologize our cities as, for example, Dickens mythologized London. Thanks to the description of, "Fog up the river . . . . Fog down the river," that opens *Bleak House*, reinforced by Conan Doyle's Sherlock Holmes stories, fog became an enduring element of London mythology (even though it is no longer a salient feature of London's weather). For those who tire of quaint Victorian images, a mythology of multicultural London is taking shape in the fiction of Smith, Ali, Levy, Hanif Kureishi, Hari Kunzru and others.

In Canada the mythologization of the multicultural experience is left to the media. This is not healthy. No Canadian city, with the difficult exception of Montreal, where the myths are disjointed by their expression in two linguistic traditions that pay scant attention to each other's literatures, has been imagined deeply enough to radiate a convincing literary mythologization. By turning their backs on our cities, our best-known novelists have failed to offer us myths by which to reimagine ourselves.

"Writing the City" was published in *Geist* No. 54 (Fall 2004).

7. WHITE CURTAINS

During the power cut that paralysed southern and eastern Ontario in August 2003, the residents of my townhouse condominium complex began talking to each other. It was an event that took me by surprise. Under normal circumstances human interaction in our development means someone reporting a neighbour to the condominium authorities for putting up curtains of a colour not permitted by regulations. (This means any colour other than white.) But, facing darkened apartments, darkened television screens, darkened stoves – a darkness that even pristine white curtains could not repel – we wandered out to sit on the hard cinderblock steps overlooking the parking lot. In the fading light we traded wild-eyed rumours about the power outage. People who had passed each other on the way to the mailbox on innumerable occasions without ever stopping to speak progressed from discussing the power cut to recounting stories of childhoods spent in countries where electrical power had been a luxury. I was on the point of succumbing to the illusion that the mood of communal bonding might outlast the return of our electricity when, all at once, conversation stopped.

My neighbour Dragoslav walked out to the patch of grass next to his parking spot carrying a small kerosene stove, a frying pan, some cooking implements and a steak. He sat down in the grass and coaxed a muted roaring from his stove. Crouched in the shadow of his high-fendered 1970s sedan, he began to fry the steak. The gush of kerosene and the sizzle of tenderloin carried across the parking lot. No one spoke. We did not look in Dragoslav's direction and we did not comment on what he was doing. The Dragoslav we knew was a man who drove a second-hand car, lived with a woman who spoke English less well than he did

247

and walked his dog when he came home from work. The Dragoslav who was cooking in the grass next to the parking lot was a foreigner: a Yugoslav who had learned survival skills in a grisly war.

Contrary to custom, no one reported Dragoslav to the condominium authorities. We sat on the steps in the dusk, mute and embarrassed. All of us had arrived in Canada as immigrants (even though some, such as I, had been here since childhood). We were happy to talk about the countries in our pasts, but we were mortified to see one of our neighbours acting as though he were living in the past. It was normal to be an immigrant; it was unacceptable to act like one. As proven members of southern Ontario multicultural society, we knew how to respond to Dragoslav's lurch into antediluvian behaviour: we tolerated him. We neither reproached Dragoslav nor approached him. We kept our distance and turned conversation to other subjects. When darkness fell, we all went back inside to sleep behind our white curtains. Two days later, when our television screens lighted up again, we stopped talking to each other.

In 1994 Neil Bissoondath published *Selling Illusions: The Cult of Multiculturalism in Canada*. At the time I joined the chorus denouncing Bissoondath's book as a silly right-wing tract. Since moving to southern Ontario, where the idea of multiculturalism is more dominant than in eastern Ontario or Quebec (my earlier Canadian residences), I have modified my view. There is silliness in Bissoondath's book, but there is also wisdom. Bissoondath's analysis of "tolerance," the central tenet of Canadian multiculturalism, is particularly trenchant. Tolerance, Bissoondath writes, "requires not knowledge but wilful ignorance, a purposeful turning away from the accent, the skin colour, the crossed eyes, the large nose . . . . Understanding, in contrast, requires effort, a far more difficult proposition, but may lead to acceptance . . . ." To tolerate people is to fail to engage with who they are and how they differ from you. The fact that we define our multiculturalism in terms of tolerance may help to explain why it is so rare for

Canadians who live in multicultural neighbourhoods to write multicultural novels.

According to an overprivileged globetrotter named Pico Iyer, Toronto is the global capital of cost-free multiculturalism. (Iyer bestows an honourable mention on Vancouver; he ignores Montreal.) Last winter, when I was invited to teach a "Topics in Canadian Literature" course for M.A. students, I assigned an article by Iyer in which he claims to find a laudatory shedding of cultural baggage in Canadian novels that disdain Canadian material. I was surprised (though, I'll admit, not disappointed) that my students, whom I had expected to embrace this hymn of praise to the city where most of them had grown up, disliked Iyer's vision of Toronto. They saw Iyer's omission of the ethnic retaining walls that channel daily interaction in urban Canada as superficial or naive. Iyer's article sparked a discussion of the students' experience of cultural barriers: of how little they knew their neighbours; of the scant communication among the various cultural cliques present in student life; of all that Iyer overlooked; of the doctrine of tolerance that makes us turn away from the accent, the skin colour, the man who cooks in the parking lot.

The writer, of course, faces the risk that dramatizing cultural differences may descend into stereotyping. But the literary writer must take risks: must challenge and extend popular understanding, not just mimic the status quo. By averting their creative gaze from the cultural dissonance that clatters around us in the shopping malls of Mississauga, the *ruelles* of Montréal-Nord, the street corners of Winnipeg, the leaky condos of New Westminster, writers actually may contribute to prolonging a polite, latent racism. You do not overcome racism by avoiding the issue and changing the subject. Racism dissolves only when you ask the awkward, embarrassing question: do all Chinese women behave that way, do all Yugoslav men cook in parking lots? Until you voice this gut reaction, or, better yet, dramatize it in a scene, you cannot begin to question your own chauvinism. Such uncomfortable yet revealing moments abound in our daily lives. Our fiction could be feasting on them if fewer of our writers chose to sleep behind white curtains.

"White Curtains" was published in *Geist* No. 55 (Winter 2004) and reprinted in *The Active Reader: Strategies for Academic Reading and Writing* (Oxford University Press, 2007), edited by Eric Henderson.

8.   BECOMING FRENCH

For an English-speaking Canadian who has been exposed to French from an early age, Paris is the most disorienting city in Europe. It is grandiose, but it is mundane. Arriving at the Gare du Nord, the Canadian visitor, particularly the visitor raised in Quebec, Ottawa or northern Ontario, recognizes signs familiar from home: *Sortie, Défense de fumer.* Public address system announcements recite phrases that echo in the consciousness of anyone who has boarded an Air Canada plane. My first reaction, on a recent visit to Paris, was: "Oh, this is easy, they speak a Canadian language."

Of course I couldn't have been more wrong. They didn't speak my language: I spoke theirs. My error throws into relief the unparalleled oddity of the position of the bilingual English-speaking Canadian in France: you understand the words without experiencing an emotional tie to the culture; you speak the language because France once colonized part of your country, yet, unlike the Québécois, Acadien or Franco-Ontarien, you do not arrive bristling with colonial complexes. (You can save those for your visits to London – or Washington, D.C.)

Statistics Canada suggests that about two million English-speaking Canadians are bilingual in French. This figure is pathetically small: on average, a non-Hispanic American is more likely to speak Spanish than a non-Francophone Canadian is to speak French. Still, it is safe to say that many of us experience this accessible-yet-not-ours feeling in France. Even French-speaking Canadians encounter France at an emotional remove. Unlike Algeria or Haiti, New France did not fight a war to free itself from Paris's tutelage, but was lost in a global conflict then disdained by French treaty negotiators. Even more crucially, New France was severed from Old France prior to the French Revolution, which, as you soon grasp reading Parisian place-names, is the event that defines France's national identity. It can be difficult to appreciate the immense cultural gap created by this history; it is as if English-speaking Canada had been separated from Great Britain prior to the signing of Magna Carta and sequestered on a continent where no one else spoke English. This is probably why, when the Québécois do get hot under the collar about the French, they do not invoke the injustices of the seigneurial system, but prefer to complain about the Parisian waiter who made fun of their accent.

The bilingual English-speaking Canadian may also be tripped up by his use of French-Canadian expressions. But, possessing French as an acquired, rather than a maternal language, he will winnow them out of his speech after a few days. By the end of your first week in France you become an irritating mystery to your French interlocutors, your grammar too natural to be that of a learner, your accent falling into none of the received categories for foreign accents. The most casual acquaintances will growl, "You're not Swiss, are you?"

I didn't get to that point on my most recent trip. I was still sabotaging myself with French-Canadian expressions when I left – that, and marvelling at how French culture really is different. Woody Allen remains a star in France, lauded everywhere for films that were barely released in North America. The biggest surprise was the resurrection of another film, *Monsieur Ibrahim et les fleurs du Coran*. This third-rate French tearjerker enjoyed the most fleeting of runs on the Canadian repertory circuit last year. The film's plot – a Jewish boy from a psychologically damaged family finds happiness when a kindly Turkish shopkeeper converts him to Islam – does not exactly pander to current mainstream biases on our side of the Atlantic. Yet in France *Monsieur Ibrahim* enjoyed box-office success and has spawned a popular stage adaption.

The *Monsieur Ibrahim* phenomenon offers a glimpse into how multiculturalism works in a radically secular, centralized and integrationist society. "You can't be an immigrant here," an

American friend, who moved to Paris twenty years ago, told me. "You have to become French." Frenchness is not the easiest of qualites to acquire. But if you make progress, the French will at least applaud films that are complimentary about your religion. Walk around the vast pedestrian area of Les Halles, where Paris's young people meet, and you find that many of the couples are interracial. Yet casual racist comments abound and millions of French voters support the anti-immigrant National Front. Last year's law banning religious apparel in school elicited protests, but when a group of Iraqi kidnappers included the repeal of the "headscarf law" as a condition for releasing hostages, it was French Muslim groups who told the kidnappers this internal French dispute was none of their business.

The uneven results of France's efforts to press newcomers into the national mould strike the visitor as more conflicted than the easygoing ways of nearby Holland, where integrationist demands are minimal. Yet since the murder of the Dutch filmmaker Theo van Gogh in 2004 in retaliation for his film about abusive Muslim marriages, it is Holland, not France, whose cities are torn by racial upheaval. Holland's do-your-own-thing liberalism means that nowhere are Dutch audiences applauding a play such as *Monsieur Ibrahim*; immigrants and old-stock Dutch lack a shared vocabulary.

The Dutch experience renders ominous the common complaint that in Canada it is difficult for immigrants to know what they are assimilating into. The Canadian multicultural model, like that of Holland, is laissez-faire and non-coercive; and, as in Holland, it may not give us enough in common to pull together in a crisis. One interpretation of the evidence from Europe is that Canada, like France, should be supplying immigrants with a firmer notion of what their new nationality means; if not Cartesian uniformity of outlook, then a muddled Canadian compromise on citizenship courses. You can object that European models are irrelevant; that, unlike the Dutch, we have the immigrant experience at the heart of our national character. But a national character can be retooled by events in the time a tower takes to fall. Under pressure, a multiracial society cannot cohere when its citizens, like the bilingual Canadian in Paris, have access to the country but no emotional connection to it.

"Becoming French," was published in *Geist* No. 56 (Spring 2005). In November 2005, France's failure to fulfill its promise of integration resulted in three weeks of destructive rioting that started in suburban Paris and spread to other French cities. The contrast between these riots, a sort of ethnic re-enactment of the May 1968 Paris student revolts, and the assassinations and threatened terrorist strikes that regularly bring to a standstill life in Rotterdam and The Hague, illustrates the differences between the French and Dutch attempts at integration. The French rioting was spectacular and almost entirely non-lethal; the rioters turned the liberal vocabulary of the French state against itself; they were all fluent in French and even bottle-wielding thirteen-year-old boys were able to tell reporters which cabinet ministers they wished to see resign. The rioters took to the streets as Frenchmen denied the rights promised by the French state due to their skin colour. The protagonists of upheaval in Holland, where menace hides from the Dutch state rather than appealing to it, are unassimilated Muslims hostile to an alien secular society. Not only they, but often their children, can barely speak Dutch. The French protests, whether or not they lead to the reforms that will be necessary to give French citizens of colour equitable access to employment, and to positions of power in business and government, were an internal French convulsion. Rather than threatening French culture, the rioters tried to make it live up to its own ideals. Conversely, in English-speaking Canada gun violence involving young black men, most of them from immigrant families, dominated the news, particularly in Toronto, during the second half of 2005. In contrast to the French rioters, Toronto's teenage gang members spoke in accents or versions of patois that were barely comprehensible to mainstream English-speaking Canada, possessed no political knowledge relevant to how they might better their lives, and did not claim integration into the broader society of urban Canada as being a right, or even envisage it as a possibility. Like Dutch Muslims, the Toronto gang members were invisible (or depicted as invisible) until they struck, at which point they proved deadly. Their estrangement displayed the societal diffuseness bred by English-speaking Canada's reluctance to integrate immigrants into a defined cluster of values. It is telling that in Quebec, where immigrants are "oriented" by government courses on the significance of their entry into Quebec society, the presence of large numbers of impoverished young men who are the children of immigrants of Haitian or West African ancestry did not translate into similar gang violence. In 2006 Holland abandoned its laissez-faire approach to integration in favour of measures that resemble those applied in France. How long must we wait before English-speaking Canada does the same?

9.   HOW THEY DON'T SEE US

During the 1980s the literary critic Edward Said organized occasional research seminars at Columbia University in New York. Unlike most university research seminars, Said's gatherings were not advertised: admission was by invitation, supplemented by word of mouth. One evening, when I was visiting New York, a friend offered to smuggle me into Said's seminar. I was delighted to learn that night's speaker was the respected sociologist Michael Taussig.

Taussig, an Australian who has made his career in the United States, is a specialist on Colombia. Having studied in Bogotá, I was intrigued by Taussig's reputation as a chronicler of Colombia's endless cycle of violence; some of his academic articles, I later discovered, were as claustrophobic as terrifying short stories.

That night Taussig spoke not about Colombia, but about Australia. He assessed the extent to which Australians with non-British Isles surnames such as his had succeeded in entering the Australian elite. After the talk, a woman asked Taussig whether he thought that some of his general points about Australian culture might also be applicable to Canadian culture.

"The thing about Canada," Taussig said, "is the way it doesn't have a culture. It has no history or art or – "

Feeling compelled to intervene, I asked Taussig: "But when you say that Canada has no culture, aren't you, as an immigrant to the United States, simply internalizing U.S. stereotypes about Canada rather than studying Canadian reality?"

Taussig shifted in his chair and did not reply. Irate New Yorkers turned belligerent gazes on the impertinent nobody who had asked the question. Edward Said, effortlessly in control in a navy blue suit, suggested that we all go downstairs for drinks.

"That's the last time I invite you to anything," my friend whispered.

It was not the last time I was to provoke discomfort by presuming the existence of Canadian culture. A few years ago I found myself at a High Table dinner at one of the colleges of Oxford University. In these medieval feasts, suited and gowned scholars proceed through multiple courses served in a succession of ancient rooms. That evening's guest of honour was an American Ivy League historian famous for his eccentric approach to 19th-century Europe. At the candlelit second stage of the dinner, I was seated next to the historian's wife. An imposing woman, she spoke to me about university hiring policies in the United States. In the hope of making acceptable polite conversation, I began to explain how these policies worked in Canada.

My neighbour grew rigid. "I hate it," she said, "when Canadians pretend to have some kind of difference! That's what you get with multiculturalism. First the blacks and Hispanics think they have a different culture from other Americans, and now even Canadians are pretending they're not American. It's outrageous!"

The atmosphere not being conducive to spirited rebuttals, I turned to speak to the person sitting on my left.

These two incidents have returned to my mind in recent months, when I have been living in England and travelling in Europe. A certain cheerleading Canadian journalism maintains that Canada's culture is respected throughout the world. Nothing could be farther from the truth. The cultural particularities that many Canadians cherish are invisible abroad. Our fiction is little known abroad and barely recognizable as Canadian. Our national debates about multiculturalism, bilingualism and coexistence with an omnipotent United States, which others might find illuminating, receive no international airing. In a Europe strongly opposed to the invasion of Iraq, Canada's refusal to participate passed unnoticed: every British or European academic or graduate student I have spoken to in the last six months has assumed that Canadian troops were in Fallujah. During the same period, I have seen Canada mentioned only once in the British newspapers, when *The Independent* ran a brief article on the Supreme Court's decision on gay marriage. The article stated that the Supreme Court was located in Canada's capital, Toronto. The activity for which Canadians are best known in Europe is bludgeoning baby harp seals. In Vienna I dodged an anti-sealing demonstration outside the Canadian Embassy; in Lisbon intellectuals were writing letters to protest the seal hunt. In France and Germany, harp seals are so ubiquitous that you might think they, not the beaver, were our national symbol. The sealing debacle reinforces the European image of Canada as a frigid absence inhabited by a handful of fur-muffled figures wielding clubs. In much of Latin America Canada's invisibility is even greater than in the United States or Europe. The Spanish language makes Canada invisible by using the words *Norte América* to refer to the U.S.A. When Colombian or Argentine newscasters speak of "the North American capital, Washington," it becomes a contradiction of fact to assert that another capital city, or a second nation, exists in North America. In 1995, when Canada seized Spanish cod trawlers, one Madrid newspaper explained to its readers that Canada was "this North American country that is not North America."

But parochialism is an elite privilege. A friend from Alberta, having endured condescension in Oxford, encountered a warm reception in an economically depressed town in the north of England where all the locals knew someone who had found a job in Canada. My experience has been similar. In Romania I heard admiring tales of prosperous cousins in Kitchener, Ontario; in an Arab restaurant in Paris, where every diner knew by heart which countries had invaded Iraq, Canadians were made very welcome; working people in Portugal explained to me in amazing detail Canada's policies towards undocumented construction workers. The problem may be not that we are invisible, but that the people to whom we are visible are not the movers and shakers of their respective societies. However maddening we may find the myopia of international elites, we would be wrong to disdain this destiny. To be known and well regarded among frustrated people looking for somewhere better to live is a fate most countries would envy.

"How They Don't See Us" was published in *Geist* No. 57 (Summer 2005).

10. TRANSLATED FROM THE AMERICAN

In 1999, when I returned to Canada from London, England to teach Spanish at the University of Guelph, I was handed an introductory Spanish textbook and told that two-thirds of my teaching load was basic language instruction. The textbook was American. This fact, which seemed unimportant at first, became an irritation and an impediment.

I wasn't surprised by the map of North America that ended at the forty-ninth parallel, the two Mexicans conversing in Mexico City who spoke of the temperature in degrees Fahrenheit, or the line-drawings showing eager students saluting the stars-and-stripes. But other examples of American insularity dispatched class discussion into time-consuming detours. Dialogues in which characters debated paying in-state versus out-of-state fees necessitated mini-lectures on how U.S. universities worked. The textbook taught students Spanish expressions to describe the weather – "It's hot," "It's cold," "It's raining" – then provided prompts to elicit the desired response. My students knew how to respond to "You are in Alaska in January," but what was the answer to "You are in Indiana in May"? Dates, presented in a similar fashion, provoked equivalent problems. The student was asked to say in Spanish the date of George Washington's birthday. Canadian students, I discovered, do not know George Washington's birthday. I began to wonder whether I was imparting Hispanic culture, or that of the United States.

The textbook's procedures were based on the premise that students had no previous experience of studying another language. In Canada the majority of students who enroll in introductory Spanish bring with them the cargo of high school French classes. The assumptions they make as a result of this experience raise a tangle of pedagogical and cultural issues that U.S. textbooks fail to address. And then there was politics. The Spanish-speaking countries featured in our textbook varied with the whims of U.S. foreign policy. Cuba may be one of our two closest Spanish-speaking neighbours, visited by 500,000 Canadians in 2004, but not even the word "Cuba" is allowed to appear in most U.S. textbooks. When Venezuela elected a socialist president, one of the most popular U.S. texts replaced the chapter set in Venezuela with a chapter in which students savoured the culture of Texas. The North American Free Trade Agreement, a subject on which Canadian students have diverse and often well-informed opinions, is not acknowledged as a source of controversy. One U.S. textbook dismisses NAFTA with a photograph of a harried-looking Mexican woman leaning over a sewing machine, accompanied by the caption: "This woman is happy because she owes her job to NAFTA."

One day a man I didn't recognize appeared at my office, pointed to the book on my desk and said, "What do you think of that textbook?" I lashed out with a diatribe about how humiliated the book made me feel. "You've written a few books," he said. "How'd you like to write one for us?"

I had blown up at the representative for the publisher Thomson Nelson. My outburst led to intensive discussions. I invited my friend Professor Antonio Velásquez of McMaster University to join these discussions. Thomson Nelson's copious market research indicated that Spanish professors across Canada shared my exasperation; but the Canadian market wasn't large enough to offset the high cost of producing a complete Canadian textbook "package," including a video, DVD and interactive CD-Rom. Chris Carson, then acquisitions editor at Thomson Nelson, suggested an ingenious solution: Tony Velásquez and I would translate a popular U.S. textbook into "Canadian."

It must have looked so simple. "This will be a light Canadianization," a company memo stated. The illusion collapsed as soon as Tony and I started tearing apart the American textbook to which Thomson Nelson had acquired Canadian rights. Our efforts disabused us of the popular misconception that swapping names around is enough to transform one culture into another. It was easy to change "Hi, I'm from New Jersey," to "Hi, I'm from Saskatchewan," but anything more serious required a thorough overhaul. The dialogues in the U.S. textbook followed a student from Wisconsin in her travels through the Hispanic world. American students, whether Boston liberals or Dallas conservatives, could identify with a Midwesterner. Canada has no neutral Midwest. Whichever region I chose as my protagonist's home, other Canadians would feel alienated. After wracking my brains, I decided that the best compromise was to weave new dialogues around three central characters of different ethnic backgrounds, one each from Montreal, Toronto and Vancouver. Tony wrote ground-breaking spots on Hispanic culture in Canada. Again, new material was required. The most influential Hispanics in U.S. society are the ultra-conservative Miami Cubans; the founders of the Hispanic community in Canada were liberal Chileans and Argentines who fled military dictatorships during the 1970s.

The American textbook was drenched in the ideology of empire. Each example of a Spanish saying was offset by a line informing students that all cultures had the same "universal" (i.e. U.S.) values. A culture spot explaining the Mexican university system extolled Mexico's new private universities but did not mention the state universities attended by at least two-thirds of Mexican students. A note on the novelist Carlos Fuentes insisted that the only theme in his work was "freedom of speech," an assertion that might make Fuentes blink. The capsule history of how Teddy Roosevelt brought the Panama Canal into being was an unspeakable whitewash. A chapter set in Arizona even boasted about the superiority of the U.S. health system! We took particular pleasure in replacing this chapter with one set in Cuba, which enjoys a lower infant mortality rate than the U.S. and provided an apt background for the introduction of medical vocabulary.

We amended many other assertions to provide a more balanced view of cultural difference, Mexican universities, Fuentes's explorations of cultural history, the creation of Panama, NAFTA and other topics. And that was before we began revising the grammar lessons to better fit Canadian university curricula.

The most obvious lesson I learned from my two years of work on *Intercambios: Spanish for Global Communication, First Canadian Edition* is the depth of the ideological debt we incur by inflicting U.S. textbooks on our students. But another lesson may be more important: to avoid analogies when imagining Canada. Analogy is our national disease ("The Liberals are Canada's Democrats," "Vancouver is Canada's Seattle"); it is the rotten heart of our sloppy intellectual culture. In translating our textbook, Antonio Velásquez and I learned to resist facile equivalencies and seek out precise information. Like other translators, we had to accept that translation was impossible, that the U.S. and Canadian cultures are as different as separate languages, before we could convert an expression of American dominance into a Canadian introduction to the Hispanic world.

"Translated from the American" was published in *Geist* No. 58 (Fall 2005).

11. NATIONS WITHOUT PUBLISHERS

In 2002, when my essay collection *When Words Deny the World* was published, people started behaving strangely. Ambitious young writers scurried out of sight when I entered a room, as though afraid that irate authors might banish them from Toronto for having spoken to me. By contrast, many general readers, journalists, students and writers not resident in Toronto, and some (though definitely not all) academics expressed their support.

Strangest of all, literary agents suggested that we meet for coffee. These cups of coffee were not productive, as I had little interest in being groomed as the next imitator of Michael Ignatieff or Mark Kingwell (invariably the agent's plan for me) and intended to continue writing novels and short stories, as I had been doing before my essays were published. But I did learn a few things. One agent asked me where I wanted to be in twenty years' time. When I faltered in my reply, the agent said: "Of course twenty years from now there won't be any Canadian publishers. But there will be Canadians who write for American publishers. And I shall be representing them."

If the agent is right, we are currently living through the dismantlement of Canadian publishing. Evidence supporting this view is not in short supply. Publishers, to survive, need bookstores. The 2004 statement of Heather Reisman, whose Chapters-Indigo chain controls nearly 70% of the Canadian bookselling market, that "our goal has always been to get as close to the Wal-Mart level of excellence as we could," suffices to tell us where our bookstores are going. The dominance of Chapters-Indigo forces independents and smaller chains to reproduce the "Wal-Mart level of excellence" in order to compete. During three quick trips to Alberta, Saskatchewan and Manitoba in 2004 and 2005, I observed that the selection of books for sale in the once well-stocked and engaging stores of the McNally Robinson group was growing thinner and thinner, just like the selection in Chapters.

The depleted shelves of our larger bookstores pose obvious problems, such as the omission or under-representation of literary press books, which leads to the suffocation of these presses. As the aesthetic challenge provided by the smaller presses falters, the big publishers' literary standards drop: middlebrow entertainment predominates, often dressed up in pretentious pseudo-literary trappings. But the more insidious consequences of the Reisman model leave far deeper scars on our culture. In the past a young reader who discovered a writer whose work spoke to him or her could find a thorough selection of the writer's books on the shelves of a good bookstore. The bookstore trained new readers by presenting the full arc of writers' careers and the evolution of the reading experience. In this way, bookstores recruited diehard readers committed to exploring life through literature. Today, a young reader who identifies with a novel by V.S. Naipaul or Nadine Gordimer (two writers I discovered in my teens) will find only their most recent book, and perhaps one other well-known title, on the shelves of Chapters. The sense of chronology, of literature itself as a narrative with its own historical trajectory, has been erased. Chapters shrinks literature to one more flashy distraction that is destined to lose the battle for the reader's attention to television or computer games. The message, underscored by the relegation of fiction to the back of big-box stores where candles, mugs and calendars have pride of place, is that books are of secondary importance to the primary forms of merchandising and the media. By extension, only books promoted by the media – for example, books validated by having the Oprah Winfrey stamp of approval on their covers – need command the reader's attention. The chain bookstores, by their nature, train servile intermittent readers rather than self-directed addicts. Their dominance sets in motion a downward spiral in which every year fewer young people are inducted into the reading obsession, leading inexorably to lower and lower sales.

Plummeting sales, already a reality, will bring us eventually to the future anticipated by that literary agent. One vision of how writing might look without Canadian publishers is available via a backward glance at the 1940s, when Sinclair Ross suppressed Canadian references from *As For Me and My House* in order to find a publisher in the United States and Morley Callaghan's short stories drained Toronto of its street names and history to satisfy U.S. magazine editors with a faceless Anytown. In a nation without publishers, writers create work that does not reach its full potential by abandoning the telling detail for the convention the metropolis expects.

In the summer of 2005 I glimpsed another version of the future when I visited Angola. From the time of its independence from Portugal in 1975 until 1990, Angola's state-supported publishing industry was admired throughout Africa. In spite of poverty, illiteracy and civil war, books were abundant and cheap. Angolan writers became well known in Portugal and Brazil – two countries with which they shared a language – and widely translated in Europe. In 1990, the government withdrew funding: overnight the publishing industry disappeared. For almost a decade no books were published in Angola. Established writers continued to publish in Portugal, but, in the absence of an indigenous industry, no new writers emerged. Only in the late 1990s, when the state publisher was revived, along with two private companies, did new literary voices begin to be heard. The fiction of the young Angolan writer Ondjaki is becoming known in both southern Africa and southern Europe; but without the resuscitation of the Angolan publishing industry he would not have a career. A nation without publishers cannot foster its own literary talent, record its distinctive experience of literary language, host aesthetic debates, thrash out its personal and collective demons, express its regional identities, teach its children their history, or project its myths into the global ether. A nation without publishers loses the ability to define itself, and is destined to be defined by strangers, and ultimately, ruled by them. That is the sort of nation Canada may become.

———————————

"Nations Without Publishers" appeared in *Geist* No. 59 (Winter 2005/2006).

12. ATWOOD'S INTERVENTIONS

1. A Pen Too Far

On March 5, 2006 a group of people gathered in a small Ontario city in the expectation of having books signed by an author who was not present. The formal inauguration of LongPen, the technology developed by Margaret Atwood and members of her family to enable a writer on one continent to sign books on other continents, had been scheduled for 11 AM on Sunday morning in the Green Room, at the back of the second floor of The Bookshelf, the bookstore-cinema-café-restaurant-bar that is the epicentre of literary activity in downtown Guelph. Those of us who arrived on time found that the doors leading to the second floor were locked. The set-up was behind schedule but, we were assured, there was nothing to fear: LongPen had been tested twice, once late at night at The Bookshelf (a signing filmed for a video on the LongPen website) and once in Ottawa. The technology would not fail.

When we entered the Green Room, a small, plush space that is a popular venue for book launches, camera lenses and computer terminals peered at us from all angles. A movie-sized projection screen covered one wall. One of the tables where students habitually drank beer was occupied by a desktop computer. Behind the computer, wired up to a laptop and various other bits of technology, stood the glistening steel LongPen: an apparatus that hybridized the Canadarm used on American space shuttles with a menacing surgical instrument fitted with a nib where one might expect a blade. Customers, we were told, would sit in front of the computer. The face of Margaret Atwood, who was in England to attend the London Book Fair, would appear on the screen in "interactive form." Our copies of *The Penelopiad* and *The Tent*, meanwhile, would be carried to the table where the LongPen stood. Like a customer providing a signature specimen to retrieve a registered letter from Canada Post, Atwood would sign her greetings on a signature pad. The LongPen would inscribe a simulacrum of Atwood's writing on the reader's book. After the Guelph signing, a second session of ninety minutes was scheduled at the McNally Robinson bookstore in New York.

The event attracted substantial media attention. In the Green Room, four different television networks had their cameras aimed at the LongPen. At a charity auction, Patrick Boyer, the Toronto lawyer, writer and former Progressive Conservative Member of Parliament, had purchased the right to be the first official recipient of a book signed via LongPen. A tall, distinguished-looking man with white hair and a blue suit, Boyer paced in the wings while The Bookshelf's owner, Doug Minett, fielded media questions. Forty numbered tickets were available to members of the public. I had ticket number one and I knew what, in interactive form, I was going to ask: "Ms. Atwood, is LongPen an attempt to extend stand-offish southern Ontario WASP culture into the new millennium?"

No doubt she would have put me in my place with a withering riposte. But I think the point is a serious one. As anyone who followed the news reports knows, the technology failed on March 5. After two hours of delays, we were all sent home. Atwood was unable to sign books in either Guelph or New York (although the New Yorkers, unlike the Guelphites, were treated to a video apology). In the afternoon Atwood succeeded in signing a book in the exhibition hall in London for her British publisher, who was in another part of the hall. But the problem with LongPen is not the technology, which is bound to become more reliable. The flaw is in the way in which the technology is imagined.

Virtual culture exerts a wide appeal when it brings us into contact with those who are far away. Westerners who read the blogs of young people living under the mullahs of Iran, or young Iranians tapping into Western newspapers, feel that they have broken through the boundaries that confine them. They have expanded their humanity by connecting with those whose views are normally mediated for them by authority. Atwood, it seems to me, has forgotten that literature is already a mediated form: the words written in the author's room of her own are refined, rewritten, edited, printed, bound, packaged, fitted with an alluring cover. The reader who is intrigued by the author's books attends a reading or signing in order to glimpse who the author is behind the screen erected by the publishing process. Watching the author's hand moving across the page we are privileged, for a second, to see the writer *writing*. We witness the act that created the book that enthralled us. It is this promise of authenticity, however fleeting, that brings crowds to readings and signings: the brief return to the oral roots of storytelling, followed by the tantalizing mirage of witnessing the instant of literary creation.

The proof of this can be seen in the sparse turnout for the LongPen launch in Guelph. The forty numbered tickets designated for the general public were not exhausted at the time the event was called off. If Margaret Atwood came to Guelph in person, The Bookshelf could not contain the crowd. The reading would have to be held in the church across the street and the organizers could charge admission and still fill the building. (This happened when Ann-Marie MacDonald came to Guelph.)

LongPen, by Atwood's own admission, is the brainchild of a jet-lagged superstar who wants to spend more time at home. By enshrining the author as a remote talking head, it harks back to an older vision of the writer as inaccessible authority figure. The device's conception is counter-intuitive to the logic of virtual culture. LongPen reiterates the yearning for distance rather than engagement, ironic detachment rather than emotional involvement, that characterizes Atwood's fiction; it evokes the diffidence of traditional southern Ontario WASP culture. LongPen seems likely to go the way of quadrophonic sound because our ever less WASPish society craves emotion and disdains artificial barriers, and even art itself, preferring the "real story" – even if, as on reality television, the result is often ersatz emotion fuelling mediocre melodramas. Contrary to its claim to be a "democratizing force," LongPen will be perceived as elitist and anti-democratic. The reader who seeks connection will respond to the promise of an automated signature by imitating the author and staying home.

2. Kingmakers

The Giller Prize is the most conspicuous example of the corporate suffocation of the public institutions that built our literary culture. True, the Giller hasn't done as much damage as the throttling of the book market by the Chapters-Indigo chain. Until the early 1990s, a Canada-wide network of independent bookstores made it possible for a well-received small-press short story collection to sell 700 to 1000 copies, and sometimes more. Today the omnipresent outlets of Chapters-Indigo make it possible for a well-received small-press short story collection to sell 250 copies. But if Chapters-Indigo is the disease, the Giller Prize is the symptom. Nothing signalled the collapse of the literary organism as vividly as the appearance of this glitzy chancre on the hide of our culture. Year after year the vast majority of the books shortlisted for the Giller came from the triumvirate of publishers owned by the Bertelsmann Group: Knopf Canada, Doubleday Canada and Random House Canada. Like the Three Musketeers, this trio is in fact a quartet since Bertelsmann also owns 25% of McClelland & Stewart, and now manages M&S's marketing. From 1994 to 2004, all the Giller winners, with the exception of Mordecai Richler, lived within a two-hour drive of the corner of Yonge and Bloor.

The 2005 Giller Prize was won by David Bergen, a skilful writer who conformed to type in that his winning novel, *The Time In Between*, was published by M&S and took place in an exotic foreign locale (Vietnam). Bergen's earlier – and, in my view, stronger – novels, such as *The Case of Lena S.*, were set in and around Winnipeg, where, to the horror of the Toronto media, the author still lived. "Winnipeg Schoolteacher Wins Giller Prize," read the baffled *Globe and Mail* headline announcing Bergen's victory. This outrageous breach of etiquette was compounded by the fact that Bergen, a very tall Mennonite who looked like a serious fellow in photographs, did not fit the teddy bear image – think W.O. Mitchell, think Farley Mowat, think Timothy Findley, even think Richler in his final, mellower years – expected of male Canadian writers with a wide readership.

At first glance, the 2006 Giller shortlist looked like a recanting: four of the five nominated books were published by smaller presses; three of the five authors were from Montreal and a fourth was from Vancouver Island; two of the titles were translations of Quebec novels originally published in French. Numerous people asked me why Vincent Lam's *Bloodletting & Miraculous Cures*, which many readers thought clichéd and sloppily written, was on the list when it obviously didn't attain the literary level of the books by Gaétan Soucy, Rawi Hage and Carol Windley. He's published by Doubleday, I replied; they have to make one concession to the Bertelsmann Group. I should have paid more attention to the significance of Alice Munro and Margaret Atwood withdrawing their 2006 titles from consideration for the Giller. This canny strategy enabled the old guard to become kingmakers.

In 2003, an almost certain victory for Atwood's novel *Oryx and Crake* was derailed when *The Globe and Mail* detailed two of the jurors' close personal ties to Atwood, drawing particular attention to the fact that Atwood's publisher, McClelland & Stewart, had never failed to win in a year when David Staines was on the jury. The adverse publicity, rendering an Atwood triumph potentially damaging to the Giller's credibility, led to the uncomfortable compromise of giving the Giller to M.G. Vassanji for the second time. Choosing Vassanji instead of Atwood did not dispel the growing impression that Giller night was the preserve of a small clutch of anointed insiders. Even the nearly beatified Munro faced a ripple of discontent in 2004, when she won her second Giller Prize.

Giller night 2006, which found Atwood in the audience and Munro sharing jury duties with Adrienne Clarkson and Michael Winter, displayed the Canadian establishment at its most repellent. Host Justin Trudeau and correspondent Ben Mulroney swapped complacent quips about the pleasures of being a Prime Minister's son. Four of the nominees were introduced by Canadian actors. As soon as Atwood stood up to introduce Vincent Lam, anyone who understood power in Canadian culture knew that Lam had won. Margaret Atwood does not introduce losers. By placing her authority behind Lam, she was giving the equivalent of the *dedazo*, the jab of the finger with which a Mexican president signals his successor. The image was so powerful that the next day's *Globe and Mail* misreported the event, stating that Lam had received his Giller Prize from Atwood when, like every previous winner, he was handed his cheque by the Giller Prize's founder, Jack Rabinovitch. But in political terms, *The Globe*'s initial report – later retracted – was accurate.

The peculiarly Canadian feature of Atwood's intervention was her astonishing decision to tell in public the story of how Lam had approached her to read his manuscript while working as the ship's doctor on an Arctic cruise on which Atwood was a passenger. The Family Compact takes for granted that advertising pre-existing links between old and new members of the establishment legitimizes the next generation in the eyes of the public. Our bourgeoisie, being weaker than that of other Western countries, must assert its cohesiveness in public. In the United States, the story of Atwood's role in finding Lam a publisher would have remained the property of a small group of acquaintances educated at private colleges. In Great Britain the story would have surfaced weeks later in a tabloid newspaper. Only in Canada could it have been broadcast on national television, prior to the awarding of the prize, to enable the old WASP establishment to claim parentage over the new multicultural establishment. In an instant Vincent Lam, in contrast to previous "multicultural" Giller winners Vassanji, Rohinton Mistry and Austin Clarke – all of them relative loners, none of them born or raised in Canada, none of them able to boast of an exemplary interracial marriage such as that between Lam and his Anglo-Greek-descended wife – became a member of the Family Compact and a potential teddy bear.

But the real future of Canadian writing lay on the banquet tables of the 2006 Giller dinner, where each guest was invited to take home an individually wrapped party favour provided by Chapters-Indigo. When the guests opened their favours, they found that all the packages contained the same remaindered Stephen King novel. The tragedy of Canadian culture is that power brokers such as Atwood, Clarkson and Munro do not use their influence to rebuild a less monopolistic, more effective system for selling Canadian books. Without such an effort, the current generation's legacy will be future Canadian readers who know nothing of either Margaret Atwood or Vincent Lam but are intimately acquainted with Stephen King.

3. Witch Hunt

In a letter of 350 words, published in *Geist* No. 65, Michael Redhill calls me a racist once and implies that I am a racist on at least four other occasions. Redhill's repetition of the ultimate insult of the postmodern era offers a fascinating, if depressing, window into how certain Canadian writers betray their responsibility to the society in which they live. In an earlier column, I examined Margaret Atwood's advocacy of Vincent Lam during the 2006 Giller Prize ceremonies as evidence of the WASP cultural establishment's need to diversify its ethnic alliances in order to shore up its dominance in the 21st century. This prompted the writer Lisa Moore to accuse me of a variety of sins, including, by implication, racism. Now Redhill, rushing to Moore's defence, repeats the racism cry.

Redhill's cynical invocation of racism belittles the pain caused by racist acts, just as people who liken everyone they disagree with to Adolf Hitler banalize the monstrous reality of Nazism. An observer of colour would be justified in finding ridiculous the spectacle of three overprivileged white people such as Moore, Redhill and me squabbling over who is a racist. We may all claim our own forms of marginalization – Redhill is Jewish, Moore a Newfoundlander, and I am an immigrant – but none of us has to contend with the distrustful stare on the street, the nervous hostility of the attendant at the drugstore counter, that are the daily currency of, for example, Canadians of Afro-Caribbean descent. All three of us draw on the European cultural tradition whose development fed on the wealth Europe accumulated by classifying the inhabitants of much of the rest of the world as subhuman in order to colonize them. It would be suicidally foolish to repudiate the European cultural heritage; it would be naive, however, not to recognize that racism is fatally interwoven into that heritage. The issue is not that some white people are racist and others aren't. We are all the inheritors of a culture drenched in racist assumptions. The question is: to what extent can we examine these assumptions, explore and analyze the ways that interracial interactions play themselves out in our multiracial society, and, in this way, understand and better appreciate the multicoloured patchwork of our daily lives?

The conversation about interracial dynamics is, arguably, the most important one that can take place in contemporary Canada. Michael Redhill decries the discussion of race as "disgusting." His position is reactionary because without debate about interracial dynamics, these dynamics will not change. It's true that a debate of this sort requires a freewheeling openness that is un-Canadian; it is undeniable that such debate will provoke some stereotyped, or even racist, remarks. But it's only once such biases have been flushed into the open that they can be addressed. We must have this debate, to which my "Kingmakers" column contributes, because, increasingly, we all live multiracial lives.

Yet the burden of racial pigeonholing for people who our society defines as racially (or even culturally) different is unlikely to disappear any time soon. The representation, manipulation or exploitation of race in the public culture sets boundaries and influences the way people treat each other on the street. Knee-jerk defences of the token promotion of a few selected individuals do not address this problem; indeed, by trivializing it, such propaganda makes the situation worse. Even in countries where public discourse – the words of politicians, business people, television channels and tabloids – is overtly racist, this blatant racism provides a target for those who oppose it; the covert version, enshrined in liberal pieties and strategic tokenism, is more difficult to combat. In a multiracial society such as Canada's, which deflects confrontation with its multiracial make-up through the euphemism of "multiculturalism," anyone who raises the issue of the public manipulation of race, or tries to analyze the significance of race in public contexts, becomes susceptible to attack as a racist merely for commenting on racial difference.

In such a climate Michael Redhill can say, sarcastically, that he would "love to hear Henighan's ideas about Jews" because anyone who attempts to analyze the public manipulation of race can be smeared with all forms of racism. If Redhill had done some research before writing those words, he might know already about my vision of Jews through the depiction of the Sephardic family in my novel *The Streets of Winter*, the descriptions of the vestiges of the Jewish community in Chisinau, Moldova in my travel book *Lost Province*, or the discussion of the Holocaust in my new book, *A Grave in the Air*. His little clique is as transparent as it is puerile. Lisa Moore has spoken in public about eating dinner at the home of her good friend Michael Ondaatje; Redhill is a long-time employee of the Ondaatje family. Ondaatje and Atwood have been supporting each other for decades. These people are old friends who share an interest in limiting discussion about the dynamics of literary power in Canada. Racism is the most effective accusation with which to carry out this witch hunt; it's the magic word with which to discredit someone who evokes the spectre of open debate. But these shock tactics also hurt people far beyond the literary world by curtailing a potentially fruitful conversation about how race is exploited in our society. As long as the Toronto literary cocktail parties which Redhill imagines me attending remain thronged with sloganeering pawns who mimic the wooden pieties of the status quo, fail to challenge the encrusted assumptions that surround us and, through their subservience, reinforce a polite, self-congratulatory form of oppression that closes down debate, thoughtful people will look elsewhere for the passion for language, literature and ideas that keeps a culture alive.

"A Pen Too Far" was published in *Geist* No. 60 (Spring 2006), "Kingmakers" in *Geist* No. 63 (Winter 2006) and "Witch Hunt" in *Geist* No. 66 (Fall 2007). The controversy over "Kingmakers" continued for months on blogs and in newspapers. The line which attracted the most criticism was my mention of Lam's wife, Margarita Antoniades, and her ethnic background. Some of these comments were made by people who sincerely, although in my view mistakenly, regard noticing an individual's ethnicity to be in poor taste; others simply leapt on the "racist" accusation as the easiest way to discredit my criticism of the flagship institution of corporatized publishing. To the former group, I would say that the dominance of the ideology of multiculturalism obliges us to develop a flexible, natural, non-racist language for talking about racial difference. Without such a language, we can't even address the social conundrums of our present and future, many of which do or will centre on inter-ethnic difference or problems which impact specific communities in particular ways. Cultural life, too, will be susceptible to being defined or manipulated in terms of racial differences that will remain powerful, if unspoken, lines of definition – unless we face up to these issues by learning how to talk about them in public. In our racially diverse future, traditional Anglo-Canadian politeness will not be an option.

As for the Lams, it is worth remembering that the first journalist to pay them serious attention was not a literary critic, but *The Globe and Mail*'s Maria Jiménez, who quoted Lam in two articles, one about medicine and the other about real estate, published at a time when the doctor's creaky short story collection had not yet begun to sell by the truckload. The second article, which appeared on May 20, 2006 – months before Giller season – was about how the exclusive cottage country of Ontario's Muskoka region was ceasing to be a WASP preserve. To illustrate the "multicultural" incursion into this bucolic domain of the old elite, the article, which detailed the family histories of both Lam and Antoniades, featured a photograph of the couple and their infant son relaxing on a beach near their Muskoka hideaway. Having offered up his family as a poster for multiculturalism, Lam can hardly complain when his Giller victory is interpreted in this light.

Atwood, meanwhile, continues to promote LongPen. What Vincent Lam and this lethal-looking piece of technology have in common is Atwood's concern for her legacy, both cultural and financial. An Atwood intimate confided that he was startled by the single-mindedness with which Atwood was pushing her invention. Atwood's campaign to make LongPen an indispensable tool for booksellers has led her into further miscalculations which have been almost as disastrous as her introduction of Lam during the 2006 Giller Gala. The most unwise of these was her decision to collaborate with the convicted felon Conrad Black. Having been forced to surrender his passport to the U.S. authorities, Black could not enter Canada to promote his biography of Richard Nixon. Atwood arranged to purchase the first copy of the Nixon biography – blasted in *The New Yorker* as a sloppy right-wing tract full of slanted presentations of history – signed at a Toronto bookstore on October 15, 2007 via LongPen by Black, who was in Florida.

"I know how much you both admired Nixon," Black snickered over the video link prior to signing a copy for Atwood and her partner, Graeme Gibson. As Philip Marchand pointed out, Black, unlike Atwood, had not forgotten that "both Atwood and Gibson were famous for their Canadian nationalist and anti-war views during the Nixon administration." Black is a reprehensible character, but at least he demonstrated a sense of perspective. The magnate-turned-convict also may have recalled that many critics believe Zenia, the she-devil figure of Atwood's novel *The Robber Bride* (1993), to be based on his wife, the conservative columnist Barbara Amiel. Atwood's most recent interventions suggest that what once appeared to be her core values as a writer and activist have been sacrificed in order to polish her image and promote a piece of metal.

13. AN ENDING FOR ALICE MUNRO

The narrator of "Material," in Alice Munro's early collection *Something I've Been Meaning To Tell You* (1974), says of her hunger for short stories with good endings, "I am not moved by tricks. Or if I am, they have to be good tricks. Lovely tricks, honest tricks [. . .] It is an act of magic, there is no getting around it; it is an act, you might say, of a special, unsparing, unsentimental love." Munro and her publisher have announced that her most recent book will be her last. Even if this statement turns out to be a "lovely trick" – as it may, given that Munro continues to publish and a new collection is said to be taking shape – the decision to make the announcement betrays a quest for a perfect ending, a conclusion both satisfying and suggestively open, appropriate to the ambitions of one of the world's most accomplished short story writers. Munro has always displayed a sharp awareness of the narrative shape of her own career. In the past she has spoken of giving up the short story to work on her memoirs; in *The View from Castle Rock*, she has written a family history divided into short-story-sized units.

Munro's compact early stories were fashioned to be read on the CBC radio program "Anthology" or published in small Canadian literary magazines such as *The Tamarack Review* (1956-82). The constraints of space made Munro dexterous in the honing of the lovely trick that contained a dose of "unsparing, unsentimental love." "How I Met My Husband," from the same early collection as "Material," lures the reader into the romantic fantasy of a farm girl's infatuation with an aviator whose plane makes an emergency landing in a nearby field. After the flyer's departure, Edie waits for the letter he has promised to send her. She gets to know the mailman – "The mailman was a Carmichael . . . there were a lot of Carmichaels living out by us and so many of them have a sort of sticking-out top lip" – and ends up marrying him. The trick is in the title, which misdirects the reader, since the story's internal evidence insists that the naive narrator has failed to grasp that the aviator's romantic interests lie elsewhere.

The struggle to overcome the insularity of country life is the first major theme of Munro's fiction. Her own route out of rural poverty, by way of high achievement in secondary school and a scholarship to the University of Western Ontario (which she left after two years to marry), sometimes weighs heavily on her portrayals of those, such as Edie, who fail to escape. The tongue-in-cheek diffidence veers into an irony that is tainted with disdain. In *Lives of Girls and Women* (1971), Munro's most autobiographical fiction and the one that is sometimes classified as a novel, bright Del Jordan drifts away from brainy Jerry Storey, who satisfies her intellect but to whom she does not feel attracted, in favour of Garnet French, the young lumber worker with whom she loses her virginity. Jerry and Garnet recapitulate the pairing of the aviator and the mailman, the difference being that Del, unlike Edie, uses her intelligence to extract what she needs from each – intellectual companionship from Jerry, sexual initiation from Garnet – then goes on her way to an idealized version of Munro's own success, gaining admission to Canada's most elite undergraduate institution, Trinity College at the University of Toronto. The breadth of perspective that lends Munro's later stories a temporal sweep exceptional in short fiction, yet which also marks them with an emotional self-protectiveness that sometimes limits their capacity to reveal, is visible in embryo in Del's cool calculation of her own self-interest.

The watershed book in Munro's career is *Who Do You Think You Are?* (1978), which bridges the gap between the rural past and the second central theme of Munro's writing: the ways in which women seek both freedom and security in the aftermath of the social upheavals of the 1970s by negotiating divorces, affairs and second marriages. Rose, the protagonist of this collection of linked short stories, is a small-town scholarship girl of artistic ambitions who leaves university to marry an heir, moves to Vancouver (as

Munro did with her first husband), divorces, then returns to Ontario to become an actress, then a television personality in Toronto. Munro's eye for detail has never been keener, her contradictory insights into the emotional costs of ambition closer to the surface, than in this, arguably her most revealing work. The title is a phrase, common in rural Ontario, used to deride people whose ambitions cause them to be accused of thinking that they are better than their neighbours; here it acquires the second meaning of a search for identity. Margaret Atwood observed at the time that Alfred A. Knopf's decision to change the title of the American edition to *The Beggar Maid* encapsulates an important difference between Canadian society, where the upwardly mobile are seen as disrupting social cohesion, and that of the United States, where ambitious people are looked down upon from the perspective of those who are already rich or famous.

Two of the stories in *Who Do You Think You Are?*, "Royal Beatings" and "The Beggar Maid," appeared in *The New Yorker*, initiating Munro's association with the magazine that has published most of her fiction over the last thirty years. *The New Yorker*'s tolerance for very long stories freed Munro from the compressed forms of her early work, encouraging her to experiment with layerings of times and places that bypassed "lovely tricks" in favour of endings that resonated with ambiguity. The depiction of Canadian reality in Munro's fiction also underwent an adjustment. The harsh rural poverty of the early collections gave way to a sardonic, distanced outlook that portrayed rural life as narrow, sometimes vindicative, yet reassuring in its quaint familiarity. Munro's language shifted to accommodate her American readership. In *Lives of Girls and Women*, Jerry Storey asks Del Jordan: "You're still going to university, aren't you?" The later Munro replaces the Canadian "university" with the American "college," repeated in story after story, even when the characters are attending or working at recognizable Ontario universities that no Canadian would call a "college." In *Runaway* (2004), the CBC, the institution that gave Munro her start, is downgraded to "the national radio network," suppressing the call letters that would have been unfamiliar to American readers. In *Hateship, Friendship, Courtship, Loveship, Marriage* (2001), rural Ontario children of the 1960s address their mother with the American "Mom" rather than the "Mum" that was standard among Canadian children at the time and remains common in small-town Canada today. Munro's later stories retain Canadian place names, satisfying the *The New Yorker*'s obsession with precision, but the rough edges are buffed off the culture of the places named to satisfy the export market.

The structural inventiveness of Munro's later stories, particularly those in *The Progress of Love* (1986), *Friend of My Youth* (1990) and *Open Secrets* (1994), is both made possible and to some extent hobbled by this stylization of the settings of her fiction. Experiments with foreign locales, such as Australia, having proved only moderately successful, Munro appears to have resigned herself to being stuck with rural southwestern Ontario (with Toronto as an escape-hatch) and the mildly counter-culture fringes of Vancouver. In contrast to the realism of the early work, the later stories shuffle place as they shuffle time: Munro's heroines no longer perceive provincial society as being capable of suffocating their development. Merely one stopover in the long arc of a life, the rural world becomes plastic, susceptible to being presented satirically, sexually or as a setting for postmodern pastiches of Gothic romance. Stories set in 19th-century Ontario, such as "Meneseteung" in *Friend of My Youth* or "Carried Away," in *Open Secrets*, comment on colonial literary language in order to poke fun at contemporary literary conventions. Yet these stories, like those set in the more recent past, remain detached from the impact of history. Munro's fascination with the ways in which chance opportunities and casual misunderstandings telescope into contour-lines defining a life contains an implicit refutation of the role of larger historical forces. Diminished authorial attention to the historical realities of setting is almost a precondition for the writing of these stories. "Open Secrets," in the collection of the same title, ties together in a suggestive manner the disappearance of a local girl on a nature hike and a former secretary's self-sacrificing marriage to an ailing small-town lawyer. By the end of the story the attentive reader feels that most of the characters have missed the crucial details; the wife, who may see what happened, is unable to articulate her insights. In "Tricks" in *Runaway*, Nancy, the devil-may-care protagonist, shrugs off her responsibility for changing the course of her friend's life by having introduced her to her own stolid fiancé's dangerously alluring brother. Fifty years later, Nancy, now widowed, meets the brother by chance. She knows he is lying when he, too, claims to be widowed, but says nothing. The tension in these stories arises from seeing lives run inexorably off course; the reader, who often knows more than the characters, waits in vain for the misunderstanding to be straightened out. The resonance Munro achieves by juxtaposing scenes set decades apart gives the reader a sense of deep insight into the shape of a life. The female protagonists in these later collections, while still yearning for independence, are less emotionally complex and revealing of themselves than Rose in *Who Do You Think You Are?* Lacking the historical engagement that lends thematic range and variety to the stories of Mavis Gallant, the other prolific Canadian short story writer who enjoyed a long relationship with *The New Yorker*, Munro's themes can become repetitive. Regardless of their impeccable crafting, collections such as *The Progress of Love* and *Friend of My Youth* leave the reader with the impression that people in their forties and fifties do little other than plot, commit and endure the consequences of marital infidelity. Two recent collections, *The Love of a Good Woman* (1998) and *Hateship, Friendship, Courtship, Loveship, Marriage*, were uneven, but the highly successful *Runaway* raised expectations that Munro had returned to the top of her form. Unfortunately, by the standards of Munro's earlier work, *The View from Castle Rock* is a disappointment.

A very private writer who prefers not to comment on her work, Munro takes the unusual step of equipping her new book with a foreword. The foreword wrestles with how to define the middle ground between memoir and fiction that these pieces occupy: "You could say that such stories pay more attention to the truth of a life than fiction usually does. But not enough to swear on. And the part of this book that might be called family memoir has expanded into fiction, but always within the outline of a true narrative." The "I" voice of the author hovers over the first half of the book, which offers an account, midway between fiction and family history, of the lives of Munro's ancestors, a severe Lowland Scottish family named the Laidlaws. To describe the Laidlaws' world, Munro cites the writings of their cousin, the author James Hogg. Her fascination with Scotland has been evident before, in her inclusion of two stories with Scottish settings in *Friend of My Youth*. Here the approach is almost as dour as the characters, low-church people who immigrated to Canada in 1818. The restrained, almost flat language lacks the originality of Munro's best prose. Moments of fictionalized action are pulled up short by intrusive citations from letters and diaries; Munro quotes from the manuscript of an unpublished historical novel written by her father. The story of her ancestors' emigration and the early generations' difficult lives as pioneers stresses the resurgence, from one generation to the next, of the unstoppable impulse to tell stories. It is not surprising that this book was originally announced under the title *Power in the Blood*: Munro attributes her lifelong fictionalizing to ancestral inheritance. Yet while these stories may be factually close to "the truth of a life," with rare exceptions they are less inventive, witty, linguistically surprising or emotionally authentic than the "pure" fictions of her earlier collections.

The second part of *The View from Castle Rock* concentrates on the span of Munro's own life, moving from childhood to her early seventies in seven stories. Munro's effort to understand her life as an extension of her ancestral heritage means that large sections of her experience vanish: her three children, for example, do not appear in these stories, even though other family members are referred to by their real names. Munro's famously difficult relationship with her mother, which has nourished her fiction with mother-daughter anguish as far back as the much-anthologized

"The Peace of Utrecht" in her first collection, *Dance of the Happy Shades* (1968), shrinks to the logistical problems of living with a woman suffering from a chronic illness. The narrative sweep in this collection is so vast that emotions barely register. People contribute to the family tree, then pass into history. The penultimate story, "What Do You Want to Know For?", casts the search for ancestry in an almost despairing light against the immeasurably larger movements of geological time. The two best stories are those that grow out of individual experience. In "Lying Under the Apple Tree" the adolescent Munro learns two contradictory lessons about deceit in love. The rural background of apple orchards, barns and old-fashioned religion is vividly evoked. The best story in the collection, "Hired Girl," details the author's emerging awareness of her own sexuality during a season spent working in the kitchen of a wealthy family's summer house on a wooded island in Lake Huron. The brisk, unhappy mother, the grandmother in the early stages of Alzheimer's disease who inadvertently reveals family secrets, and the unrequited sexual pact between the youthful narrator and the family's father, expressed through a shared interest in Gothic literature, mesh with effortless resonance. These two stories, whose achievements surpass mere "lovely tricks," give this placid, meandering book, satisfying neither as fiction nor as memoir, instants of vigorous insight. The "concluding work" in a remarkable career, *The View from Castle Rock* is not the ending that Alice Munro would have chosen.

"An Ending for Alice Munro" was published as "The Sense of an Ending" in *The Times Literary Supplement*, 27 October 2006.

14. ONDAATJE'S PEOPLE

In a pivotal early scene of Michael Ondaatje's novel *Divisadero*, a California farmer in the 1980s surprises Coop, the farmhand he has raised from an orphaned child, making love with his sixteen-year-old daughter. The farmer hurls Coop through a glass wall, beats him with a stool and leaves him for dead. The daughter, Anna, runs away; her adopted sister, Claire, rescues Coop and cares for his wounds. Early in Coop's recovery, the reader is told, "When he woke he realized he had been asleep at the table." More than 200 pages later, in the novel's final sequence, Lucien Segura, a fictional early-20th-century French writer, hobbles back to his country house from the First World War to spend a night fantasizing that he is caring for the woman who is both his informal adopted sister and occasional lover. "He woke in the morning, his head on the kitchen table," Ondaatje writes. The repetition of the image of a battered man asleep at a table stresses the often tenuous thematic continuities in this diffuse work, which insists on the sibling-like kinship bred by proximity even as it flings its characters into orbits so separate that *Divisadero* reads less like a novel than a series of discrete narrations.

The guiding intelligence is Anna, who reveals herself as the narrator in the opening sentence and returns to close the book in its final paragraphs. After running away from home, Anna changes her name and becomes a literary scholar. Her preoccupation with French literature is reflected in recurring allusions to the works of Stendhal, Balzac and Flaubert. A panoptic intelligence, Anna recreates the fates of herself, Coop and Claire, who scatter and lose touch with each other after her father discovers her with Coop. She is the *divisadero* of the title; this Spanish word, which is also the name of a street in San Francisco, means a lookout point which offers access to a broad view. Less accurately, Ondaatje also teases out of the word the connotation of division, a reference both to the day that the non-traditional family on the California farm falls apart, and to Anna's own life, divided between a rural childhood and an academic adulthood, and finally between the roles of scholarly researcher and of artist.

The symbol which towers over the novel's final section is also a *divisadero*. This section moves from an account of Anna's affair, whilst doing research on Lucien Segura in the south of France, with Rafael, a man of gypsy background who met the aging Segura as a boy, to the lengthy biography of Segura with which the novel closes. A minor character works on the renovation of a fifty-metre-high church tower of a peculiar twisted form "created originally by a sudden and perverse wind or by the madness of a roofer in love." The church tower looms over the final 100 pages, much as the descriptions of the viaduct built across a Toronto ravine by immigrant workers loomed over Ondaatje's earlier novel, *In the Skin of a Lion* (1987). The church tower's power to unify *Divisadero*, however, is diminished by comparison with the role of the governing symbol of the earlier novel. Ondaatje's romanticism and residual modernism coexist with an ever stronger postmodern ethos of fragmentation, evident in the cumbersomely self-conscious discontinuities of the latter half of his previous novel, *Anil's Ghost* (2000). *Divisadero*'s structure is centrifugal, as the lives of Anna, Claire and Coop are propelled farther and farther apart; yet vestigial modernist devices, such as the repetition of the image of a man asleep at a table and the symbol of the church tower, fret against this drift towards shapelessness, reasserting the authority of the artist to order the narrative world. The result is a novel which titillates the reader with the promise of a coherence which it is structurally incapable of delivering.

Ondaatje hedges his bets against fragmentation by allowing the lives of Coop and Claire to cross briefly in adulthood. Coop becomes a professional poker player in the resort town of Lake Tahoe. The pared-down passages describing his relations with other gamblers, and his boldness in making off with a large sum of money in violation of the gamblers' code, are among the most narrative-driven pages Ondaatje has written. The California and Nevada settings of most of the first two-thirds of the novel, Coop's immersion in a world of male camaraderie and Claire's obsession with riding horses over dangerous mountain terrain, lend these sections a curious similarity of tone to the novels of Cormac McCarthy. Men, in Coop's universe, relate to women or other men through almost arbitrary acts of violence. The beating Coop suffers at the hands of his adoptive father, for which the novel provides no psychological preparation, foreshadows his later ordeals. The gamblers whom he has betrayed lure him back to Lake Tahoe by placing a beautiful, self-destructive young woman in his path. After suffering terrible tortures, which cause him to lose his memory, Coop is rescued by Claire, whom he meets by chance after years of separation. Like the father in the opening section, and like Coop himself, Claire is a character whose motivations remain invisible; she becomes an investigator for a public defender in San Francisco, has no perceptible emotional life and devotes her weekends to horses and her adoptive father.

The conception of character, in *Divisadero* as in Ondaatje's earlier novels, is the most problematic aspect of his fiction. His novels may even owe part of their popularity to his very contemporary definition of human beings as the meeting point of strong visual identities and specialized information. Ondaatje's characters perform acrobatics, committing burglaries naked like Caravaggio in *The English Patient* (1992), or swimming at great speed like Anil in *Anil's Ghost*. They master obscure trades. Kip, in *The English Patient*, is an expert at dismantling bombs, Anil is a forensic scientist who specializes in skeletal remains. In *Divisadero*, Coop's card-playing strategies are described with similar attention to detail. Ondaatje revels in the gamblers' language: "The plan is for him at some point to double-duke .... He will place this riffle-stacked slug of cards beneath a crimp, about where the man on his right usually cuts the cards." A poet before he turned to fiction,

Ondaatje ransacks his research for fresh words. Yet the three central characters, Anna, Coop and Claire, all emanate the same lack of a persuasive emotional or psychological life, the same passivity and absence of self-awareness. Ondaatje's romanticism requires his characters to take lovers, but at bottom they are solitary beings. Citing Friedrich Nietzsche and French literature, and brandishing their specialized talents as they suffer in isolation, they feel like the creations of a much younger writer. Lucien Segura, whose work Anna is researching, is the only significant character in Ondaatje's last three novels with an active marriage. But Segura's wife is never named; the only explicit references to his family life appear in accounts of his daughter's extramarital affair with a young poet.

Anna, as much of a cipher as the others, is plagued by inconsistencies. Last seen as a homeless runaway hitching a lift on the streets of a California town, she reappears without explanation as an established professor, an almost unimaginable transformation in a country where higher education costs as much as it does in the United States. Twice she is shown conversing in "her mother's Spanish," even though her Mexican-American mother died the week she was born and she grew up in an English-speaking household. When she travels to France, it is not with the fascinated yet diffident posture of the American in that country that descends from Henry James and Edith Wharton, but with a stunned colonial reverence for the achievements of European high culture more reflective of Ondaatje's own experience as a Sri Lankan sent to be educated in Britain and Canada.

Two-thirds of the way into the novel, Ondaatje abruptly abandons Anna, Coop and Claire, leaving many narrative threads unresolved, to concentrate on what really interests him: the life of an artist. The lengthy digression about Segura with which the novel concludes gives the book an unsatisfyingly unbalanced form, but it also contributes the few moments of honest emotion. A woman whom Segura meets in a railway car evolves into a character who takes over his creative life. At home "he already missed her . . . He began to invent the days and nights of this woman without having taken a single step into her life. For more than a year he wrote of Claudile and her belligerent companion . . ." While the novel's three central characters remain opaque, Segura's acts of creation radiate vitality. If the passion Ondaatje feels for the creator extended to his own creations, *Divisadero*'s glistening surfaces might be amplified by emotional depth.

<hr>

"Ondaatje's People" was published in slightly different form as "Divided We Fall," *Times Literary Supplement*, 14 September 2007.

15. LEAVING CANADA: GENERATIONAL
CHANGE IN AN HISTORICAL VACUUM

On December 23, 2004 Danny Williams, Premier of Newfoundland and Labrador, became furious with the Canadian government. Canada's founding document, the British North America Act, a bill passed by the British parliament during the 19th century, assigns Canada's provinces control over natural resources, requiring the federal government to negotiate with its regions as to how the revenue from oil, gas and minerals will be shared. Newfoundland has oil. In December, when negotiations over oil revenues between Mr. Williams and the Canadian Minister of Finance, Ralph Goodale became, in Mr. Williams's words, "frustrating," Mr. Williams decided to protest. What did Mr. Williams do? As Premier, he ordered the Canadian flag removed from all public buildings in Newfoundland. The movement spread to private businesses and family homes, and by Christmas Canadian flags had almost disappeared from Canada's easternmost province. Some flagpoles remained bare; others raised the pink, green and white flag flown by Newfoundland during a brief period in the early 20th century when it was an independent nation.

Canadians in the rest of Canada were enraged by Mr. Williams's actions. But they should not have been. The Newfoundland story could have happened in almost any one of Canada's ten provinces and three territories. Threatening to leave Canada is Canada's national sport. Only the reasons for wanting to leave differ from province to province. Newfoundland wants to retain control of its oil, Quebec wants to leave to preserve the French language, Alberta wants to leave to indulge its conservative socio-religious leanings, and British Columbia, cut off by the

Rocky Mountains and strongly influenced by the culture of Asia and the U.S. West Coast, with its two largest cities deprived of the defining experience of the chilly Canadian winter, believes that it has left already. The small Maritime provinces would threaten to leave, except that no one would notice, while Saskatchewan and Manitoba, with their decaying agricultural economies, see no point in leaving because, in their eyes, the Canadian government has abandoned them. Only in Ontario do Canadians not threaten to leave Canada as a unit, preferring to leave as individuals. One month after Danny Williams ordered the Canadian flag to be raised again in Newfoundland on January 10, 2005, two of the most famous entertainers from Ontario, the pop singer Alanis Morrissette and the comedian Jim Carrey, confirmed their departure from Canada by becoming citizens of the United States of America.

Literature, we are sometimes told, is an expression of a shared history, shared language, a shared cultural memory or longstanding common reference points. This definition, which originates in Europe, has to be twisted in various ways to capture the dynamics of literature in Canada. Canadians do not share a single language, often know little about the history that they do share and lay claim to a bewildering variety of regional or ethnic cultural reference points. One of our Prime Ministers said that the problem with Canada was that it had too much geography and not enough history. Yet I don't think this completely captures our dilemma. It is not that we lack history: in some parts of Canada, the ancestors of many of today's Canadians have been living together, and elaborating the institutions in whose clasp we all live, for three hundred, four hundred, or, as in Newfoundland, five hundred years. This is a long time by comparison with the relatively short common histories of superficially more integrated countries such as Singapore, Argentina, Australia, or Costa Rica. The tensions in Canadian culture do not spring from a lack of history, but from the many competing forms that history acquires according to whom you are talking and which part of the country you find yourself in. This is both an old and a new problem. It is an old problem because it forms part of the long process of deriving a nation from a series of former British and French colonies spread over an extension so enormous that if you placed Canada in Europe it would cover the entire area from the West Coast of Ireland to the Ural Mountains. It is a new problem because developments over the last fifteen years – what is usually referred to as "globalization," although more accurately we could call it the decisive acceleration of a globalization process that has been underway for centuries – has undermined many Canadians' confidence in a single Canadian nation, leading them, whether they are politicians or writers or doctors or truck drivers, to threaten every once in a while, to pull down the Canadian flag and leave for somewhere else.

Recently, while arguing about literature with a friend from Scandinavia, I began to complain about the difficulty of being a writer from a small country – and in terms of our influence in the world, we remain a small country. I had barely uttered this complaint when my friend said: "A small country with two big languages!" This, of course, is the core of the problem. My friend was pointing out that a writer writing in English or French has access to a global readership in a way that a writer who writes in Danish or Swedish does not. This is a huge privilege; but in the absence of an integrated historical tradition it can also be a curse. Ireland, for example, has produced writers such as W.B. Yeats and James Joyce, and, in recent decades, John McGahern and William Trevor, not only because colonization by Great Britain suppressed the Irish language and replaced it with English, but also because the Irish share a perception of the impact of this experience on their literary language and national preoccupations. Canada lacks this sort of shared perception. Among French Canadians, the Québécois, like the Irish, write in a French that reflects shared assumptions about a shared historical experience of colonization; even writers who are not ethnically Québécois adopt this language if they are brought up in Quebec, as can be seen, for example, in the recent fiction of Stanley Péan, a black Francophone writer born in Haiti and raised in provincial Quebec. Yet Quebec French could never be mistaken for the Acadien French of Canada's Atlantic provinces, which reflects the Acadiens' different experience of colonization, defined by their deportation to the southern United States in 1755 and their inexorable return to Atlantic Canada over a period of more than a century. The result is that the major Acadian writers, such as Antonine Maillet, who won the Prix Goncourt, France's most prestigious prize for a novel, in 1979, or a more recent, avant-garde novelist from Atlantic Canada, such as France Théoret, write in versions of French that people in Quebec recognize as "different." In a similar vein, the prim, buttoned-down colonial irony that one hears in the prose of writers from southern Ontario, the part of English Canada that identified most closely with the British crown when Canada was a colony of London, saturates the prose rhythms of Margaret Atwood and Alice Munro. Western Canada, sparsely populated at the time of British rule, has a different history. Here dreams take the form of doomed grand projects. From the Utopian Selkirk settlement in Manitoba in the early 19th century to the two armed rebellions of the Métis political leader Louis Riel in 1869 and 1885, to the left-wing Utopianism of the Winnipeg General Strike, culminating in the founding of the short-lived "Winnipeg Soviet" in 1919, to the social democratic Commonwealth Cooperative Federation's dream of bringing electricity and agricultural cooperatives to the prairies and the conservative populist Social Credit Party's "funny money" theories of overcoming economic hardship during the Depression of the 1930s, Western Canada has a more radical, even evangelical history of the use of language. It is hardly surprising that the fiction of Western Canadian writers who emerge from these traditions, from Rudy Wiebe to Aritha van Herk to Robert Kroetsch, are sometimes perceived in Central Canada as preaching too much. Unlike Atlantic Canada, Quebec and Ontario, Western Canada did not fight for its survival against the United States military at any point during the 18th or 19th centuries, with the result that Westerners are more likely to see the United States as a collaborator in their development than as an obstacle to the expression of their identity. About a year ago I turned on CBC Radio to hear an interviewer asking questions to someone I immediately identified by his voice and preoccupations as an American writer. At the end of the interview I learned that this "American" was in fact the Western Canadian writer Mark Anthony Jarman, whose accent and cultural references had struck my Central Canadian ear as foreign. To me, Jarman did not sound Canadian.

This is another way in which Canadians "leave" Canada: whichever part of the country we come from, we sometimes insist that people from other parts of the country are not "really Canadian" or do not understand our part of Canada; or that, in some indefinable way, their Canada is less authentic than ours. In recent years, some writers have turned this suspicion of difference to their advantage. At a time when much Canadian fiction, profiting from the fact that most of us write in a language understood all over the world, has appeared to abandon the quest for art rooted in local experience in favour of a more commercial register oriented towards international publishing markets, a group of younger writers from Newfoundland has resuscitated the badge of regional identity. The success of the Newfoundland author Wayne Johnston established a precedent that enabled a group of writers now in their early forties to become well-known outside Newfoundland. This group, known as the Burning Rock, after the creative writing workshop in which they critiqued each other's stories, includes writers such as Michael Winter, Lisa Moore, Michael Crummey and Ramona Dearing. First published by small literary presses in Ontario, these writers stretch language in ways that feel refreshing to some readers and strained to others. The Burning Rock writers are significant because they are the only identifiable group of prose writers in English-speaking Canada today who claim to be united by an aesthetic search. (Whether this is actually the case, or simply an astute marketing ploy, is a more complicated question.) Burning Rock's success in Ontario proceeds in part from the perception, which its members have helped to foster, that, coming from Newfoundland, they are exotic, and more "real" than Ontarians themselves, who see the traditional elements of Ontario culture dissolving into the postmodern, multicultural haze of contemporary urban and suburban Ontario. If a Western Canadian may sound American to a radio listener from Ontario, a Newfoundlander, particularly a rural Newfoundlander, can sound almost Irish. Yet nostalgia for the disappearing Newfoundland of hardbitten fishermen and authoritarian Catholic priests plays only a minor role in the fiction of the Burning Rock group; part of their achievement has been to put on display, in an unselfconscious fashion, the cosmopolitanism and contemporaneity of the regional.

The Burning Rock group provides perhaps a partial answer to the question I am trying to raise: that of generational change in a context in which a palpable sense of history is less and less accessible to us. If present-day Canada, where different regions brandish different literary versions of English and French, filtered through dozens of ethnic variations on each regional focus, is united largely by the pervasiveness of difference, it is important to note that this is not where we expected to find ourselves forty, thirty or twenty years ago. In order to frame this predicament more clearly, I would like to take a swift look back at English-language Canadian writing.

As recently as the late 19th century, the idea of creating a literature that was Canadian would not have been axiomatic to most writers in the country. Unlike the United States, or the Spanish-speaking countries of Central and South America, Canada never rose up against the colonial power in a bloody war of independence propelled by nationalistic slogans. For this reason, our public language lacks ringing phrases that valiantly define Canadian nationhood. The only wars Canada has fought for its survival consisted of defending itself against attempted invasions by the United States in 1775-1776, 1812-1814 and during the Fenian raids of the 1860s; in these campaigns we were assisted by British colonial power. In contrast to other larger colonies in our hemisphere, with the notable exception of Brazil, Canada relied on its colonial master as its collaborator and protector. Our amble towards independence is so inconspicuous that it is difficult to know when we actually became a separate country from Great Britain. The tradition of dating Canadian independence from the year 1867, when four British North American colonies united, is a useful fiction. One could, with equal validity, mention 1844, when the British colonies in North America attained responsible government; 1931, when the Statute of Westminster gave Canada's Parliament full law-making authority; 1949, when the Supreme Court of Canada replaced the Judicial Committee of the Privy Council of the British Parliament as Canada's highest court of appeal; 1982, when the Canadian constitution finally came home to Ottawa; or some unknown future date when all ten of Canada's provinces will have signed the constitution. What is certain is that for 19th-century Canadian writers, national identity was a weaker imprint than it was to become later in the country's history. The group of landscape poets, sometimes called the Confederation Poets, who dominated late-19th-century English-Canadian literature, employed a late-Romantic British literary language in an uphill battle to describe the much harsher Canadian physical environment. Listen to these lines by Bliss Carman, one of the best-known Canadian poets of the period, in a poem published in 1893, called "Low Tide on Grand Pré." Here Carman's narrator looks on "Grand Pré" (which is French for "big meadow"), and, observing this beach on Canada's Atlantic Coast well known for its exceptionally high tides, indulges in a typical Romantic conceit of associating the landscape with a lost lover. For Carman's narrator, the tide is:

> A grievous stream, that to and fro
> Athrough the fields of Acadie
> Goes wandering as if to know
> Why one beloved face should be
> So long from home and Acadie

One can hear the stress placed on Carman's British Romantic phrasing by the Canadian landscape. Denominating the residue of the tide as a "grievous stream" displays an almost hostile estrangement from the natural processes that create his environment; the pathetic conceit that unites the "wandering" river to the narrator's quest for his lover reveals the limitations of Carman's perception of his surroundings. He lacks the vocabulary to speak with familiarity and understanding of Canada's rivers and streams. Likewise, the French place-names such as "Grand Pré" and "Acadie" demonstrate the mixed, bilingual culture of this region, which Carman's language does not in any other way acknowledge. Employing a literary language that responds neither to the landscape nor the history of the place he is describing, Carman creates rhythms and a kind of music that sound like literature but are not fully invested with the power of literature because the narrator's language condemns him to speak *about* a place rather than *from* it.

French-language poetry in late-19th-century Canada suffered from similar disjunctures. The two principal schools of poetry opposed each other, but shared a dependence on the language and literary fashions of Paris. Octave Crémazie and his friends wrote a nationalist, religious poetry that drew heavily on French Romanticism, but failed to identify French-speaking Canada as its epicentre; the shape of Crémazie's idea of the nation derived from the incompatibly different history of France. Opposed to Crémazie was the École Littéraire de Montréal, exemplified by Émile Nelligan, which emphasized aesthetic concerns, seeking beautiful images rather than striking religious or political statements. Yet until the 1920s, the writers of the École paid little attention to the realities or language of French-speaking Canada, striving to imitate a foreign idea of what a good poem sounded like. The notion of melting down the language and experiences of their daily lives into poetry did not form part of their artistic vision.

A third group of poets living – or perhaps more accurately, dying – in Canada at this time would not have defined themselves

as Canadian, either. These are the poets belonging to Canada's
indigenous cultures, which faced crisis and destruction at the end
of the 19th century. These poets did not write their works; they
sang or chanted their compositions in their own subtle and complex languages. Fortunately for us, a few of these oral poems were
written down at the time. In the year 1900, the poet who is sometimes called Skaay, or occasionally known by his English name,
John Sky, recited a 5000-line oral poem, known as the *Qquuna
Cycle*, to a group of linguists. Regarded for decades as mere
anthropological curiosities, First Nations oral poetry has begun to
be translated into literary English in recent years and to be taken
seriously as literature. The *Qquuna Cycle*, for example, displays an
individualized artistic sensibility filtered through a defined cultural context. Skaay belonged to the Haida culture of the British
Columbia coast. At the time of his upbringing in the mid-19th century, European diseases were killing the Haida people. After
almost everyone in Skaay's native village died of smallpox, he
moved to another village. When the second village, too, was wiped
out by smallpox, Skaay began to compose his epic poem, employing the traditional structures of Haida mythology to portray the
holocaust of the Haida people and suggest the possibility of their
rebirth. Critics such as Robert Bringhurst, who has translated
Skaay's work into English, claim Skaay as one of the best writers of
late-19th-century Canada in spite of the fact that he did not write,
used neither English nor French as his literary language and, in
political terms, would not have considered himself a Canadian.

Only in the middle of the 20th century did Canadian writing
become visible as possessing the contours of a defined national literature. The British-born humorist Stephen Leacock, who lived in
Montreal and southern Ontario, set some of his books, such as
Arcadian Adventures of the Idle Rich, in the United States; but his
Sunshine Sketches of a Little Town mythologized small-town Ontario
in an affectionate, mildly ironic way that for many became
emblematic of Canada. In later years critics would claim that
Leacock had invented a "distinctively Canadian" genre: the linked

short story collection. This is an exaggeration, since many literatures include collections of linked short stories or sketches. But the
mere fact of Leacock's being identified in this way shows us that
from somewhere around the 1930s, English-speaking Canadian
writing is laying the foundations of a literature in the sense of current writers writing out of an awareness of the works of those who
have preceded them. By the 1940s, Montreal had become the centre of literary activity in both English and French. Poetry was the
dominant form. In French the manifesto of "Refus global,"
launched by both visual artists and writers, broke with the Catholic conservatism of Quebec's hierarchy and sought a cosmopolitan
modernity capable of adapting the techniques of the European
avant-garde to a French-Canadian context. In English, movements
such as First Statement heralded the birth of a distinctively Canadian form of literary modernism in the dense, Latinate verse of
A.M. Klein. The novel, having developed later, was more traditional in form. The dominant English-language Canadian novelist
from the early 1940s until the mid-1960s was the serious, intelligent, long-winded and stuffy Hugh MacLennan. The quest for
Canadian national identity dominated the novels of MacLennan,
who today seems almost like a 19th-century writer in his untrou-
bled adherence to social realism. In retrospect, MacLennan's work
is important because it signals the consolidation of a tradition of
writing *from* Canada; the British heritage, in MacLennan's work, is
depicted as obsolete. MacLennan's best novel, *The Watch That Ends
the Night*, contains a section where the protagonist gets a job in a
boy's school outside Montreal populated by British schoolmasters
who are absurdly out of touch with Canadian life and still live in
England during the school holidays. These scenes depict the dwindling influence of the imperial tradition, here reduced to an object
of ridicule.

MacLennan was able to parody the decline of the British
empire's influence in Canada, but his own extremely traditional
training as an historian of Ancient Greece did not equip him to be a
literary innovator. *The Watch That Ends the Night* was published in

1959, on the brink of a tidal shift in the way that Canadians wrote and published and promoted their works. The period from the mid-1960s to the mid-1970s is the most decisive decade in the development of Canadian writing, because it is the period when the idea of Canadian literature as a concept moved beyond the desks of a tiny group of isolated writers and entered common parlance and the mainstream media. It is the first decade in which a durable readership for Canadian writing, particularly Canadian fiction, emerged among the English-speaking Canadian middle class. By the 1960s Canada had slipped free of the weight of colonial authority that had lumbered much English-language Canadian culture with a second-hand Britishness. History, as we know, abhors a vacuum; but, where the United States might have been expected to step in to assume the reins of cultural control in Canada, during the 1960s, the U.S. was too preoccupied with its internal problems to notice that Canada was developing its own distinct cultural infrastructure. Amid the racial strife of the civil rights movement, the student revolts over the Vietnam War and the assassinations of prominent public figures, the U.S. became increasingly inward-looking, which enabled Canada, too, to look inward and build from within. The rise of Québécois nationalism brought with it the magnificently complex novels of Hubert Aquin and the innovative work of important younger writers such as the novelist Marie-Claire Blais and the playwright and novelist Michel Tremblay. But the increasing force, and even violence, of Quebec nationalism sapped the vitality of English-language culture in Montreal, causing many English-speaking Quebec residents to leave the province. The beneficiary of much of the social upheaval of the 1960s and 1970s was Toronto. The city became a crossroads where displaced English-speaking Quebeckers, economic migrants from less prosperous regions of Canada, American draft dodgers fleeing the war in Vietnam, recent immigrants from Italy, Greece and Portugal, political refugees from Hungary, Czechoslovakia and Poland, and, by the 1970s, new immigrants and refugees from Asia, the Caribbean and Latin America, rapidly converted what had been a quiet Anglo-Saxon city popularly known as "Toronto the Good" into the defining site of multiculturalism. Most of these migrants were attracted to Toronto by its reputation for peace, quiet and political stability. This may be the origin of the frustrating sense conveyed by the city that, no matter how many Brazilians, Pakistanis or Trinidadians one mixes together in its streets, within a generation or two their children sound like the prim, cautious, concerned yet somewhat parochial inheritors of the social mores of 19th-century Anglican colonials.

Yet merely by coming into contact with each other, these more recent Canadians and their children posed the question of what sort of country Canada was going to become. The contribution of immigrants remained submerged during the 1960s and 1970s, when, partly in response to United States actions in Vietnam, and partly in celebration of the centenary of Canadian nationhood in 1967, public energy concentrated on the expression of a distinctive yet traditional Canadian identity. One of the obstacles to the dissemination of Canadian culture lay in the relatively small number of publishing houses available to produce and market Canadian books. The founding of new Canadian literary publishers such as Coach House Press and House of Anansi Press inspired the creation of other small publishers in other parts of the country, such as Oberon Press in Ottawa, Talon Books in Vancouver, and Goose Lane Editions in Fredericton. In the expansive economic climate of the late 1960s, all of these publishers soon began to receive, and rely on, grants from the Canada Council, as did many individual writers. This government support was handed out on an apolitical, arm's-length basis; even so, there is little doubt that, at some level, it fostered the debatable assumption that the writer's task was to represent Canada. Margaret Atwood and Michael Ondaatje both began their careers as poets and small-press publishers and evolved later into novelists. Yet for many years Atwood's most successful book was a work of literary criticism, *Survival: A Thematic Guide to Canadian Literature* (1971). Published by House of Anansi Press, *Survival* sold 140,000 copies, an astonishing number for a work of literary criticism. The book's subtitle – *A Thematic Guide to Canadian Literature* – illustrates one of the weak points of the literary nationalism of the 1960s and 1970s: its concentration on a work of literature's theme to the detriment of its language, structure or technique. Influenced by the archetypal criticism of Northrop Frye, her professor at the University of Toronto, Atwood proposed that the theme of "survival" – the survival of the Canadian nation and, in Quebec, the survival of the French language – was a single, multi-purpose lens through which all Canadian writing could be understood. This simple formula became enormously influential, creeping into university lectures, newspaper articles and political speeches. The criticism that the "Survival" mantra overlooked huge tracts of Canadian experience, and that other nations, such as, say, the Ukrainians or the Vietnamese, had had to work much harder to survive than people in Canada, appeared only gradually. The focus on "Canadian themes," often in a rather ahistorical way, resulted in a writing that lacked the technical innovation that was spurred by, for example, Latin American writers' rediscovery of their history during the 1960s and 1970s. Even so, the decade between the mid-1960s and the mid-1970s saw the publication of many pivotal English-Canadian novels and short story collections. Canada's two best-known writers of fiction of the generation then in its early forties, Mordecai Richler and Margaret Laurence, both of whom had left the country in youth in response to the parochialism of Canadian literary life during the 1950s, returned to live in Canada, their returns more or less coinciding with the publication of important new works such as Laurence's *The Stone Angel* and *The Diviners*, and Richler's *St. Urbain's Horseman*. An older writer, Robertson Davies, reinvented himself in a more modern guise and experienced international success with the novel *Fifth Business*. New, mainly southern Ontario-based writers, such as Alice Munro and Timothy Findley appeared, and Margaret Atwood, already established as a poet, launched her highly successful career as a novelist. By 1980 even Mavis Gallant, a Montrealer who lived in Paris and published her work primarily in the United States, started to receive some of the attention she deserved as probably Canada's most accomplished 20th-century writer of fiction. For the first time, French-language Canadian fiction began to be consistently translated into English.

In retrospect this period is seen as an expansive time, when Canadian writers explored and exalted the nation, put down an early layer of what might become an enduring national literary canon, and institutionalized the structures of Canadian literature through the founding of literary publishing houses, granting systems, a Writers' Union, newspaper book review columns and literary prizes. Yet if we look at the fiction, what is striking is the precariousness of the whole enterprise of consolidating a national culture: a precariousness that seeps down into the novels themselves. Margaret Atwood's *Surfacing*, one of the emblematic novels of this era, is about a small group of Torontonians spending the summer in northern Quebec. They are a beleaguered, neurotic and insecure crew, trapped between the aggressive ethnic assertion of the local Québécois, who treat them with hostility, and the brutal power of the American mining company that controls much of the area, blasting huge holes in the ground and polluting the environment. The fragility of a bilingual, multicultural, federalist Canadian nation, teetering between ethnic nationalism and what today we might call globalized industry, leaps out from the novel's pages.

It is important to remember, though, that Canadian nationalism was not the only force at work during the 1960s and 1970s, nor were writers such as Atwood, Munro, Davies and Ondaatje the only trendsetters. In contrast to the nationalism of most prose fiction, the major developments in poetry stemmed from sources such as the minimalist Tish movement, based in Vancouver, and the sound poetry of the Four Horsemen in Toronto, both of which tapped into the energy of the spoken language of the United States. While fiction dwelt on the regional and the national, poetic language tended more in the direction of continentalism. And, even in fiction, diverse tendencies persisted. The Montreal

Storytellers, based around John Metcalf, Clark Blaise and Hugh Hood, developed an aesthetic that emphasized shorter fiction, surprising language and public performance. The 1970s, in particular, were also the time when the women's movement entered the middle-class mainstream and divorce began to rearrange the traditional structure of the family, imposing more responsibility on women but also offering them greater freedom than they had enjoyed in the past. Much of the fiction of the writers who established themselves during the 1970s, particularly that written by Alice Munro, Margaret Laurence, Margaret Atwood, Marian Engel, Audrey Thomas and Elisabeth Harvor, drew on the difficult choices between family and career, self-sacrifice and the search for fulfillment, traditional roles and sexual freedom, that came with these changes. A minority of conservative writers, such as Carol Shields, resisted the changes, promoting the more traditional values of the 1950s.

The influence of immigrants took longer to register in fiction. Only in 1991 did two novels written by Canadians who were neither English nor French nor Jewish appear on the country's bestseller lists: *Such a Long Journey* by Rohinton Mistry, who had immigrated to Toronto from Bombay as a young man, and *Lives of the Saints* by Nino Ricci, a Canadian born in small-town Ontario to Italian immigrant parents. Neither of these books was set in Canada. One of the telling contradictions of Canadian fiction over the last fifteen years is that the rise of what might be called the fiction of multiculturalism has coincided with the increased commercialization ushered in by globalization. Indeed, it's possible to argue that the intensification of globalization after 1990, *created* the trend in ethnic fiction in Canada. Unable to earn the profits necessary to sustain their businesses in the relatively small Canadian market, larger publishers and literary agents promoted books with "international appeal": books in which engagement with Canadian reality was usually minimal. The result is that the best-known Canadian novels of the 1990s, such as Michael Ondaatje's *The English Patient*, Anne Michaels's *Fugitive Pieces*,

Rohinton Mistry's *A Fine Balance*, Barbara Gowdy's *The White Bone* and Carol Shields's *The Stone Diaries*, addressed international themes such as the Second World War, the Holocaust, strife in India, or the extinction of African wildlife; occasionally, as in the case of Shields, these novels were set largely in the United States. The new theory of publishing was to streamline books so that rights could be sold in as many foreign countries as possible and, in that way, to earn profits that could not be accumulated in Canada alone. This commercial imperative had the paradoxical result of making larger publishers accessible to immigrant writers who felt more comfortable setting their stories outside Canada. The patterns imposed by the global economy spilled over into university English Departments, where older white authors such as Laurence and Richler were dropped from the curriculum and replaced by writers of recent immigrant stock. Many writers who came from minority backgrounds followed the example of Rohinton Mistry in writing widescreen historical extravaganzas about the countries they or their parents had come from rather than accounts of their own experiences as newcomers, or the children of newcomers, confronting life in Canada. In this way, so-called "immigrant literature," far from being an "authentic" emanation of cultural difference, as a certain neo-Romantic strain of CanLit academic criticism pretends, was even more unremittingly conditioned by the globalized market than were other tendencies in Canadian fiction. A few novels that engaged with the actual experiences of immigrants did appear, such as the East African-Indian-Canadian writer M.G. Vassanji's early novel, *No New Land*, or the Caribbean Canadian writer Dionne Brand's lush epic, *At the Full and Tide of the Moon*, which brings Caribbean history to Toronto. A few writers from Atlantic Canada, such as David Adams Richards and Wayne Johnston, continued to write novels whose action took place in Canada (though Johnston's two most ambitious novels, *The Colony of Unrequited Dreams* and *The Navigator of New York*, each had significant sections set in the Big Apple). Atlantic Canadian novels featured the regions of Canada that had been least transformed by immigration and globalization. Their appeal to readers in Ottawa, Toronto or Vancouver depended on the ability to supply nostalgia for a traditional Canadian life. Significantly, almost no one was writing about the Canadian present. The most internationally successful Canadian novel of the new millennium, *Life of Pi* by Yann Martel, which won Britain's Booker Prize in 2002, extends this flight into the ether. Written in English by a Québécois raised overseas, whose diplomat-poet father is a friend of influential English-Canadian cultural figures such as Michael Ondaatje and Margaret Atwood, *Life of Pi* initially enjoyed only modest success in Canada, finding its vindication in the international market. The novel is a fantasy about a young man from India who tries to immigrate to Canada, finds himself marooned outside human society and washes ashore in Mexico. The story is clogged with undigested research about the flora and fauna of the Pacific Ocean. The research throttles the reader's imagination; the story is bereft of human interaction. In the tried and true fashion of middlebrow Canadian sentimentalists from Timothy Findley to Barbara Gowdy, human relations are displaced by an animal protagonist with a cute name, in this case a Bengal tiger with whom Pi finds himself adrift. Martel was later contracted to represent Canadian culture in Europe by teaching a course on "Animals in literature" at the Free University of Berlin, an event which did little to challenge European perceptions of this country as a wilderness rather than an urbanized modern society. Reading *Life of Pi* is like sitting at home late at night watching the Discovery Channel and feeling that this is what the rest of your life will be like: solitude interspersed with great gobs of information about a natural environment with which you have lost touch. The novel evokes a world many of us recognize, even as it skirts the societies in which we live.

* * *

The irony of globalization in Canada is that, in economic terms, it has made us less global. As a result of NAFTA, more than 85% of our exports now go to the United States. In proportional terms, we exchange far less with other countries, particularly in Europe, than was the case prior to the implementation of NAFTA in 1993. Canadians have more contact now with Americans, more Canadians are married to Americans and Canadians are more knowledgeable than before about Americans and less knowledgeable than they used to be about the rest of the world (although still far more knowledgeable than are Americans). Our neighbours, on the other hand, still don't know the name of Canada's Prime Minister or its capital city; but they may have acquired a liminal awareness of Canada's existence. In my book *When Words Deny the World* (2002), I linked these trends to the disappearance of Canadian society from the Canadian novel, the proliferation of genre fiction and sentimental historical novels, and the almost total lack of productive, creative engagement with daily Canadian life or spoken Canadian language in a way that might generate a challenging literature. My explication of these views earned me furious personal denunciations from writers whose work I analyzed within this framework, yet not one made a consistent case that my analysis was wrong.

Since 2002, however, a number of contradictory developments have occurred. I'm not certain how to interpret these changes, but I will close by offering them as an indication of our present confusions. First, it has become clear that the generation of Canadian writers who built Canada's literary institutions and shaped our idea of what Canadian fiction was like is disappearing. Many have died: Margaret Laurence in 1987, Robertson Davies in 1995, Mordecai Richler and Timothy Findley in 2001 and Carol Shields in 2003. Mavis Gallant, now in her mid-80s, has not published a book of new fiction in more than a decade. Alice Munro is in her seventies and her recent work has been disappointing (although the usual parrots who pass for critics have not yet summoned up the gumption to scrutinize the empress's latest wardrobe). Margaret Atwood's career rolls along as inexorably as ever, although with a little less verve than in earlier times. The waning of these writers' influence raises the question of whether we may expect such commanding literary figures to emerge from the generations that succeed them. At present, certainly, it is difficult to predict who among current writers will acquire a commensurate stature, combining literary respect with public popularity. One may gesture in the direction of Wayne Johnston or Guy Vanderhaeghe or Dionne Brand or David Adams Richards or Rohinton Mistry or M.G. Vassanji, but the gesture is not thoroughly convincing because most of these writers play to limited constituencies, enjoying respect without great popularity (Brand, Vassanji) or great popularity without vast respect (Richards, Mistry), or else they enjoy both popularity and respect but are plying a literary form, the historical novel, that tends to be conservative and resistant to innovation (Johnston, Vanderhaeghe). What this may suggest is that our notion of a "major author" has to be scaled back for a society that has become terminally fragmented. Having arrived as a culture on the world scene later than many other nations, at a time when the idea of nationhood has grown problematic, we may have to accept that we will not have a "great novelist" – a Tolstoy or Balzac or Dickens or, in the case of newer, less central nations, a Joyce or a García Márquez or an Ngugi wa Thiong'o – but rather that once the generation that institutionalized our literature in the 1960s and 1970s is gone, Canada will have commercial writers who produce no-name blockbusters for the international publishing industry and "niche" writers whose books are read by Edmontonians or short story lovers or avid gardeners or video game buffs or Punjabi Vancouverites or Celtic Nova Scotians or Montreal feminists, but not by all of these groups at once. This anomaly of a traditional form of artistic expression, such as literature, outlasting the context that nourished it belongs to what I call the afterlife of culture.

The second paradoxical development is that since 2001 the intertwining of Canada's economy with that of the United States has not prevented the growth of resistance to U.S. norms. In what might be seen as a final 21st-century rebuke to Marxist determinism, the two societies appear to be diverging. The public rift over the United States invasion of Iraq may be attributed in part to the fact that France exercises greater influence in Canada than in the three English-speaking countries (the United States, Great Britain and Australia) which rushed into the quagmire in Babylon; but even more important was the growing force, particularly among young Canadians, of multiculturalism and multiracialism as the glue of Canadian society. More and more, what Canadians have in common is that we are all different from each other. A war that is perceived as a revenge attack on a particular race is a war most Canadians refuse to support.

The divergences extended well beyond different policies on the Iraq war. In the November 2004 U.S. presidential elections eleven U.S. states had a question on the ballot about legalizing the right of homosexuals to marry. In all eleven states, voters defeated the legalization of gay marriage. But within two months of the U.S. election, gay marriage had become legal in seven of Canada's ten provinces. Similar patterns are evident elsewhere: Canadian public opinion supports the legalization of marijuana and abortion, while U.S. opinion remains strongly opposed; Canadians, like Western Europeans, rarely go to church, while Americans are becoming more religious; Americans have a high birthrate while Canadians have a low birthrate; roughly 60% of immigration into the United States comes from Mexico while no single country accounts for more than 15% of the immigration Canada receives. More extensive business contacts with the United States and greater exposure to American television news have done little to erode Canadians' traditional support for health care and university education remaining in the public sector.

The social question which has the greatest influence on the literary representation of our society is that of racial tolerance. Indeed, the extreme care Canadians take when discussing racial and cultural difference may explain why so few contemporary

Canadian novels are set in Canada. Our cities have become so ethnically diverse that almost nobody knows what the neighbours
think, or what they eat for dinner – and, being polite Canadians,
we don't dare to ask. In multicultural Toronto or Vancouver, English is the language of advertising and business and education, and
is being extended in a slapdash way to express intercultural
intimacy; it is not a unifying glue freighted with shared cultural
resonances or the potential to express a heritage or a vision conditioned by a shared history. The family across the street is from
Bosnia, the people two doors down are from China, the Greeks on
the corner still speak Greek after forty years in the country, Soma-
lis and Sri Lankans and Jamaicans and Guatemalans are moving in
at the end of the block. No one is sure what kind of place the people next door imagine when they murmur the word, "Home." The
children all play and fight together, go out together in the evenings
and, when they grow up, will have children together. The cultural
coordinates of the children's lives will be the pidgin of commerce,
its governing mythology inscribed in a strange conglomeration of
video-game personalities, American television images and a cautious Canadian care not to offend people who are different from
you. Canadian history will not play much of a role in these kids'
imaginations. As a number of commentators have noted, in order
to preserve social peace in a radically diverse society, Canadians
have begun to pay less attention to history. In a sense, we live in an
historical vacuum. In the midst of this void, we continue to write
and paint and sing, producing works that are one step beyond
postmodern pastiches of traditional cultural forms; works that are
ghosts, or after-images, of an entity known as culture.

I would like to mention one final contradiction. And that is
that the commercialized publishing networks set up during the
globalizing, free trade 1990s no longer seem to work very well.
Chapters-Indigo barely turns a profit; the Toronto literary agencies
are dropping clients; the big publishers have cut their fiction lists
and banished short story collections, unless written by Alice
Munro, from their editorial desks. Rumour insists that the owners

of Chapters-Indigo would like to sell the chain, but nobody in Canada has enough money to buy it. The owners are hoping that the government will change the law to enable them to sell to an American chain, a development which could be fatal to the publishing industry; this danger makes governments reluctant to authorize such a move. It appears, then, that we are stuck with a monument to the failure of the big-box, globalized bookselling model. The model of promoting books designed to sell outside Canada has also stagnated. Many of our foreign-rights sales were to the United States, and since September 11, 2001, the U.S. has no interest in the outside world. European sales are also down, even in Germany, traditionally the best European market for Canadian fiction. All of this may be simply a temporary phenomenon, as the apparent divergence of U.S. and Canadian social norms may be a short-term aberration in a long-term trend towards uniformity. But there is a chance that this interval may serve as a period in which to take stock of our relationship to language and society, to the fact that multiculturalism has replaced bilingualism as the trait that most people feel makes Canada different from other countries (even though "multiculturalism" is often more about race than culture). There are hints of a stock-taking of this sort in a tentative trickle of engaged urban fiction that has been published in the last two years. And, strangely, history has not vanished: events constantly remind us of it. Think back to Danny Williams, ordering the Canadian flag lowered in Newfoundland. As is so often the case, the best way to enter history is through literature; the best way to understand Danny Williams's anger with Canada is to read . . . . Wayne Johnston, perhaps?

The multiculturalism of the present is the historical bedrock of the future. I was reminded of this last year when, in the company of a sister I hadn't seen in many years, I drove around rural southwestern Saskatchewan, a region that was settled in the early 1900s by peasants from Eastern Europe and is now falling into ruin as people move away. We drove into towns where a corner store, a gas station and a few well-maintained houses were surrounded by streets of empty houses lacking windowpanes or doors, the once whitewashed wood turned black with rot. We drove back out onto the prairie, where the bulbous domes of Ukrainian orthodox churches and the double towers of Romanian orthodox churches rose out of the endless grass like mirages of another world. Once, we got out of the car and walked across a stretch of flat prairie. Suddenly I felt something beneath my feet that was harder than earth; scraping with my boot, I realized that it was pavement. This emptiness had once been a town: the houses, the people, their culture and languages had all vanished. I listened to the wind flattening the short grass. When I came back from Saskatchewan, I looked differently on the cities of central Canada, streaming with people from all over the world. All this will one day disappear, I thought, and that's why we have to concentrate our artistic energy on what it is and where it came from while it's still alive in front of us.

"Leaving Canada: Generational Change in an Historical Vacuum" is based on lectures given in March 2005 at Petru Maior University in Tîrgu Mures, Romania, University of the North in Baia Mare, Romania, Pázmány Catholic University in Budapest, Hungary, and the University of Innsbruck, Austria, and also incorporates material from a talk given at the Université de Moncton in New Brunswick, November 6, 2002.

16. THE AFTERLIFE OF CRITICISM

1: In-Box (1)

Hi Mr. Henighan,
My friends and me have to do a presentation in
class tomorrow on your book When Words Deny the
World. We're wondering if you thought all that
stuff you said was still true. You can write me
back anytime tonite. Don't worry if it's late,
we're pulling an all-nighter....

2: Afterlives

Bob Dylan – I've blown my credibility already by using a popular culture reference that's decades out of date – once sang: "He not a-busy being born is a-busy dying." Times evolve and, if you're lucky, so do you. These days I think a lot about a concept I'm calling "the afterlife of culture." It's starting to look as though the next stage beyond the "Free Trade Fiction" I talked about in *When Words Deny the World* is total severance from past cultural tradition. We write or read or go to art galleries or listen to music not because we are capable of engaging with artistic tradition, but out of a kind of sleepwalking adherence to our roles as people of a certain social status. Most of us, though, are no longer capable of paying the scrupulous attention to detail that good art demands; among other impediments, few people still have the habit of concentrating in silence for hours on end. One example of this can be seen in the way in which the classical music recording industry has collapsed. The majority of those who listen to classical music these days are people like me, who can't tell a superb rendition of Vivaldi from an indifferent one and usually play CDs as background music while completing household chores. This has bolstered the market for cheap recordings of the classics, many of them made in the former Eastern Europe, and has undercut the accomplished productions of the major orchestras of Germany, Austria, France, Great Britain and the United States, where unionized musicians make recordings which, in the absence of a substantial audience with a discerning ear, are too expensive to compete with less meticulous work. In literature, Free Trade Fiction, which subordinates history to the primacy of metaphor, has evolved into book-club novels that package history in ways that institutionalize its remoteness and disconnection from contemporary events. The eternal present of the electronic world in which young readers and writers grow up makes the mere concept of historical chronology a difficult one to grasp and certainly not the natural way in which they conceive experience. Where privileged young intellectuals of earlier eras embarked on the "Grand Tour" of Europe in order to consolidate their acquaintance with the chronological, political and linguistic development of a cultural tradition by connecting the ruins of Rome with the Latin texts they had studied in school, or to improve their French or German or Italian, or savour contemporary artistic debate in Paris or Vienna (which invariably sprang from competing interpretations of past achievements), today's travellers prefer to limit their encounters with other countries to "seeing" the "sights" (often from the seat of a tour bus or the deck of a cruise ship). "Have you seen Florence?" (or Rio de Janeiro or Kuala Lumpur) is the vital question. Competition among national tourist industries requires the packaging of each country's attractions as items that can be summarized in visual form in photographs placed in enticing brochures or websites. Our experience of other nations becomes visual and one-dimensional; the appreciation of national historical particularities occurs in ways which, shrinking history to the difference between two very similar day-trips, asserts their un-importance. The multifaceted drenching of the individual in a culture whose assumed centre is writing evaporates. Visual culture, buttressed by a nearly identical apparatus of tourist hotels, beaches, excursions and scrambled-egg-and-orange-juice breakfasts, supplants historical difference with a monochrome present. In the absence of the bedrock consciousness of history and language, it is difficult to imagine future generations sustaining the literary enterprise. The fabric that carried literature from one generation to the next has been torn. And a much bigger tearing may lie ahead of us.

Since the 1960s, the Club of Rome has been tracking how the depletion of natural resources, the rise in the world's population and the pollution of the planet will interact in shaping our future. Access to more information and more sophisticated computers have refined their initial predictions: the lifestyle of well-off people in wealthy countries, they predict, will reach a peak of comfort and convenience around 2020, and will then go into very rapid decline. By 2050, wars and famines induced by the scramble to seize dwindling sources of water, food, oil and electrical power will have reduced the world's population to about one-fifth its present size; the people who survive will be living at a level of comfort roughly equivalent to that of medieval Europe. Many of the world's scientists subscribe to this scenario, with the caveat that it could be rendered less cataclysmic by a dramatic voluntary reduction in the birth rate. These predictions, which are fleshed out in various ways in books such as Jared Diamond's *Collapse* (2004), Ronald Wright's *A Short History of Progress* (2004) and Jane Jacobs's *Dark Age Ahead* (2004), are so frightening that it seems almost petty minded to wonder what will happen to literature. Yet, given that we may have only about a dozen years of rabid consumption left, it's difficult not to pose the question. It is not inconceivable that by about 2035 the internet will have sputtered into oblivion and publishers, libraries and most universities will have closed. Our headlong rush towards a technological future blinds us to the fact that history regresses as often as it advances: the Phoenicians, who visited Great Britain in vast ocean-going warships in 350 BC, would have laughed at the three ridiculous little tubs in which Christopher Columbus crossed the Atlantic Ocean eighteen centuries later. We forget that Europe needed more than a thousand years to recover from the collapse of the Classical civilization of Greece and Rome. The fact that we are losing our literary heritage, even while we still possess the tools to retain it, bodes ill for the future. In the world of 2075, the struggle for survival through basic agriculture may have reinstilled the gift of concentration to the point where, if people have any leisure time, or light to read by in the long evenings, they may be more disposed to the pursuit of literature than we are today. But it is also possible that most of the literary tradition of the past two or three thousand years will have been lost. Or it may have to be imported from overseas, as the culture of classical Greece was preserved by Arab scholars and restored to the knowledge of Europeans in the late Middle Ages. In the 23rd century, when international travel again becomes possible, the tradition of English-language literature may have to be brought back to us from India or South Africa.

I'd answer your question by saying that we live during the onset of "the afterlife of culture," but that this idea of an afterlife has to be interpreted in different ways: as the present time, when we are losing touch with the historical-literary traditions that allow us to grow and renew ourselves through art and the written word; as a coda to the civilization we inhabit, which may be on the brink of collapse; as speculation about what will happen to literature and culture after the structures that have sustained them in our civilization are swept away. Virginia Woolf once lamented that, "The merest pebble on the beach will outlast Shakespeare." Plangent and personal when they were written, these words encompass our collective condition today.

3: In-Box (2)

```
Hi!
Well that's cool, I guess, but I'm not thinking
about 2075, I'm worried about tomorrow. My
prof wants a presentation on CanLit - like do
you still agree with what you said? I don't
care about the afterlife of culture, I want to
know about the afterlife of criticism....
```

4: Two Afterlives

Criticism, like culture, has a variety of afterlives. Two afterlives are unavoidable. One is the subsequent evolution of the institutions, textual interpretations and structural bottlenecks that are discussed in a book of literary or cultural analysis. A second, often more personal, afterlife lies in the responses of some readers, including writers who have been objects of criticism.

5: First Afterlife: Prizes and Bestsellers

In *When Words Deny the World* I described our literary culture as split between the state-fostered institutions (the Canada Council, the CBC, the Governor General's Awards, small literary presses, independent bookstores) built up during the cultural consolidation of the Canadian nation-state between the 1950s and the 1970s, and the invasive presence of a corporate sector (literary agents, the Giller Prize, publishers who are branch plants of German-U.S. megacorporations, the Chapters-Indigo chain stores) encouraged by conditions during the post-1990 free trade era. The split remains, yet each side of the equation is becoming more like the other. Government institutions try to act like corporations, and corporations try to improve their image by wrapping themselves

in the flag ("The World Needs More Canada," boast inscriptions
on the walls of the Indigo bookstores, even as the chain's
book-ordering policies ensure that, in the future, the world will
hear a lot less from Canada).

A central trait of globalization is that all institutions, whether
public or private, become more like each other. In 2005 the Giller
Prize became the Scotiabank Giller, putting paid to the sentimental
myth of the kind-hearted individual patron by unveiling the corporate underpinnings of this peculiarly Toronto-centric institution. Yet, paradoxically, in the year of overt corporate sponsorship
the prize was won for the first time by a writer who neither lived in
southern Ontario nor belonged to the pre-1990 literary elite (as did
Mordecai Richler, the only previous winner from outside the
Toronto commuter belt). David Bergen's victory for *The Time in
Between* left the Toronto media in a quandary, unable to resort to its
habitual touting of familiar local heroes. "Winnipeg schoolteacher
wins Giller Prize," reported *The Globe and Mail*, in a condescend-
ing, if almost fetchingly baffled, vein. (In fact, Bergen, the author of
four previous books, had not taught school for three years at the
time he won the Giller.) As the Giller migrates towards the Canadian standards of the regional and the multicultural (exemplified
by the victories of Austin Clarke in 2002, M.G. Vassanji in 2003 and
Vincent Lam in 2006, interrupted by the statutory re-crowning of
Alice Munro in 2004), the Governor General's Awards continue
their peregrination in the direction of corporate glamour, with the
recent introduction of high-profile Toronto readings for the
shortlisted writers.

Our bestseller lists, by contrast, underwent a facelift in 2005,
when Chapters-Indigo changed its ordering system and pared
down the display space for fiction in its stores. Canadian fiction,
unless it is by Margaret Atwood, Alice Munro or this year's Giller
winner, was erased from the bestseller lists. The problematic category of the "literary bestseller" became less viable, causing publishers to rethink their lists. In the long run, this truncation of the
overlap between the literary and the commercial may be healthy,

diverting literary fiction from the easy emotional choices and flowery-yet-unchallenging language that characterize the upper-middlebrow Canadian bestseller. In the short term, the reorganization of Chapters-Indigo has given us tackier fiction bestseller lists that are barely distinguishable from those in the United States. It has caused the branch plant publishers to begin cropping their fiction publishing programs, discarding writers who, with some reason, believed that their careers were secure.

The situation is complicated by the fact that contemporary Canadian bestsellers do not always appear on bestseller lists since many of them make the majority of their sales through steady book-club purchases in paperback two or three years after publication. A good example of this sort of "invisible bestseller" is *A Blade of Grass* (2002), a first novel by the South African-born, Toronto-based writer Lewis DeSoto which, according to publishing industry gossip, has sold thousands of copies across Canada, many of them to book clubs. *A Blade of Grass* is the perfect book-club novel. It revolves around a public issue with which nearly all middle-class people are familiar – apartheid in South Africa – and presents this issue from a perspective that is emotive, superficially progressive (we're all against racism, aren't we?), yet, beneath this veneer, is deeply, comfortingly reactionary, suppressing the revindications of a people by sentimentalizing an individual. The melodrama opens somewhere in the high *veldt* in late apartheid South Africa, close to the border of an unnamed Marxist African state (a conglomeration of early 1990s Zimbabwe and Mozambique). A young couple, Ben (English) and Märit (liberal urban Afrikaans, but mainly English speaking) take over a farm. The local Boers are ultra-conservative; Märit is lonely, Ben is idealistic. They have great sex until "terrorists" from across the border blow up Ben, leaving Märit to run the farm. She befriends her black female servant Tembi, provoking the racism of the Boers. The novel's popularity is inseparable from its identification of a cosmopolitan white English-speaking middle class with the summit of civilization, in contrast to the racist regionalism of the

lower-middle-class Boers, the primitive savagery of the "terrorists" running the neighbouring independent African nations and
the sleepy passivity of the local blacks. For black people, it seems,
the main options are to be slaves or terrorists; the only exception
is the odiously romanticized Tembi. Otherwise, Märit and a black
man who has been brutally mutilated are the sole characters depicted as meriting the reader's sympathy. *A Blade of Grass* is complacent in its refusal to scrutinize the social dynamics of pre-1994
South Africa: the suffering of black people is airbrushed out of
the picture, as are South Africa's murderous military assaults on
its neighbours, which provoked those "terrorist" reprisals DeSoto
finds so scandalous, but so is the complexity (there must have
been some!) of the Boers. The story rattles along and the writing
is less clichéd than the plot, but ultimately this is Wilbur Smith re-
packaged for upper-middle-class North American female sensibilities. *A Blade of Grass*, unfortunately, may tell us more about the
future of Canadian writing and publishing than either works of
greater literary merit or those which receive more media
attention.

That's one of the afterlives I see for the arguments I made. The
other sort of afterlife is of a more personal nature.

6: A Second Afterlife.   I: Oxford Literary Festival, Oxford,
    England, April 5, 2003.

In 2003 the Oxford Literary Festival featured an event dedicated
to Canadian writing. The three panel members were Yann Martel,
author of *Life of Pi*, Michael Crummey, author of *River Thieves*, an
historical novel set in Newfoundland at the beginning of the 19th
century, and a British academic specializing in Canadian literature. Discussion proceeded in an affable tone until the academic
brandished a copy of *When Words Deny the World*. What, she
asked, did the two authors think of the arguments made in this
book?

Martel bowed his head. "I don't want to talk about Henighan's book."

The academic turned to Crummey.

"I don't want to talk about Henighan's book," Crummey said.

After an awkward pause, conversation resumed. Martel, whose novel was better known in the U.K. than Crummey's, received most of the questions. Near the end of the session, a young Oxford faculty member addressed Martel. "I'd like to come back to Henighan's book. Henighan says that the present has disappeared from Canadian fiction and that most Canadian novels are set either in the past or in faraway places. Now it seems to me that one of you has written a novel set in the past and the other has written a novel set in a faraway place, so I'd like to know whether you think this is an accurate description of Canadian fiction."

Tension stifled the room. Martel drank his glass of water. He got to his feet, walked to the end of the stage, filled the glass again from a pitcher and returned to his seat. The silence continued. At last, Martel spoke. "I have two things to say," he said. "I don't know and I don't care."

7: Neo-Vulgarity

The essay that earned *When Words Deny the World* much of its media attention was "Vulgarity on Bloor: Literary Institutions from CanLit to TorLit." Daniel Richler described this chapter as "the hit single that made the CD popular." I did not foresee the tempest (admittedly in something of a Torontonian teapot) stirred up by this chapter. It seemed obvious to me that anyone who observed the workings of the book business in Toronto would reach the conclusion that the Toronto publishing industry had been retooled to serve the global market, and that the consequences of this restructuring included a disdain for the national material that feeds most good novels in most other countries, the erosion of literary institutions and the debasement of literary standards as writers rushed to devise no-name fantasies that Canadian agents and editors judged according to the likelihood that their subject matter would elicit interest in the "international market."

This era is passing as globalization enters a more uncompromising phase. The delusion that publishers could make a profit in the modest English-language Canadian market by bringing out long lists of novels by relatively little-known Canadian authors, however chic, ethnic or beautiful they might be, in $35 hardcover editions is fading. This 1990s chimera always depended on the wilful suspension of the knowledge that, in spite of media blitzes, alluring author photographs displayed in full-column ads, festival appearances and television interviews, many of these elegant, empty novels sold only 500 or 600 copies – about the same number as an equivalent novel published in softcover at $19.95 by a literary press with only nickels and dimes to spend on publicity. A small-press novel by an author with an established track record – someone like Bill Gaston, for example – was capable of outselling by a factor of three or four many of the glitzy, overpriced concoctions of TorLit. (Whether this will be the case in the future is uncertain. Since the reorganization of Chapters, the smaller presses are experiencing Herculean difficulties placing their books in the chain stores or getting paid promptly for the books that Chapters sells. Tim Inkster of the Porcupine's Quill, for example, reports that in 1999 his net sales through Chapters and Indigo stores were 9,241 copies; by 2004 this figure had fallen to 1,382 copies. The even harsher "restructuring" that occurred in 2005 will make this situation worse.)

The difference, in theory, between the TorLit author and the CanLit author was that the former, enjoying the prestige of large-press, hardcover publication, widespread media attention and the support of a literary agent, would make foreign rights sales that would swell his or her recognition and bank account. Foreign publication, furthermore, in a gesture of painfully Canadian neo-colonial self-abasement, was seen as an achievement that would reinvigorate the author's Canadian reputation and sales just as the national media campaign was winding down. This Free Trade Fiction model of profit through export is being choked off in the new millennium as globalized culture becomes increasingly uniform. In striving to conform to a perceived "international market," Free Trade Fiction novels accelerated the onset of an even more rigid uniformity in which, as corporate logic would dictate, a single burger is eaten ever more widely all over the world: for children, the Harry Potter with cheese; for adults, the Dan Brown with lettuce. (The saddest people in the world today are adults who read Harry Potter.) The combination of populism and mass market-style restriction of choice enforced by the one-book-fits-all model of capitalism seeps into public literary institutions, such as CBC radio and television's irresistible, if hugely reprehensible, "Canada Reads" competitions. The notion that all of Canada *should* be reading a single book corrupts the anguished Canadian quest for national coherence with the mono-product presumptions of corporate marketing. The fact that occasional fascinating rogue choices, such as Hubert Aquin's *Prochain Épisode* (1965) and Frank Parker Day's *Rockbound* (1928), have won the contest is a reminder of the value of wrenching taste-making away from the usual taste-makers; but the contest's underlying univocal assumption, nullifying the interplay between different books from varying schools that is essential to the weaving of a literature, erases the vital concept that literature consists of a series of complex *relationships between books*, rather than a single book that can be waved as a triumphant banner of national identity or stunning first-quarter sales.

The opportunities for selling Canadian fiction in foreign markets have been debilitated by other factors, such as the wariness towards the outside world that characterizes the post-September 11, 2001 United States, the concentration of bookstore ownership in Great Britain, the never-ending economic sluggishness induced by western Germany's absorption of the former East Germany, the end of the Japanese economic miracle, the collapse of literary markets in the former Soviet Union, and the crumbling of public universities in Latin America. But was the foreign rights bonanza ever as big as it was touted as being? Many of these much-vaunted foreign sales reaped whopping profits of $400 or $500 for translations of Canadian novels in Quebec or Croatia or Denmark. (I received foreign rights of US$150 for the translation of one of my books into Romanian.) There is no doubt that such experiences are gratifying and form part of the essential diffusion of literatures beyond their cultures of origin, but, in general, literary translation is a specialized activity. To pretend that glossy literary agencies can pay downtown Toronto overheads on a 20% commission on a few foreign-rights sales of US$150 is to waft up into la-la land. (And the big sales were too infrequent, and went bad too often, to pick up the slack. Frances Itani's First World War blockbuster *Deafening* (2002), for example, racked up more than a million dollars in foreign rights, but the U.S. edition, in particular, failed to sell, reportedly leaving bad blood between Itani's agent, the Westwood Agency, and Grove Press in New York.) This mistaking of an intense literary activity, such as translation, for one of the economic pillars of the publishing industry reveals the confusions inherent in the hybridized model of the "literary bestseller" that lay at the heart of Free Trade Fiction. It also helps to explain why, over time, these "literary bestsellers" became more bestsellerish and less literary, and why the literary agencies representing their authors began assessing manuscripts as platforms for film rights.

All that is behind us now. The landscape ahead is one of unremitting commercialized bleakness. In late 2005, the Toronto agent Denise Bukowski announced that she was switching her agency's emphasis to non-fiction. It is not clear where or how fiction or poetry will be sold in the future. Globalization's propulsion of all institutions towards a form of mixed-mode convergence dictates that, as Chapters and Indigo sell more candles and mugs, so Costco, Wal-Mart, Zellers and even the supermarket chains, are beginning to sell more books. Amazon is known as an on-line bookseller, but as a quick glance at the pull-down menu on an

Amazon homepage reveals, books represent only a sliver of their sales. Few privileged spaces for books remain: most of the independent bookstores are now cafés and art galleries or repertory cinemas in addition to being bookstores; in 2006, the chain that controls most of Canada's university bookstores replaced these stores' fiction sections with enlarged displays of souvenir T-shirts.

The leavening of the literariness of the venues in which books are sold means that books that are very literary will have more and more difficulty finding hospitable environments in which to be presented to the public. Novels that succeed in the future will be less those aimed specifically at export markets than those which contain a component that makes them appear significant within the framework of a highly commercialized, mixed-mode environment. In the future, look for more novels that contain recipes, novels that are war-gamed, novels that purport to provide crucial information about dominant global institutions (the U.S. government, the Catholic church), novels that include advice on furniture-building or home decoration or investment strategies, novels that contain pictures (the rise of the graphic novel represents the logical extension of this impulse), novels that come with accompanying DVDs tucked inside the front cover, novels that interface in as-yet-unimagined ways with email, computer games, cellphones, Blackberries or virtual reality; above all, novels that are written in language that is accessible to the broad swathe of the population, which includes young people whose grasp of written language has been weakened by their submersion in visual culture and many recent immigrants who speak English as a second, third or fourth language.

That's the afterlife of my criticism.

8: In-Box (3)


```
Hey, thanks! I guess you don't mind if I use
that in my presentation? And what about that
```

```
second afterlife you talked about? Did you get
any ugly reviews....?
```

9:   A Second Afterlife. II: Rave Culture.

There were more than thirty reviews. Many were good, some were mixed, a couple of them were really bad. My larger concern is for the state of Canadian reviewing in a highly commercialized environment that construes literary analysis as a threat to entrenched commercial interests. The individual who incarnates this degeneration of the culture of literary criticism is T.F. "Rave" Rigelhof, Canada's least respected book reviewer. Rave Rigelhof earned his sobriquet by writing sunny book reports, which focused on key literary elements such as author biography, for the Montreal *Gazette*. Tiring of his intellectual inability to analyze works of literature, the *Gazette* dropped Rigelhof as a reviewer. To general amazement, he was snapped up by *The Globe and Mail*. The role Rigelhof plays at *The Globe* is indicative of the state of Canadian publishing. *The Globe* succeeds in reviewing more books than other Canadian newspapers because it retains a freestanding books section. In contemporary newspaper publishing, books sections contained within the body of the newspaper must withstand remorseless space pressure from more lifestyle-oriented sections. In this context, book reviewing invariably gets squeezed, as has happened in recent years at the once-expansive books section of the Montreal *Gazette*; or the books section is cut completely, as happens intermittently at *The National Post*. The survival of *The Globe and Mail*'s freestanding books section is a significant achievement, but it comes at a cost: keeping the advertisers happy. The separate books section remains financially viable by attracting advertising. Since the Bertelsmann Corporation owns Doubleday Canada, Knopf Canada and Random House Canada, and holds a 25% stake in McClelland and Stewart (which, having closed down its marketing department in early 2006, has its marketing strategy dictated by Bertelsmann), the continuation of *The Globe*'s separate books section depends, at least to a certain extent, on how much advertising the Bertelsmann quartet (and other large publishers) buys in its pages. This is where Rave Rigelhof comes in. With uncanny frequency, highly promoted novels receive one of Rigelhof's patented raves, known to editors and journalists as "a Rave Rigelhof blow-job."

Rigelhof is of no interest as a writer. He is simply the point at which converging market forces intersect: if he vanished tomorrow another willing lackey would replace him. It is important to signal the defining characteristics of the Rigelhof rave. Foremost among these is a hortatory insistence on including within the review a call for the reader to buy the book under discussion. Rigelhof dispenses with the premise that literary judgement has any intrinsic value: his reviews are commercial enterprises that are designed to sell books. "Buy *Galveston* now, but save it for a rainy day," begins Rigelhof's review of Paul Quarrington's novel (May 15, 2004). "There's very little a reader really needs to know in advance about the things that happen in *Crow Lake*," Rigelhof writes as he prepares to fawn over the next middlebrow book-club favourite – and exempt himself from attempting any serious evaluation of the book's strengths and weaknesses (March 2, 2002). Rigelhof's advertising pitch for Kevin Patterson's novel *Consumption* concludes with the statement that the novel's epilogue "is, in itself, reason enough to buy [the] book" (September 23, 2006). The second sentence of Rigelhof's rave of Jane Urquhart's *The Stone Carvers* opens, "All you want and need to know is that Jane Urquhart's latest book is now available at bookstores and that it's as rich and rewarding a reading experience as her last two . . ."; by the next paragraph Rigelhof has told his reader not to bother with the rest of his review: "You're excused and can start propelling *The Stone Carvers* up the bestseller list" (April 7, 2001). Reviewing Dennis Bock's *The Ash Garden* – arguably the book that completes the transition from "literary bestseller" to bestseller pure and simple – Rigelhof concludes: "And so, at the end, a skill-testing question for the thousands who have read Jane Urquhart's *The Stone Carvers* and kept it on the bestseller lists: Which is the greater literary accomplishment, that book or this one? Buy and read *The Ash Garden . . .*" (August 25, 2001). Neither of these books, of course, can be ranked as much of a *literary* accomplishment: they are middlebrow commercial novels. But the readership must be flattered (by "a skill-testing question") into believing they are proving their social, intellectual and artistic superiority by purchasing works by Urquhart and Bock. Occasionally Rigelhof takes a stab at literary subtlety by making the command to buy almost implicit: "*The Navigator of New York . . .* ought to attract Richard B. Wright's fans and many more readers besides" (August 31, 2002). In one unexpected case Rigelhof appears to be satirizing his own assigned role in life. His review of an Alberto Manguel anthology opens with a flash of almost postmodern ironic self-awareness: "Don't buy a single copy of *The Penguin Book of Christmas Stories* – get at least two" (December 17, 2005).

Buy buy buy! Literature, in the Rave aesthetic, is useful because it generates profits. This Gradgrindian outlook, which emanates from corporate headquarters, cannot be presented quite this nakedly, of course, and so the Rigelhof rave garbs itself in self-absorbed pontifications that substitute for criticism. To bolster his advertising copy, Rigelhof often quotes the blurbs on the book's back cover as though they were independent critical opinions, a habit that has been known to induce agonizing embarrassment in the blurbers, who have often provided these quotes as a result of substantial corporate arm-twisting. Rigelhof's innate inability to assess literary language, style or structure limits the content of his own pontifications to unctuous references to other authors whose books it is Rigelhof's mandate to promote, usually channelled through the question of whether their central female characters are appealing (this, not coincidentally, tends to be a pivotal concern for book clubs). Books are grouped together not on the basis of literary tradition or shared aesthetic qualities, to which Rigelhof is impervious, but according to what is recent and needs to be promoted. This makes for incongruous bedfellows, as, for example, when Rigelhof concludes a review of Frances Itani's *Deafening* with this comparison: "Itani creates as deeply affecting a central character in Grania O'Neill as [Austin] Clarke's Miss Mary-Mathilda or [Barbara] Gowdy's Louise Kirk or Mary Lawson's Kate Morrison – and that's very good company indeed" (September 6, 2003). These four books – an historical blockbuster, an avant-garde postcolonial novel (Clarke's *The Polished Hoe*), an inert Gothic love-story (Gowdy's *The Romantic*) and a flat-out bestselling melodrama (Lawson's *Crow Lake*) – do not share *literary* traits. What they have in common is that they are the books Rigelhof feels he should be promoting at this point in time: the corporate imperative crushes any sensitivity to the books' artistic qualities or literary distinctiveness. Aware of his own intellectual limitations, as I'm almost certain Rigelhof is, he discourages his readers from thinking too deeply. His frequent repetition of the phrase "all you need to know is . . ." aims to deflect readers from concentrating hard enough to perceive the superficiality of his "buy buy buy" mantra (or, in some cases, the superficiality of the books under review). "What do you need to know about the writer before you pick up a first novel? Not much, usually," Rigelhof asserts, in defiance of publishing realities, as he prepares to praise Colin McAdam's *Some Great Thing* (April 3, 2004). His need to impose his authority is evident in his curious penchant for clogging his reviews with lists of "best" books or "most important" writers: lists that are incoherent because their unifying principles are not aesthetic criteria but Rigelhof's perception of whose approval he should seek, whose reputation is on the rise, and which books he should be promoting. Rigelhof never justifies these lists: they are more or less unjustifiable according to any rational literary standard; rather the

Words for Our World

lists are there to convey to you, the reader, that Rave Rigelhof knows what he's talking about and you do not, and that therefore you should follow his recommendation by buying the book he tells you to buy. This is bookchat aimed at the servile reader sought by a big-box bookselling culture.

As they are not based on literary criteria, Rigelhof's lists exclude many of the country's best writers. The lists are Rigelhof's technique for erecting a pallisade around a commercial publishing elite; they close out scrutiny of the comparative literary merits of different works of fiction by enshrining an anointed clutch of middlebrow novels as the only permissable points of reference in what remains of public literary discourse, of which *The Globe and Mail*'s books section is by far the most influential surviving vestige. In this way, Rigelhof completes the work of the globalizing transnational corporation by shattering literary tradition (which is based on relations between books on the basis of their literary language or technique) and shrinking the stock of books available for public discussion: Urquhart, Bock and a small number of others become for Canada what J.K. Rowling and Dan Brown are for the world.

In spite of being for many years *The Globe*'s principal fiction reviewer, Rigelhof has almost never given negative reviews to literary books (his reviews of books on religion are a separate matter) and when he has done so it has been with a clear motivation. Virtually his only full-bore negative literary review for *The Globe and Mail* (September 3, 2000) was of a book co-authored by Bryan Demchinsky – not coincidentally the editor who dropped Rigelhof as a reviewer at the Montreal *Gazette*.

10: In-Box (4)

But what about reviews of When Words Deny the
World? You sure dished it out. Did you have to
take it, too?

11: Blindness

Many of the reviews were extremely gratifying, but it's difficult to think of one of them that engaged in any depth with the book's central aesthetic contention. The core of my argument was that due to Canada's off-centre position in the world, attention to local detail and literary innovation are inseparable from one another; that, when your reality doesn't quite match the dominant models, you have to twist and reweave and invent new forms. I suggested that if Canadian writers spurned the no-name commercialism of Free Trade Fiction and returned to observing Canadian reality in meticulous detail, circumstances would oblige at least some of them to generate inventive, avant-garde narrative because the contorted particularities of Canadian life, colliding with the levelling assumptions of an English-language literary tradition institutionalized by the two greatest empires in the history of the world, would leave them no alternative. *When Words Deny the World* closes with this plea, which is also made in vigorous form at other points in the book. The prevailing indifference to this important dimension of the book's argument represents a cognitive roadblock: another example of our inability to see ourselves; to recognize that we are on the edge of things, however much we may yearn to be viewed as dwelling at the heart of the globalized world.

The misreadings of *When Words Deny the World* are revealing because they illustrate how, in a conspicuous case of neo-colonial false consciousness, the "high art versus bad political fiction" dualism promoted by critics in 19th-century Great Britain and the 20th-century United States, the two imperial societies that exercised the greatest influence on Canada's cultural development, have been grafted onto the "urban multicultural versus rural WASP" split portrayed by the Canadian media as a central axis of tension in the country. (This Manichean characterization is grossly oversimplified: rural Western Canada is inhabited by, among others, First Nations people and the descendants of Slavs,

Mennonites and Scandinavians; rural Nova Scotia and parts of southern Ontario have significant populations of African-diaspora extraction; in the Ottawa Valley today you can rent a Cantonese-language DVD or meet third-generation Valley residents with local accents and Lebanese ancestries; in Sainte-Clothilde-de-Beauce, in the Quebec heartland, you can immerse yourself in a vibrant Colombian community, and you can hear Punjabi spoken in the B.C. interior.) Yet the "art versus social commentary/ multicultural cosmopolitanism versus rural whiteness" dichotomy, a warped legacy from past empires that could make assumptions which we cannot make, retains such dominance that the argument that was at the core of my book, no matter how emphatically I reiterated it, remained invisible to many readers. In the mainstream view, if I was criticizing current Toronto trends, I *must* be arguing for a return to the rural, univocal simplicities of the past. No other attack on Toronto was imaginable. The notion that I was suggesting surpassing a neo-colonial subservience to transnational market mechanisms with a cosmopolitanism nourished by national history and local detail – the localism of *The Tin Drum*, *One Hundred Years of Solitude* or *Midnight's Children* – did not register. Hence, when Russell Smith satirized me in his novel *Muriella Pent* (2003), he placed a few of my words, in slightly distorted form, in the mouth of a figure described as being a sweating CanLit nationalist from Regina and Winnipeg; to ascribe my challenge to the status quo to an immigrant who has spent half his life outside Canada and is by profession a specialist on Latin American literature, would have required Smith to acknowledge the complexities I was stirring up. This would have spoiled the satire. What is more frustrating is that the same mistake was made by people whose intentions were not satirical.

We must rupture this dualism by breathing life into the cross-pollination of that which is political and that which is aesthetically innovative, of the rural and the urban, of all the curious cultural permutations Canada has bred. The Irish writer John McGahern, a courageous interpreter of his own fraught marginalized country, spoke for writers in many countries when he said: "Ireland has changed more in the last twenty years than it did in the preceding two hundred years . . . . I think that it is by focusing on the local that you can best capture that change. If you were to focus on the universal, you'd end up with vagueness."

Let the local resonate! Listen to the rural local and the urban local and all their points of interconnection. The vast changes that will overtake us once the oil and the water run out may mire us in local life. Now is the time to forge our aesthetic of the cosmopolitanism on our doorstep.

12: In-Box (5)

> Sweet! That's enough for my presentations for the rest of the semester. You've been awesome. Now I can get through my English requirement. Then I'm done with reading. I was worried for a while there, but with the stuff you gave me it's in the bag. I'll never have to crack open a book again! Thanks a lot, man. I never could of done it without you.

Sections of "The Afterlife of Criticism" were published in different form under the same title in *Canadian Notes & Queries* No. 70 (Fall-Winter 2006).

ACKNOWLEDGEMENTS

My largest debt is to two editors: Lindsay Duguid, for unwavering support over a dozen years at the *Times Literary Supplement*; and Stephen Osborne, who invited me to write a column for *Geist*. At the Montreal *Gazette*, I'm grateful to Bryan Demchinsky, who assigned a number of these pieces. Thanks for stimulating assignments are also due to Ray Beauchemin, Rupert Shortt, Chris GoGwilt, Josh Jones, the late Robert Allen, Martin Levin and Scott Anderson. I'd like to thank Steven Heighton for an extended dialogue on Ian McEwan, Andrea Ruthven and Heather Keyes for research assistance, Amanda Jernigan for Maritime logistical expertise, Michael Darling for help with Mordecai Richler, and Jenny MacDonald and David McClellan for introducing me to rural southern Saskatchewan. For help and hospitality in making possible my 2005 Central European lecture tour, I'm particularly in the debt of Ana Olos in Baia Mare and Mária Palla and Ákos Fárkas in Budapest; I'd also like to thank Anda Stefanovici, Tania Iaţcu, Krisztina Kodó, Verena Klein, Magdalena Stiftinger and Ursula Moser.

Special thanks are due to Daniel Wells and John Metcalf, for encouraging me to put this book together, and for good-humoured support and ferocious editing along the way.

PHOTO: LORENA LEIJA

Stephen Henighan (www.stephenhenighan.com) is the author of ten previous books, a columnist for *Geist* magazine, and a contributor to publications such as *The Walrus* and *The Times Literary Supplement* (London), where a number of these essays first appeared. Henighan has won a Potter Short Story Prize and a McNally-Robinson Fiction Prize and has been nominated for a Governor General's Award, a National Magazine Award and a Western Magazine Award. His popular following increases with each book.

Marquis Book Printing Inc.

Québec, Canada
2008